为梦想加速

U0612116

长难句闪过

主　　编　张国静

副 主 编　葛倩茜

编　　委　（以下按姓氏笔画排序）

卫璐瑶　马娟娟　王明飞　王　萌

刘　丹　张君芳　钟爱丽　薄艳丽

世界图书出版公司

西安　北京　广州　上海

图书在版编目（CIP）数据

长难句闪过 / 张国静主编 . —西安：世界图书出版
西安有限公司，2017.7（2022.1 重印）
ISBN 978 -7 -5192 -3189 -7

Ⅰ . ① 长… Ⅱ . ① 张… Ⅲ . ① 英语—句法—研究生—
入学考试—自学参考资料　Ⅳ . ① H319.35

中国版本图书馆 CIP 数据核字（2017）第 153715 号

书　　名	长难句闪过	
	CHANGNANJU SHANGUO	
主　　编	张国静	
责任编辑	陈康宁	
内文设计	徐欣欣	
出版发行	世界图书出版西安有限公司	
地　　址	西安市锦业路 1 号都市之门 C 座	
邮　　编	710065	
电　　话	029 - 87234427　029 - 87233647（市场营销部）	
	029 - 87234767（总编室）	
网　　址	http://www.wpcxa.com	
邮　　箱	xast@wpcxa.com	
经　　销	新华书店	
印　　刷	北京盛通印刷股份有限公司	
开　　本	787 mm × 1092 mm　　1/16	
印　　张	14	
字　　数	220 千字	
版　　次	2017 年 7 月第 1 版	
印　　次	2022 年 1 月第 10 次印刷	
书　　号	ISBN 978 -7 -5192 -3189 -7	
定　　价	49.80 元	

前 言

传统长难句辅导书为什么无法帮你搞定长难句？

长难句的复习是考研备考过程中虽然基础但非常重要的关键环节，对于我们理解阅读、翻译、作文等题型有着举足轻重的作用。如果不能快速攻克长难句，便会严重影响我们的英语复习。

在备考长难句时，很多考生采用传统书籍中的复习方法，费尽周折，却没有明显的提升。究其原因，是因为传统的长难句书籍存在两大缺陷。

一 不注重长难句分析过程

用传统的长难句书籍复习时，大多数考生常常发出这样的感叹：这个句子原来是这样分析的，我怎么没想到！它们将句子结构的分析结果直接呈现给考生，使其看后恍然大悟。然而，考生再遇到新的长难句时，却又无从下手，一筹莫展——主句在哪？从句在哪？哪些是修饰成分？出现这种情况的原因是传统长难句书籍只给出结果，却没有展示解析句子的过程和方法，导致考生虽看得懂解析，却依旧不会举一反三。

二 句子分析方法不成体系

在传统的长难句书籍中，我们经常可以看到，同一本书在讲解不同的语法结构时，会使用不同的分析方式。这其实有很大的缺陷：一方面，没有系统的句子分析方法，就会导致考生需要不断去熟悉和适应不同的分析模式，严重影响复习效率；另一方面，不同的句子分析方法交替使用，会使得书籍内容混乱，缺乏条理，同时也会影响考生的复习思路，使其难以掌握破解长难句的有效方法。

《长难句闪过》有哪些特点？

针对以上传统长难句书籍存在的两大缺陷，我们力图打破传统的长难句解析方法，为考生提供一种新颖、准确、精辟、快速的分析方式，因而研发出这本独树一帜的《长难句闪过》。相较于传统的考研长难句书籍，本书有以下特色。

一 详解句子分析过程——锁定谓语动词，抓住句子主干

在破解长难句的过程中，抓住主干部分是一大难点，而锁定谓语动词则最为关键。本书突破性地为考生总结了寻找主干谓语动词的方法，并将其精炼为三个步骤。书中所

有完整分析的真题例句均使用这一方法进行分析，帮助考生通过辨别主干谓语动词理清句中的主从关系，并剥离掉各种修饰成分，从而提取出句子的主干部分。相较于把成分分析的结果直接展现出来，我们更希望教给考生破解长难句的方法，让他们面对任何长难句，都能直接上手分析，一闪而过，瞬间搞定，大大提高复习效率。

二 句子分析体系完整——找主干、理修饰、看标点

为了弥补传统长难句书籍的缺陷，本书在分析完整真题例句时，全部使用了我们的"九字真经破解法"—— 找主干、理修饰、看标点，并采用【难句破解】和【结构分析】的讲解模式，帮助大家细致掌握破解长难句的方法，提高学习效率。

在【难句破解】中，我们首先通过锁定谓语动词找出句子主干，并分析其句型构成；其次，梳理找主干过程中被剥离掉的各类修饰成分；最后，分析句中影响结构的标点符号。将这三个步骤通过图表的形式呈现出来，展示出本书分析长难句的统一方法体系。本书中所有完整分析的真题例句都使用了这一方法进行解析，足见该方法对考研长难句具有普遍适用性。

在【结构分析】中，我们采用了句子图解的形式，与【难句破解】相对应，将破解长难句的结果用图解的方式，简洁直观地呈现给考生。图解中将句子主干与各级修饰分别标示出来，并指明各层级之间的关系，使句子结构更加清晰明了。这一部分能够帮助考生巩固"找主干、理修饰、看标点"的方法，有效提升快速理清句子结构的能力。

总结起来，破解长难句的关键就是重视过程，而该过程的重点就是通过辨别谓语动词找主干。这也是本书最大的特色 —— 强调找主干的方法和过程。我们希望考生能够通过本书中的真题原句解析，掌握"九字真经破解法"，在破解长难句时直接套用。考生可以通过本书中难度递进的前四个章节，节节攀升，再利用第五章进行实战演练，最终达到"闪过"的效果。

最后，祝大家都能闪破长难句，闪过考研英语。

目 录

第三章　提高篇

第四章　挑战篇

第五章　演练篇

宣言

我将坚持复习，至考方休

我将不求职，不出国，不考公务员

我将不耽玩乐，不猎新奇

我将悬梁刺股，孜孜不懈

我是图书馆的雕像，自习室的幽灵

我是唤醒黎明的闹钟，闪耀午夜的台灯

守望课本的双眼，追寻知识的灵魂

我将把所有的耐心和坚持献给考研

日日如此，考上为止

为梦想加速

时间不足用"闪过"，划重点，省时间！我是"闪过"，你的"省时小能手"。

关于长难句复习，若你准备好了，请在此郑重签下你的名字。

风里雨里，"闪过"会一直陪着你……

守护人：<u> 闪过 </u>　　宣誓人：<u>　　　</u>

本书将采用一些符号来表示不同的句子成分，主语——加<u>双下划线</u>；谓语／系动词——加<u>单下划线</u>；宾语／表语——加<u>波浪线</u>；宾语补足语——加<u>虚线</u>；从句引导词——[**加粗**]；省略——（ ）。

注　本书（除第一章外）将采用一些符号来表示不同的句子成分

符号表示的含义	符号
主语	双下划线
谓语／系动词	单下划线
宾语／表语	波浪线
宾语补足语	虚线
从句引导词	[**加粗**]
省略	（ ）

我们通过两个例句来说明上述符号的具体使用方法。

实例 1

Every month on pay day, she banks hundreds of dollars into a savings account she keeps from her husband. 每个月发工资的那一天，她都瞒着丈夫将几百美元存入一个储蓄账户。【英语（二）2008 Text 3】（详见 P165）

一级修饰　Every month on pay day,

时间状语

句子主干　she banks hundreds of dollars into a savings account

省略关系词（that/which）的定语从句，修饰 a savings account

一级修饰　**(that/which)** she keeps from her husband.

实例 2

Research on animal intelligence also makes us wonder what experiments animals would perform on humans if they had the chance. 对动物智力的研究也使我们想弄明白：如果动物有机会的话，它们会对人类做什么样的实验。【英语（一）2009 完形】（详见 P55）

一级修饰　**on** animal intelligence

介词短语作后置定语，修饰 Research

句子主干　**Research**…also makes us **wonder**（主＋谓＋宾＋宾补）

what 引导的宾语从句，作 wonder 的宾语

[what] experiments animals would perform on humans

if 引导的条件状语从句

一级修饰　**[if]** they had the chance.

1

第一章 基础篇

考生经常会抱怨，"考研英语中，单词意思我大概都知道，可怎么就是读不懂文章呢？"为什么会出现这种情况，是句子太长，还是句子太难？实际上，长句不一定难，而难句也不一定长，真正让考生搞不清楚状况的是那些既长又难的句子。我们通常认为，是句子中出现了倒装、省略、虚拟等特定的语法现象导致句子很难。其实，在考研英语中，倒装、省略以及虚拟是较少出现的，而真正的长难句一方面是句中出现了多个动词，我们无法辨别真正的谓语动词是什么；另一方面，由于各种从句互相嵌套，导致句式繁杂凌乱，让人无法一下子触及主干。

在有限的时间里，要判断出复杂的长难句的主干成分是什么，修饰成分是什么，主干的主要成分是什么，只有具备深厚语言功底的英语专业考生才能快速辨别，而多数非英语专业考生，只有通过掌握正确有效的方法才能做到。

目前市场上可见的讲解长难句的方法都是直接体现主干句如何划分，比如告诉考生哪些是主语，哪些是谓语，哪些是宾语，这种做法直接将结果告诉考生，却没有说明这一结果是怎么得来的，也就是说，他们都忽视了如何获取主干这一思维过程。本书旨在探究如何把不是谓语的动词剥离出来，并辨认出从句，进而找出真正的谓语动词，又如何从众多成分中剥离出主干句。这是一种思维过程的具体呈现，而非结果的直接展现。这种做法会助力考生真正学会自行分析长难句（而不是我们把分析好的长难句成分指给考生看）。

一个句子的核心成分是主谓宾或主系表，可仅靠主谓宾或主系表又无法将句子变长，因此要让句子变长，少不了各种修饰成分，比如定语和状语。也就是说，长难句的特点就是修饰成分多，句子结构复杂。那么，反过来也可以说，如果要理解一个长句，我们需要先把修饰成分去掉，掌握句子的最基本构成，然后再整理修饰部分；而要掌握句子的最基本主干，关键是要找到谓语动词。也就是说，长难句的要害和难点，就是谓语动词和主从关系，而破解长难句的核心方法，就是从谓语动词入手，理清主从关系和修饰成分。

本书所呈现的语法分析只是一种帮助考生理解并掌握长难句规律的手段，并无意指导大家依靠语法在考场上句句分析。我们要做的是，让大家明白长难句的构成，提取最核心部分，明白语义。考生不必非常清楚定语的概念、补语的概念等等，大家只需在看到其他长难句的同样结构时，能正确做出判断即可。

破解长难句的要害、难点和步骤

在考研英语中，最容易对考生造成理解障碍的是句子的修饰部分。这个修饰部分有时是简单的成分修饰，比如形容词作定语充当修饰部分，或者是插入语充当修饰部分等等，有时也会用一个完整的句子来充当修饰部分，后者多见于长难句。

我们将句子构成图解如下：

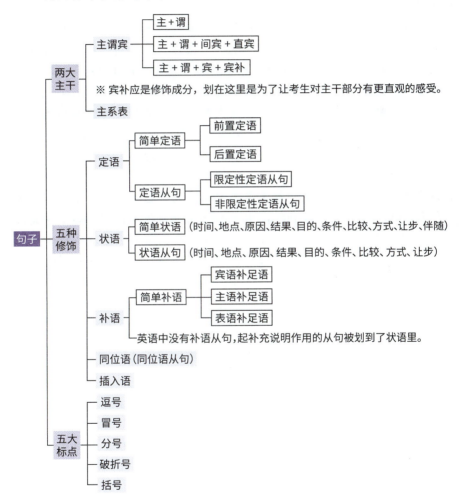

※ 主语、宾语和表语既可以由简单成分构成，也可以由句子构成，即主语从句、宾语从句和表语从句。

一 句子构成的三大元素

由上表可看出，在考研英语中，句子＝主干部分＋修饰部分＋标点符号。按照谓语动词有实义还是无实义，可以将句子主干分为主谓宾结构和主系表结构，其余皆为修饰成分。下面我们对句子中的各个部分逐一进行解读。

（一）两大主干

1. 主谓宾

主谓宾是一个句子的主要构成部分。但如果谓语动词是不及物动词，那么其后就不需要跟宾语，主干部分就可简化为"主＋谓"结构；另外，一个及物动词后可能牵涉两个宾语，根据直接涉及对象和目的对象的不同，可分为直接宾语和间接宾语，那么主干部分则转化为"主＋谓＋间宾＋直宾"结构；而当及物动词后的单个宾语无法表明完整意义时，则需要补语来补充说明宾语的状态或意义，那么主干部分则转化为"主＋谓＋宾＋宾补"结构。主语、宾语、表语可以是一个单词或词组，当这些成分是一个句子时，就出现了主语从句、宾语从句、表语从句。

（1）主语＋谓语（不及物动词）

实例	Stratford cries poor traditionally. 哭穷是斯特拉特福德镇的传统。【英语（一）2006 Text 2】
结构	主语（Stratford）＋谓语（cries poor），traditionally 作状语，修饰谓语动词。可以将 cries poor 看作一个动词短语，意为"哭穷"。
说明	不及物动词后面不需要接宾语，也就是说，如果主谓结构完整，那么句子核心也就掌握了。在考场上，如果不是考查细节题，那么除了主干部分，其余修饰成分则可以选择不看，这样可以提高做题速度，而且可以避免因修饰成分较难而造成的解题困扰。

（2）主语＋谓语（及物动词）＋宾语

实例	Similarly, the physical act of laughter could improve mood. 同样，笑这一身体动作也可以改善情绪。【英语（一）2011 完形】
结构	主语（the physical act）＋谓语（could improve）＋宾语（mood）。介词短语 of laughter 作后置定语，修饰主语；句首的副词 Similarly 作状语。
说明	在这个句型中，因 improve 是及物动词，所以宾语不是可有可无，而是必须存在。要找到宾语，才能看懂句子。宾语通常由名词或代词充当，如实例中的名词 mood 就充当了宾语，或者由相当于名词的其他形式，比如非谓语动词 to do 或 doing 来充当。需要注意的是，简单句中也会有多个宾语并列的情况，各个宾语之间会由并列连词或词组来衔接。

4

(3) 主语 + 谓语（及物动词）+ 间接宾语 + 直接宾语

实例	He taught himself shorthand to get an even better job later as a court stenographer and as a reporter in Parliament. 他自学速记，从而得到了一份更好的工作——法庭速记员和议会记者。【英语（一）2017 新题型】
结构	主语（He）+ 谓语（taught）+ 间接宾语（himself）+ 直接宾语（shorthand）。
说明	1. 指"人"为间宾，表示动作是为谁而做；指"物"为直宾，表示动作的承受者。直宾与间宾没有逻辑上的主谓关系。 2. 直宾和间宾均可以是名词或代词。

(4) 主语 + 谓语（及物动词）+ 宾语 + 宾语补足语

实例	This allows the TSA to focus on travelers who are higher risk, saving time for everyone involved. 这能使美国运输安全管理局将精力集中到高风险的旅客身上，节省每个人的时间。【英语（一）2017 Text 1】
结构	主语（This）+ 谓语（allows）+ 宾语（the TSA）+ 宾语补足语（to focus on travelers）。to focus on travelers 这一动作的发出者是 the TSA，二者在逻辑上是主谓关系。
说明	1. 宾语补足语是对宾语的补充说明，宾语和宾语补足语一起构成复合宾语，它们通常有逻辑上的主谓关系。 2. 宾语补足语可以是名词、形容词、不定式、分词或介词短语。

2. 主系表

　　当句中的谓语动词没有实际意义，是系动词或者半系动词时，该句子是主系表结构。

实例	Of course, the basics of using any computer these days are very simple. 当然，目前计算机使用的基本操作是非常简单的。【英语（一）1999 Passage 3】
结构	主语（the basics）+ 系动词（are）+ 表语（very simple）。介词短语 of using any computer 作后置定语，修饰 the basics；these days 作时间状语；介词短语 Of course 作插入语。
说明	1. 表语表示主语的特征或状态，可以是名词、形容词、副词、介词短语、现在分词、过去分词或不定式。 2. 英语中有些动词有系动词的用法，可称为半系动词，分为以下四类： （1）表感官: feel, look, taste, sound, smell, notice, hear 等，在表示"……起来怎么样"时，后跟形容词作表语； （2）表状态变化: get, turn, become, grow, make, come, go, fall, run 等； （3）表状态依旧: remain, stay, keep, stand, continue, rest, lie, hold 等； （4）表好像/似乎：seem, appear 等。

3. 从句作主干（在宾语从句、主语从句和表语从句的构成中，括号中内容表示从句与主句的关系）

（1）宾语从句

	宾语从句
构成	宾语从句 =（主句谓语动词 / 介词 / 特殊形容词 /doing/to do+）引导词 + 陈述句
实例	Many argue that it is a flawed concept. 许多人认为它是一个有缺陷的概念。【英语（一）2017 Text 3】
结构	该句的宾语从句 =（主句谓语动词 argue +）引导词 that + 陈述句（it is a flawed concept），句中谓语动词 argue 之后紧接着出现 that 引导的宾语从句。
说明	1. 考研英语中，宾语从句常常省略 that，详见标准篇省略结构。 2. 常考查的是动词后的宾语从句和介词后的宾语从句。 3. 不只是及物的谓语动词之后会接宾语从句，及物的非谓语动词 doing 或 to do 之后也会接宾语从句。

（2）主语从句

	主语从句
构成	主语从句 = 引导词 + 陈述句（+ 主句谓语动词 + 其他）
实例	That the seas are being overfished has been known for years. 众所周知，多年以来，海洋鱼类被过度捕捞。【英语（一）2006 Text 3】
结构	该句的主语从句 = 引导词 That + 陈述句（the seas are being overfished）（+ 主句谓语动词 has been known + 介词短语 for years），句中 That 为引导词，引导一个主语从句作主语，在从句结束之后主句的谓语动词随之出现。
说明	1. 引导词 that 即使不作成分，也不能省略。 2. 表示"是否"时，只能用 whether，不能用 if。 3. 实际上，为避免句子头重脚轻，考研英语中通常将主语从句后置，而用形式主语 it 来代替真正的主语。一般以两种形式出现： （1）It is/was + 过去分词 + 主语从句（如，It is said/suggested that...） （2）It + 系动词 + *adj./n.*+ 主语从句（如，It is strange/a pity that...）

（3）表语从句

	表语从句
构成	表语从句 =（主句系动词 +）引导词 + 陈述句
实例	The lesson from dams is that big is not always beautiful. 建造水坝的教训是：大的未必就美。【英语（一）1998 Passage 1】
结构	该句的表语从句 =（主句系动词 is +）引导词 that + 陈述句（big is not always beautiful），句中系动词 is 之后紧接着出现 that 引导的表语从句。
说明	考研英语中，对表语从句的考查难度不大，掌握其用法即可。

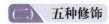 **五种修饰**

1. 定语

（1）简单定语

	分类	举例
前置定语	形容词作前置定语	an interesting story 一个有趣的故事
	限定词作前置定语	another room 另一个房间
	名词所有格作前置定语	the author's name 作者的名字
	代词作前置定语	her bicycle 她的自行车
	动名词作前置定语	a swimming pool 一个游泳池
	现在分词作前置定语	a developing country 发展中国家
	过去分词作前置定语	fallen leaves 落叶
后置定语	不定式作后置定语	the way to solve the problem 解决问题的办法
	现在分词短语作后置定语	a boy playing the football 一个踢足球的男孩
	过去分词短语作后置定语	something needed for the meeting 会议需要的东西
	介词短语作后置定语	the memory of my childhood 我童年的记忆
说明	1. 定语修饰名词或代词。 2. 后置定语在很多情况下可以改写为定语从句。（如：a boy playing the football = a boy who is playing the football）	

（2）定语从句

　　定语从句在主句中充当定语，相当于一个形容词，修饰限定名词或代词，放在所修饰的名词或代词之后。

		定语从句
要点		1. 定语从句的每一个关系词都在句中作成分，包括 that。 2. 限定性定语从句的关系词在某些情况下可以省略，详见标准篇省略结构。
限定性定语从句	构成	先行词 n./pron. + 关系词 + 陈述句
	实例	There will eventually come a day when *The New York Times* ceases to publish stories on newsprint. 终有一天，《纽约时报》会停止发行印刷版报纸。【英语（一）2016 Text 4】
	结构	先行词（a day）+ 关系词（when）+ 陈述句（*The New York Times* ceases to publish stories on newsprint），句中 when 引导的定语从句修饰 a day；when 在定语从句中作时间状语。

非限定性定语从句	构成	先行词 *n./pron.* + ⟨,⟩ + 关系词 + 陈述句
	实例	The crash of EgyptAir Flight 804, which terrorists may have downed over the Mediterranean Sea, provides another tragic reminder of why. 埃及航空 804 号航班疑遭恐怖分子袭击，坠毁于地中海，这一悲剧再次提醒人们为什么必须进行安检。【英语（一）2017 Text 1】
	结构	先行词（EgyptAir Flight 804）+ ⟨,⟩ + 关系词（which）+ 陈述句（terrorists may have downed over the Mediterranean Sea），这一定语从句对先行词 EgyptAir Flight 804 起补充说明作用。关系词 which 在定语从句中作宾语，代替 EgyptAir Flight 804。
重要说明		1. 限定性和非限定性定语从句的区别首先在于是否有逗号。 2. 本质区别在于先行词的范围是否明确，是否真的需要限定（限定的意思就是修饰）。 3. 非限定性定语从句中关系词不能用 that，且关系词不能省略。 4. 考研英语的试题中，非限定性定语从句往往较易辨析。

2. 状语

（1）简单状语

分类	举例
地点状语	I live in Xi'an. 我住在西安。（介词短语作地点状语）
时间状语	He was born in 1996. 他于 1996 年出生。（介词短语作时间状语）
伴随状语	The dog entered the room, following his master. 这条狗跟着主人进了屋。（现在分词短语作伴随状语）
目的状语	She got up early to arrive on time. 为了准时到达，她起得很早。（动词不定式短语作目的状语）
原因状语	They stop the project for the lack of money. 由于缺乏资金，他们终止了这个项目。（介词短语作原因状语）
结果状语	They left together, leaving me alone. 他们一起离开了，留下我一个人。（现在分词短语作结果状语）
条件状语（从句）	If it rains tomorrow, we won't go on a picnic. 如果明天下雨，我们就不去野餐了。（条件状语一般是以从句的形式出现，If 引导的条件状语从句表示在某种条件下某事可能发生）
比较状语	My sister is taller than me. 我姐姐比我高。（介词短语作比较状语）
方式状语	You can't do it in this way. 你不能这样做（这件事）。（介词短语作方式状语）
让步状语	Having been told many times, he still made the same mistake. 即使被告知了很多次，他仍然犯同样的错误。（现在分词短语作让步状语）

说明	1. 状语修饰动词、形容词、副词和句子。 2. 状语分为时间、地点、目的、结果、方式、比较、让步、原因、条件及伴随十类。

(2) 状语从句

一个句子作状语，补充说明句中的某个成分，可修饰动词、形容词、副词或句子，相当于一个副词。值得注意的是，作状语的句子表达的是"描述性的信息"。状语从句的种类则是由其从属连词（即引导词）来决定的，从属连词表示什么关系，从句就是什么类别的状语从句。

时间状语从句	
构成	时间状语从句 = 引导词（when, while, as, until, before, since, as soon as 等）+ 陈述句
实例	Most of us give in to a demoralization of spirit which we usually blame on some psychological conditions, until one day we find ourselves in a garden and feel the oppression vanish as if by magic. 大多数人会陷入精神萎靡的状态，并常常将此归咎于某些心理疾病，直到有一天置身花园，才顿觉压抑感好像神奇地消失了。【英语（一）2013 翻译】
结构	主句（Most of us give in to a demoralization of spirit which we usually blame on some psychological conditions）+ 引导词（until）+ 陈述句（one day we find ourselves in a garden and feel the oppression vanish as if by magic），句中 until 表示"直到……的时候"。
说明	1. 考研英语中，until 和 not until 是常考点。not until 引导时间状语从句，位于句首时，主句要倒装。 2. since 引导时间状语从句时，后面必须跟一个时间点，不能是一段时间。 3. while 引导时间状语从句，意为"正在做"，从句谓语的动作与主句谓语的动作同时发生，因此 while 后面常用进行时态。

地点状语从句	
构成	地点状语从句 = 引导词（where, wherever, anywhere, everywhere 等）+ 陈述句
实例	The Conservatives' planning reform explicitly gives rural development priority over conservation, even authorising "off-plan" building where local people might object. 保守党的规划改革明确表示，发展乡村应优先于保护乡村，甚至批准在当地村民可能会反对的地方进行"计划外"建设。【英语（一）2016 Text 2】
结构	主句（The Conservatives' planning reform explicitly gives rural development priority over conservation）+ 伴随状语（even authorising "off-plan"

	building）+ 引导词（where）+ 陈述句（local people might object），where 引导的地点状语从句修饰现在分词短语 authorising "off-plan" building，表示"在……地方"。
说明	1. 考研英语中地点状语从句考查较少。 2. 区分 where 引导的地点状语从句和定语从句：定语从句有先行词，而状语从句没有。

原因状语从句	
构成	原因状语从句 = 引导词（because, as, since, for, now that, in that 等）+ 陈述句
实例	That is no longer a problem, because there are fewer sharks around now. 但现在不会了，因为周围的鲨鱼变少了。【英语（一）2006 Text 3】
结构	主句（That is no longer a problem）+ 引导词（because）+ 陈述句（there are fewer sharks around now），because 表示"因为，由于"。
说明	1. because，as，for，in that 意为"因为，由于"；since，now that 意为"既然"。考研英语中不必详细区分，只需明白意思即可。 2. now that 引导原因状语从句，表示显而易见的事实，从句必须置于主句之前。

结果状语从句	
构成	结果状语从句 = 引导词（so...that, such...that, so that 等）+ 陈述句
实例	Indeed, homelessness has reached such proportions that local governments can't possibly cope. 事实上，无家可归者的数量已达到如此规模，以至于地方政府都无法应对。【英语（一）2006 完形】
结构	主句（homelessness has reached such proportions）+ 引导词（that）+ 陈述句（local governments can't possibly cope），句中 such...that 表示"太……以至于……"。
说明	1. so + *adj./adv.* + that，such + *n.* + that。 2. 该句型中，当 so + *adj./adv.* 或 such + *n.* 位于句首时，主句要部分倒装。以上述实例为例，需倒装为：Such proportions has homelessness reached that local governments can't possibly cope。

目的状语从句	
构成	目的状语从句 = 引导词（so that, in order that, so as that, in case, lest, for fear that 等）+ 陈述句
实例	In December 2010 America's Federal Trade Commission (FTC) proposed adding a "do not track" (DNT) option to internet browsers, so that users could tell advertisers that they did not want to be followed. 2010 年 12 月，美国联邦贸易委员会建议在互联网浏览器上添加"禁止追踪"选项，以便用户告知广告商他们不想被追踪。【英语（一）2013 Text 2】

结构	主句（In December 2010 America's Federal Trade Commission（FTC）proposed adding a "do not track"（DNT）option to internet browsers）+ 引导词（so that）+ 陈述句（users could tell advertisers that they did not want to be followed），句中 so that 意为"以便，以致"。
说明	1. so that... 既可以表示目的，又可以表示结果。区别的标准是，如果从句中有情态动词，则表示目的，如果没有情态动词，则表示结果。 2. in case，for fear that 意为"以防万一"，考研英语中考查较少。

条件状语从句

构成	条件状语从句 = 引导词（if, unless, on condition that, supposing, provided, as long as 等）+ 陈述句
实例	If we're ever going to protect the atmosphere, it is crucial that those new plants be environmentally sound. 如果我们要保护大气，那么确保这些新发电厂对环境无害就至关重要了。【英语（一）2005 Text 2】
结构	引导词（If）+ 陈述句（we're ever going to protect the atmosphere）+ 主句（it is crucial that those new plants be environmentally sound），If 引导的从句对主句进行假设，设定条件。
说明	1. if引导的条件状语从句若表示与事实相反的情况，需使用虚拟语气。 2. 考研英语中对该类从句的考查较常见，其中 if 从句是考查重点。

让步状语从句

构成	让步状语从句 = 引导词（though, although, as, even though, even if, whatever, while 等）+ 陈述句
实例	Although the figure may vary, analysts do agree on another matter... 尽管大家估计的数字可能各不相同，但分析家们对另外一个问题的看法却是一致的……【英语（一）2006 完形】
结构	引导词（Although）+ 陈述句（the figure may vary）+ 主句（analysts do agree on another matter）。Although 在句中表示"尽管"，这里可以用 Though, Even though, Even if 替换。
说明	1. as引导的让步状语从句必须倒装。 2. though 引导的让步状语从句可以倒装，也可以不倒装。 3. although，even though，even if 引导的让步状语从句不能倒装。 4. 考研英语对该类从句的考查较常见。

比较状语从句

构成	比较状语从句 = 引导词（as...as, not as/so...as, more than, than 等）+ 陈述句（或倒装句）

实例	Foreign-born Asians and Hispanics "have higher rates of intermarriage than do U.S.-born whites and blacks". 在外国出生的亚裔和西班牙裔人"比美国出生的白人和黑人有更高的异族通婚率"。【英语（一）2006 Text 1】
结构	主句（Foreign-born Asians and Hispanics "have higher rates of intermarriage）+ 引导词（than）+ 倒装句（do U.S.-born whites and blacks"）。从句使用了倒装，原语序为：U.S.-born whites and blacks do。
说明	1. as...as 表示比较的结果、程度相等。 2. not as/so...as 意为"不如……"。 3. 在 than 引导的比较状语从句中，有时会出现主谓倒装现象。

方式状语从句	
构成	方式状语从句 = 引导词（as, as if, as though 等）+ 陈述句
实例	If software promises to save lives on the scale that drugs now can, big data may be expected to behave as a big pharma has done. 如果软件有可能达到目前药物挽救生命的那种程度，那么大数据也有望像大型制药公司那样行事。【英语（一）2018 Text 3】
结构	条件状语从句（If software promises to save lives on the scale that drugs now can）+ 主句（big data may be expected to behave）+ 引导词（as）+ 陈述句（a big pharma has done），as 意为"像……一样"。
说明	1. as if, as though 意义完全相同，意为"似乎，好像"，二者可以互相替换。 2. 考研英语中方式状语从句的考查较少。

重要说明：as 作为从属连词，在考研英语对状语从句的考查中，一般有四种用法，它可以引导时间、原因、比较及方式四种状语从句。如要具体判断它代表何种含义，则需根据句意判定。但需要注意的是，它常常容易和定语从句的用法混淆。判断标准是：只要 as 后是完整的句子，那么它引导的一定是状语从句；而如果 as 后不是完整的句子，并且 as 在句中作成分，那么它引导的一定是定语从句。

3. 同位语

（1）简单同位语

举例	Bob, a critical reader, ...（鲍伯，一个批判型的读者……）	名词短语 a critical reader 作同位语，对主语 Bob 进行补充说明。
说明	1. 同位语对名词或代词进行补充说明，而不是进行修饰。 2. 很多同位语可以改写成一个主系表结构的句子。（如：Bob is a critical reader.） 3. 在考研英语中，对同位语的考查大多比较简单。	

（2）同位语从句

同位语从句	
构成	同位语从句＝（名词＋）引导词＋陈述句
实例	The idea that some groups of people may be more intelligent than others is one of those hypotheses that dare not speak its name. 人类的某些族群可能比其他族群智商更高，这一观点是众多不敢明说的假设之一。【英语（一）2008 完形】
结构	该句的同位语从句＝（名词 idea ＋）引导词 that ＋陈述句（some groups of people may be more intelligent than others）。
说明	1. 引导词 that 不作成分，但不能省略。 2. 放在抽象名词后，如：fact, news, idea, opinion, promise, evidence, question, doubt, reason, theory, belief, possibility, chance, hope, contention, guarantee, principle 等，对该名词内容进行补充说明。

4. 插入语

分类	举例
形容词（短语）作插入语	Wonderful, we have won again. 太好了，我们又赢了。
副词（短语）作插入语	This book, however, is not so interesting. 然而，这本书并不是很有趣。
介词（短语）作插入语	The new novel written by J. K. Rowling, of course, sells well. 当然，J. K. 罗琳的新书卖得很好。
分词（短语）作插入语	Generally speaking, I dislike you. 说实话，我不喜欢你。
短句作插入语	What you told me, I believe, is the truth. 我相信你告诉我的是事实。
不定式（短语）作插入语	The dishes in this restaurant, to be honest, taste terrible. 说实话，这家餐厅的菜很难吃。
说明	1. 插入语可以是一个词，一个短语，也可以是一个句子。 2. 有时插入语也会由特殊标点符号引出，这类现象详见本章五大标点部分的讲解。

5. 补语

分类	举例
主语补足语	That boy was asked to leave right now. 那个男孩被要求立刻离开。
宾语补足语	I saw my brother riding a bike in the park. 我看见我哥哥在公园骑车。

表语补足语	The driving license is really hard to get. 驾照很难拿到。
说明	1. 补语是对句子主语、宾语或表语的补充说明，通常与其说明的对象有逻辑上的主谓关系。 2. 考研英语中最常见的是宾语补足语，偶尔会出现表语补足语和主语补足语。

（三） 五大标点

1. 逗号

逗号	
概念	英语中逗号","表示句子的停顿，同类成分或逗号前后成分的分隔，及对前文内容的解释（补充）说明。要注意，与汉语不同，英语中逗号不能表示一句话的结束。
实例	In the last decade or so , advances in technology have allowed mass-market labels such as Zara , H&M , and Uniqlo to react to trends more quickly and anticipate demand more precisely. 在过去十年间，技术的进步使得大众品牌，比如 Zara、H&M 和优衣库能够快速地对时尚趋势做出反应，也能更准确地预测（消费者的）需求。【英语（一）2013 Text 1】
结构	时间状语（In the last decade or so）+ 逗号 + 主语（advances in technology）+ 谓语（have allowed）+ 宾语（mass-market labels）+ 由逗号分隔的列举内容（such as...）+ 宾语补足语（to react to trends more quickly and anticipate demand more precisely），第一个逗号分隔时间状语与主句；后面几个逗号分隔列举的品牌，表示并列。
说明	逗号用于以下情况： 1. 表示停顿，用于称呼、语气词等之后。 2. 表示分隔，用于分隔同类成分或逗号前后的成分；本书中前后成分的分隔着重讲解插入语。 3. 表示对前文内容的解释（补充）说明，本书中着重讲解同位语。 注：因逗号表示句子的停顿或同类成分的分隔这两类情况较为常见且易于识别，故我们在本书的实例中不作具体的讲解和划分，而着重讲解逗号对前后成分的分隔及对前文内容的解释（补充）说明。

2. 分号

分号	
概念	分号";"用来分隔并列的句子。
实例	Microsoft's Internet Explorer and Apple's Safari both offer DNT ; Google's Chrome is due to do so this year. 微软的 IE 浏览器和苹果的 Safari

	浏览器都提供"禁止追踪"选项；谷歌浏览器 Chrome 今年也将提供同样的功能。【英语（一）2013 Text 2】
结构	主语 1（Microsoft's Internet Explorer and Apple's Safari）+ 谓语（offer）+ 宾语（DNT）+ 分号 + 主语 2（Google's Chrome）+ 系动词（is）+ 表语（due）+ 表语补足语（to do so），这里分号连接了两个并列分句，相当于一个并列连词。注意：这里的分号不能用逗号替换，如要替换，必须用逗号 + 并列连词。
说明	分号用于以下情况： 1. 用于连接并列句，有分号时不需要并列连词。 2. 并列句中，若句子本身有逗号，为避免歧义，各句子之间用分号连接。

3. 破折号

	破折号
概念	破折号"—"常用来表示解释说明或概括。考研英语中破折号较常见，要熟悉其用法。
实例	Americans, she finds, buy roughly 20 billion garments a year —about 64 items per person —and no matter how much they give away, this excess leads to waste. 她发现，美国人每年大约购买 200 亿件衣服——平均每人约 64 件——且不管他们捐出多少，这种过剩也会造成浪费。【英语（一）2013 Text 1】
结构	简单句（Americans, she finds, buy roughly 20 billion garments a year）+ 破折号 + 插入语（about 64 items per person）+ 破折号 + 并列连词（and）+ 复合句（no matter how much they give away, this excess leads to waste.），两个破折号之间的插入语对简单句的内容进行解释说明，这里的破折号可以用括号替换。
说明	破折号用于以下情况： 1. 用于一个解释性分句或句子之前。 2. 用于解释性插入语的前后（相当于括号）。 3. 概括前面列举的内容。

4. 冒号

	冒号
概念	冒号":"的用法较多，但在考研英语中冒号不作为考查重点，了解其用法即可。
实例	These issues all have root causes in human behavior: all require behavioral change and social innovations, as well as technological development. 造成这些问题的根本原因都在于人类行为：所有这些问题的解决都需要通过行为方式的改变、社会创新以及技术发展。【英语（一）2013 新题型】

结构	主语（These issues）+ 谓语（have）+ 宾语（root causes），副词 all 修饰谓语；冒号后面的句子解释说明冒号前内容，该句子的主语是 all，谓语是 require。and 和 as well as 连接并列的宾语 behavioral change，social innovations 和 technological development。
说明	冒号用于以下情况： 1. 用于介绍或解释前面的内容。 2. 用于直接引语前，比逗号、破折号更正式。 3. 用于名单或列表之前。 4. 考研英语中常见前两种情况。

5. 括号

括号	
概念	括号 "（ ）" 常表示附加的解释说明。
实例	The bans, if fully enforced, would suggest to women (and many men) that they should not let others be arbiters of their beauty. 这些禁令如果得以全面执行，将提醒女性（以及许多男性）不应让他人决定自己的美丑。【英语（一）2016 Text 1】
结构	主语（The bans）+ 插入语（if fully enforced）+ 谓语（would suggest）+ 状语1（to women）+ 括号 + 状语2（and many men）+ 宾语从句（that...），括号中内容表示附加的说明。
说明	括号用于以下情况： 1. 用于表示附加的解释说明（单词、短语、不定式、现在分词、句子等）。 2. 考研英语中括号较少出现。

（二）破解长难句的一大要害：寻找真正的谓语动词

通常我们认为，句子中出现了倒装、省略、虚拟等特定的语法现象致使句子很难。实际上，在考研英语中，倒装、省略以及虚拟是较少出现的，而真正的长难句是因为句中出现了多个动词，我们却无法辨别真正的谓语动词是什么。

比如下面这个来源于考研英语真题的句子：Today no such severe lack exists as that ordered by Frederick.（1993 Text 1）这是一个包含了 11 个单词的句子，除去人名 Frederick 之外，剩余的 10 个单词基本都属于四级词汇。可是并非所有的同学都能很快判断出句子的大致要义，原因就在于大家无法快速判断出句子的谓语动词到底是 lack、exists 还是 ordered。换一种思路来看，如果 lack 是谓语，那么 exists 和 ordered 分别在句中作什么成分？或者如果 exists 是谓语，那么 lack 和 ordered 分别又在句中作什么成分？经过这样的一个思考过程，我们发现一个短小的句子瞬间就升级成了难句。而在考研英语中，还存在着很多又长又难的句子，但无论怎么样，找到真正的谓语动词是攻克长难句的关键所在。

容易与真正的谓语动词混淆的词有两种：1. 非谓语动词；2. 很像真正的谓语动词的词。

（一）如何辨析谓语动词与非谓语动词

考研英语中，存在着大量的非谓语动词。非谓语动词，顾名思义就是在句中不作谓语的动词。我们之所以容易将非谓语动词与真正的谓语动词混淆，是因为它的表现形式，尤其当它以过去分词的形式出现的时候，最容易混淆视听。

类别	表现形式		具体情况说明
非谓语动词	1. to do		一定不是主干谓语动词
	2. doing		一定不是主干谓语动词（其前面必须出现 be 或其变体，才可以作主干谓语动词）
	3. 过去分词	拼法同过去式	前面有冠词、系动词或该过去分词修饰其前后的名词、代词，一定不是主干谓语动词。如果该动词是缺失宾语的及物动词，那么它就不是主干谓语动词；如果该动词后面有宾语，但是前面有从句标志词，那么它也不是主干谓语动词；如果该动词后面有宾语，但前面无从句标志词，那么它就是主干谓语动词。
		拼法不同于过去式	一定不是主干谓语动词（其前面必须加上 have，构成 have done；或者出现 be，构成被动才可以作主干谓语动词）

下列例句及其分析具体体现了如何辨析谓语动词与非谓语动词。

to do	
实例	"It's just that they have so much more to cope with," says Dr. Yehuda. "只是她们有更多的压力要应对，"耶胡达博士说。【英语（一）2008 Text 1】
分析	句中动词有 is，have，cope with 和 says，但 cope with 前有 to，是动词不定式，故不是谓语动词。

doing	
实例 1	Most tests require collecting cells by swabbing saliva in the mouth and sending it to the company for testing. 大部分鉴定需要拭取口中唾液来收集细胞，然后送到公司做鉴定。【英语（一）2009 Text 2】

分析	句中动词有 require，collecting，swabbing，sending 和 testing，其中后四个分别是 collect，swab，send 和 test 的 -ing 形式，均为动名词，故都不是谓语动词。
实例 2	It is financially terrifying, psychologically embarrassing... 它（失业）是经济上的劫难、心理上的尴尬……【英语（一）2014 Text 1】
分析	句中动词有 is，terrifying 和 embarrassing。其中 terrifying 和 embarrassing 均为形容词，故都不是谓语动词。

过去分词	
实例 1	..., a society designed with other ends in mind could yield strikingly different circumstances for... ……一个以其他目的为设计理念的社会可能使……产生截然不同的境况。【英语（二）2017 完形】
分析	句中动词有 designed 和 could yield。其中及物动词 designed 后没有宾语，故它不是过去式形式的谓语动词，而是过去分词，因此不是谓语动词。
实例 2	...that such a theory would be a simplification, given the dimensions and universes... 考虑到……的范围和领域，这样的理论是否会是一个简化的程序……【英语（一）2012 翻译】
分析	句中动词有 would be 和 given。其中 given 的拼法不同于过去式，其前没有 have 或 be，故为过去分词，不是谓语动词。

（二）如何辨析真假谓语动词

1. 什么情况下会出现假的谓语动词

有一类动词，它本身也可以作谓语动词，但却不是真正的主干谓语动词。这类动词比非谓语动词更难以区分，因为我们从形式上无法辨别。我们需要思考的问题是，在什么情况下会出现这类与"真正"相对的假的谓语动词，后者又呈现出什么特点呢？

我们先看一个例句，也许会从中得到启发。例如：The truth I know is unfair. 该句中出现了两个谓语动词 know 和 is。为什么会出现两个谓语动词？到底哪一个才是真正的谓语动词呢？仔细分析之后发现，know 是及物动词且缺失宾语，所以它肯定不是主干谓语动词。因为，如果它是主干的谓语动词，动词结构必须是完整的，而不应该有缺失宾语的情况出现。所以，此句中的 know 应该是从句的谓语动词，而主干的谓语动词应是系动词 is。可见，I know 之前实际上省略了从句标志词 that，显然该从句是定语从句。

如上所述，在从句标志词被省略的情况下，会出现两个或两个以上的谓语动词，那么其中必有一个是真正的谓语动词，而另外一个或多个必然是很像真正的谓语动词的动词，也就是假的谓语动词。

我们再看一个例句，可能会对这个结论有更深刻的认识。例如：My mother knew I left home early today. 该句中出现了两个谓语动词 knew 和 left，那么必定有一个是真正的谓语动词。knew 是及物动词，但其后是一个完整的主谓宾结构 I left home，说明其作 knew 的宾语，因此它是省略 that 的宾语从句，left 是从句的谓语动词，而 knew 则是主句的谓语动词。

可见，在从句标志词被省略的情况下，会出现假的谓语动词，而这又分了以下几种情况。

(1) 定语从句标志词被省略

传统语法书中对定语从句标志词的省略情况是这样描述的：如果定语从句标志词被省略，那么该定语从句一定缺宾语，比如会缺失及物动词的宾语或介词的宾语，而宾语从句标志词省略和表语从句标志词省略则不会出现这种情况。也就是说，如果发现一个句子缺宾语，那么就要考虑是不是存在定语从句标志词被省略的情况。

一方面，需要考虑动词宾语缺失的情况。如果我们发现某一句话中有多个动词，而某个动词是及物动词，但后面又没有宾语跟随，那么这个动词肯定就是假的谓语动词，也就是说它一定不是主干谓语动词，这种情况很有可能是定语从句标志词被省略了，那么该动词所在的从句则为定语从句。

举例	The book I bought yesterday costs 50 yuan. 我昨天买的那本书花费了 50 元。
分析	句中有两个动词：bought 和 costs。其中 bought 是及物动词，但后面缺失了宾语，因此它是假的谓语动词，costs 才是主干谓语动词。实际上，I bought 是省略关系词 that/which 的定语从句，修饰 The book，关系词代替先行词 The book 作 bought 的宾语，bought 是该定语从句的谓语动词。

另一方面，需要考虑介词宾语缺失的情况。如果某个介词后缺失宾语，那么与该介词搭配的动词就肯定不是主干谓语动词，而该动词所在的从句则为定语从句。

举例	We like the city we went to for holiday last year. 我们喜欢我们去年去度假的那个城市。
分析	句中有两个动词：like 和 went to。其中 to 后面缺失了宾语，那么 went to 肯定是假的谓语动词，则 like 是主干谓语动词。实际上，we went to 是省略关系词 that/which 的定语从句，修饰 the city，关系词代替先行词 the city 作 went to 的宾语，went to 是该定语从句的谓语动词。

另外，当关系副词 when、where 和 why 引导定语从句时，在某些情况下也可以省略：当定语从句的先行词为 day, year 或 time 等少数几个词时，可以省略 when（也可将其换成 that）。如：I will never forget the day (when) I met her. 该句中出现了两个动词 will never forget 和 met。句中名词 day 后面是完整的主谓宾结构 I met her，因此这是省略 when 的定语从句，修饰 the day，met 是该定语从句的谓语动词，则 will never forget 是主干的谓语动词。

当定语从句的先行词为 place, somewhere, anywhere, everywhere 以及 nowhere 等少数几个词时，可以省略 where（也可将其换成 that）。如：The place (where) I grew up has changed a lot. 该句中出现了两个动词 grew up 和 has changed。句中名词 place 之后是完整的主谓结构 I grew up，因此这是省略 where 的定语从句，修饰 The place，grew up 是该定语从句的谓语动词，则 has changed 是主干的谓语动词。

当关系副词 why 位于 the reason 后引导定语从句时，可以省略 why。如：This is the reason (why) she did it. 该句中出现了两个动词 is 和 did。reason 之后的 she did it 是完整的主谓宾结构，因此这是省略 why 的定语从句，修饰 the reason，did 是该定语从句的谓语动词，则 is 是主干的系动词。

因为这类先行词极具辨识度，所以如果遇到这类省略情况，一般都可以直接依据先行词来给句子定性。下列例句具体体现了如何判断这种情况。

举例 1	That is the time every child rushed home after school to watch cartoons on TV. 那是一段每个孩子放学后急忙冲回家中在电视机上看动画片的时光。
分析	句中有三个动词：is, rushed 和 watch。其中 watch 前有 to，是动词不定式，不能作谓语动词；名词 time 之后的 every child rushed home 是完整的主谓结构，因此这是省略 when 的定语从句，修饰 time，rushed 是该从句的谓语动词；则 is 是主句的系动词。
举例 2	She visited the place she spent her childhood last month. 上个月，她参观了她度过童年的地方。
分析	句中有两个动词：visited 和 spent。名词 place 之后的 she spent her child-hood 是完整的主谓宾结构，因此这是省略 where 的定语从句，修饰 the place，spent 是该从句的谓语动词；则 visited 是主句的谓语动词。

（2）宾语从句标志词被省略及表语从句标志词被省略

从理论上来讲，宾语从句和表语从句都出现在主句的后面，所以判定方法是位于句子前面的是主干谓语动词，而位于句子后面的是从句的谓语动词。至于到底是宾从还是表从，只需判定主干谓语动词是不是系动词。如果不是系动词，则为宾从；而如果是系动词，则为表从。

举例1	The old man believes everything happens for a reason. 这位老人相信凡事皆有起因。
分析	句中有两个动词：believes 和 happens。believes 在前，因此它是主干的谓语动词；happens 则是省略 that 的宾语从句 everything happens for a reason 的谓语动词。
举例2	The truth is everyone can perform the magic by practice. 事实是每个人经过训练都可以表演魔术。
分析	句中有两个动词：is 和 can perform。is 在前，因此它是主干的系动词；can perform 则是省略 that 的表语从句 everyone can perform the magic by practice 的谓语动词。

2. 如何辨析真假谓语动词

我们把上述情况再捋一遍：如果定语从句的标志词被省略，那么就会出现缺失宾语的及物动词，或者与缺失宾语的介词相搭配的动词。反过来讲，如果我们发现句中出现了缺失宾语的及物动词，以及与缺失宾语的介词相搭配的动词，我们就可以肯定这是省略了定语从句标志词的情况，而这两类动词一定不是主干谓语动词，直接删除即可。如果能够通过特殊先行词定性定语从句，那么该从句中的动词也可删除。而宾语从句和表语从句的标志词如果被省略，那么位置最前的动词即为主干谓语动词。

综上所述，主干谓语动词的判断方法如下：1. 删除缺失宾语的及物动词和与缺失宾语的介词相搭配的动词；2. 删除可以通过特殊先行词定性的定语从句中的动词；3. 在剩余动词中，位置最前者即为主干谓语动词。

举例1	The news reported the place my mother saw the sea for the first time has been polluted heavily. 报道说，我妈妈第一次看海的那个地方已经遭到了严重污染。
分析	句中有三个动词：reported, saw 和 has been polluted。其中名词 place 后的 my mother saw the sea 是完整的主谓宾结构，则该句是省略 where 的定语从句，修饰 the place，saw 是该从句的谓语动词，可直接删除；剩余两个动词，reported 在前，则它是主干的谓语动词；has been polluted 是省略 that 的宾语从句的谓语动词。
举例2	The writer says the most beautiful view she had ever seen is the Great Wall. 这位作家说她曾经看过的最美的风景就是长城。
分析	句中有三个动词：says, had seen 和 is。其中 had seen 后面缺失了宾语，那么它肯定是假的谓语动词，故删除；在剩余的两个动词中，says 在前，则它是主干谓语动词；says 之后的句子作它的宾语，则 is 是 says 之后省略 that 的宾语从句的系动词。

（一）从句标志词没有被省略

从句前一般都会有从句标志词，即引导词（定语从句中一般称之为关系词），因此若一个谓语动词前有从句标志词，那么该动词就不是主干的谓语动词，而是从句的谓语动词。在考研英语中，主要考查的是陈述句，而疑问句和否定句考查得较少，所以我们重点介绍陈述句中的各种情况。

在陈述句中，如果出现从句标志词，那么在从句标志词之后，距离它最近的动词，就一定是从句的谓语动词，而不是主干部分的谓语动词。

实例 1	It is not yet clear how advertisers will respond. 广告商们对此做何回应，现在还不得而知。【英语（一）2013 Text 2】
分析	从句标志词为 how，而其后最近的动词为 will respond，说明 will respond 是从句的谓语动词。
实例 2	If good people do nothing, there is a real possibility... 如果好人无所作为，就有可能……【英语（一）2003 Text 2】
分析	从句标志词为 If，而其后最近的动词为 do，说明 do 是从句的谓语动词。
实例 3	It also means that governments are increasingly compelled to interfere in these sectors... 这也意味着：政府必须逐步加大对这些行业的干预力度……【英语（一）2000 翻译】
分析	从句标志词为 that，而其后最近的动词为 are compelled，说明它是从句的谓语动词。
实例 4	It was argued at the end of the 19th century that humans do not cry because they are sad... 19 世纪末还有人认为，人们不是因为悲伤而哭泣……【英语（一）2011 完形】
分析	从句标志词为 that 和 because，而其后最近的动词分别是 do not cry 和 are，说明它们分别是两个从句的谓语动词。
说明	上述各个例句均是从句，且出现了从句标志词，它们之后最近的动词无论是单一动词（do；are）还是复合动词（will respond；are compelled；do not cry），都是从句的谓语动词和系动词。

为了找到主干的谓语动词，进而确定主干部分，我们可考虑先将从句整体剥离，然后再单独分析从句。剥离的方法很简单，极易操作。如果知道从句在何处切分，自不必说；如果不知道从句断在哪里，可先找到从句标志词，然后找到距离该标志词最近的动词，并判断其后是否有宾语或表语，若有，至此断开；若无，则至动词断开。但仍存在一些特殊情况，我们会在【难句破解】部分具体讲解。例如，上述例句就可以剥离如下：

实例1	It is not yet clear...（is 为主干系动词，clear 作其表语）
实例2	..., there is a real possibility...（is 为主干系动词，a real possibility 作主语） 这是一个 there be 句型：there + be + 主语
实例3	It also means...（means 为主干谓语动词）
实例4	It was argued...（was argued 为主干谓语动词）

（二） 从句标志词被省略

通过上一节的分析，我们知道如果从句标志词被省略，那么就会出现假的谓语动词。也就是说，该部分实际上与辨析真假谓语动词部分论证内容相同，故此处不再赘述。

四 破解长难句的三个步骤

（一） 三个步骤

经过上述三部分的理论分析，我们知道破解长难句也是有法可循的，具体说来，可遵循以下三个步骤：

1. 找从句标志词，并剥离该从句；
2. 识别非谓语动词，同时删除非谓语动词结构及其它修饰成分；
3. 识别并删除很像谓语动词的动词。

注：对于长难句中会出现直接引语这种特殊情况，我们将在后面的章节中进行分析并以真题实例的形式具体呈现。

（二） 真题实例

我们将通过具体的真题例句将上述步骤给大家分解清楚。

实例 1

So, if the provinces want to run the health-care show, they should prove they can run it, starting with an interprovincial health list that would end duplication, save administrative costs, prevent one province from being played off against another, and bargain for better drug prices. 所以，如果某些省想全权负责医疗保健事业，他们就必须得证明自己有这个能力，首先要开一张省际医疗清单来终止重复，节约管理费用，防止省与省之间的争斗，并争取更优惠的药价。【英语（一）2005 新题型】

找主干	过程	第一步：找从句标志词，并剥离该从句。❶找到第一个标志词 if：距离 if 之后最近的动词是 want，至此将该从句剥离；❷找到第二个标志词 that：距离 that 之后最近的动词是 would end，duplication 作其宾语，并且 and 将其与（would）save，（would）prevent 和（would）bargain 并列连接，其中，administrative costs 和 one province 分别为前两者的宾语，至（would）bargain 将该从句剥离。 第二步：识别非谓语动词，同时删除非谓语动词结构及其它修饰成分。删除非谓语动词结构 to run the health-care show 和 starting with...list；删除修饰成分 from being played off against another 和 for better drug prices。全句还剩下：So, they should prove they can run it。 第三步：识别并删除很像谓语动词的动词。根据辨析真假谓语动词的方法，句中剩下两个动词：should prove 和 can run，而 prove 既没有缺失宾语，也没有与缺失宾语的介词搭配，且它又在 can run 之前，所以 should prove 是主干谓语动词，they can run it 是省略引导词 that 的宾语从句，作 should prove 的宾语，故将该从句剥离。全句剩下了 So, they should prove，这就是句子的主谓部分。
	结果	So, ...they should prove **(that)** they can run it,...（主＋谓＋宾从）省略引导词 that 的宾语从句 **(that)** they can run it（主＋谓＋宾）作谓语 should prove 的宾语，属于主干成分，故将其还原。句首的连词 So 表因果。
理修饰	状从	if 引导条件状语从句 [if] the provinces want to run the health-care show（主＋谓＋宾），其中宾语是动词不定式短语 to run...show。
	状语	第一层：现在分词短语 starting with an interprovincial health list 作方式状语。第二层：that 引导的定语从句 **[that]** would end duplication, save administrative costs, prevent one province from being played off against another, and bargain for better drug prices 修饰 an interprovincial health list，其中 and 连接四个并列的谓语。第三层：介词短语 from being played off against another 和 for better drug prices 均作状语。

---- 实例 2

Instead, we are treated to fine hypocritical spectacles, which now more than ever seem in ample supply: the critic of American materialism with a Southampton summer home; the publisher of radical books who takes his meals in three-star restaurants; the journalist advocating participatory democracy in all phases of life, whose own children are enrolled in private schools. 相反，我们目睹了精心雕琢的虚伪场面，这些虚伪场面似乎比以往任何时候都要多：美国物质主义批评家自己却拥有一幢位于南安普顿的避暑别墅；激进书籍的出版商在三星级餐厅用餐；倡导终生参与民主制度的新闻记者却把自己的子女送进私立学校。【英语（一）2000 Passage 5】

| 找主干 | 过程 | 第一步：找从句标志词，并剥离该从句。❶找到第一个标志词 which：距 which 之后最近的动词是 seem，in ample supply 作其表语，至此将该从句剥离；❷找到第二个标志词 who：距离 who 之后最近的动词是 takes，因 take 是及物动词，故 his meals 是其宾语，至此将该从句剥离；❸找到第三个标志词 whose：距离 whose 之后最近的动词是 are enrolled，至此将该从句剥离。
第二步：识别非谓语动词，同时删除非谓语结构及其它修饰成分。浏览该句子可发现，句中出现了表解释说明的冒号，且冒号后是由两个分号连接的三个并列的名词短语结构，由此可判断，冒号后内容整体上对其前前内容进行解释说明，故可将冒号后内容整体剥离掉。删除其他修饰成分 Instead 和 to fine hypocritical spectacles。全句剩下了 we are treated；这就是句子的主谓部分。
第三步：识别并删除很像谓语动词的动词。（真正的谓语动词已找到，故该步骤略。） |
| | 结果 | ..., we are treated...（主 + 谓） |

理修饰	状语	句首的副词 Instead 作状语，表转折；介词短语 to fine hypocritical spectacles 作方式状语，修饰 are treated。
	定从	which 引导的非限定性定语从句 [which] now more than ever seem in ample supply（主 + 系 + 表）补充说明主句中的 fine hypo-critical spectacles。其中，副词 now 作时间状语，more than ever 作比较状语。
	同位语	第一层：冒号后由分号连接的三个并列的名词短语作 fine hypo-critical spectacles 的同位语，对其进行举例说明。第二层：介词短语 of American materialism 和 with a Southampton summer home 作后置定语，修饰 the critic。介词短语 of radical books 作后置定语，修饰 the publisher；who 引导的定语从句 [who] takes his meals in three-star restaurants（主 + 谓 + 宾）修饰 the publisher，其中介词短语 in three-star restaurants 作地点状语。现在分词短语 advocating...of life 作后置定语，修饰 the journalist，其中介词短语 in all phases of life 作后置定语，修饰 democracy；whose 引导的非限定性定语从句 [whose] own children are enrolled in private schools（主 + 谓）补充说明 the

		journalist，其中介词短语 in private schools 作地点状语。
看标点	冒号	冒号后面三个并列的名词短语结构均是对 fine hypocritical spectacles 的举例说明。
	分号	分号连接了三个并列的名词短语结构：the critic of American materialism with...home；the publisher of radical books who...restaurants 以及 the journalist advocating...schools。

第二章 标准篇

十大必考的难句结构

在第一章我们学习了英语中句子的基本结构，考研英语中常见标点符号的用法，以及如何寻找谓语动词和梳理主从关系。下面我们就以真题为例，来学习英语句子的各种结构，看一看长难句究竟"难"在哪里？我们将按照找主干、理修饰、看标点的原则，探究如何将长难句层层剥离，还原长难句的本来面目。

一 分隔结构

（一）插入式分隔

插入式分隔是由同位语或插入语植入句中所造成的分隔。其中，同位语和前述名词或代词有关，对其进行解释或补充说明，而插入语和前后成分均没有直接关系。

1. 同位语分隔

在考研英语长难句中，对主语、宾语、表语进行解释说明的同位语常被分隔。在出现分隔时，要注意辨别动名词作同位语与现在分词作状语。

实例 1

Two of the three objecting Justices—Samuel Alito and Clarence Thomas—agreed with this Constitutional logic but disagreed about which Arizona rules conflicted with the federal statute. 三位持反对意见的大法官中，有两位——塞缪尔·阿利托和克拉伦斯·托马斯——赞同这一宪法逻辑，但是就亚利桑那州的哪些条例和联邦法冲突这个问题，他们意见不一致。【英语（一）2013 Text 4】

【难句类型】分隔结构 + 平行结构 + 从句　　　　　　　难度：★★★☆

【难句破解】

找主干	过程	第一步：找从句标志词，并剥离该从句。找到标志词 which：距离 which 之后最近的动词是 conflicted with，介词 with 后需跟宾语，故 the federal statute 作其宾语，至此将该从句剥离。

过程	第二步：识别非谓语动词，同时删除非谓语动词结构及其它修饰成分。本句无非谓语动词结构；删除修饰成分 Samuel Alito and Clarence Thomas。全句剩下了 Two of the three objecting Justices agreed with this Constitutional logic but disagreed about，这就是句子的主干部分。 第三步：识别并删除很像谓语动词的动词。（真正的谓语动词已找到，故该步骤略。）
结果	Two of the three objecting Justices...agreed with this Constitutional logic but disagreed about [which] Arizona rules...（主＋谓1＋宾＋but＋谓2＋宾从） but 连接并列的谓宾，表转折，其中 which 引导的宾语从句 [which] Arizona rules conflicted with the federal statute（主＋谓＋宾）作 disagreed about 的宾语，是主干成分，故还原。
理修饰 同位语	两个破折号中间的 Samuel Alito and Clarence Thomas 作 Two of the three objecting Justices 的同位语，对其进行解释说明。
看标点 破折号	破折号将同位语分隔出来，表示解释说明。

【结构分析】

一级修饰　　—Samuel Alito and Clarence Thomas—

　　　　　　│ Two of the three objecting Justices 的同位语
　　　　　　↓

Two...Justices...**agreed with** this Constitutional logic（主＋谓＋宾）

but 连接的并列谓宾，│ 表转折

but disagreed about

句子主干

which 引导的宾语从句，│ 作 disagreed about 的宾语　↑

[which] Arizona rules conflicted with the federal statute.

【词汇注释】

conflict with	冲突；相抵触	federal statute	联邦法规

【意群训练】

Two of the three objecting Justices //—Samuel Alito and Clarence Thomas— // agreed with // this Constitutional logic // but disagreed about // which Arizona rules // conflicted with // the federal statute.

2. 插入语分隔

　　插入语的位置较灵活，在判断插入语分隔时，要看其是否与前后成分有直接关系，如没有直接关系，则为插入语。

Far less certain, however, is how successfully experts and bureaucrats can select our peer groups and steer their activities in virtuous directions. 然而更难确定的是，专家和官员能在多大程度上成功地选择我们的同龄群体，并引导其活动朝着良性方向发展。【英语（一）2012 Text 1】

【难句类型】分隔结构 + 从句 + 平行结构 + 倒装　　　　　难度：★★★★

【难句破解】

找主干	过程	第一步：找从句标志词，并剥离该从句。找到标志词 how：距离 how 之后最近的动词是由 and 连接的并列的 can select 和（can）steer，因它们均为及物动词，故 our peer groups 和 their activities 分别作其宾语，至此将该从句剥离。第二步：识别非谓语动词，同时删除非谓语动词结构及其它修饰成分。本句无非谓语动词结构；删除修饰成分 however, in virtuous directions。全句剩下了 Far less certain is，这就是句子主干的一部分。第三步：识别并删除很像谓语动词的动词。（真正的谓语动词已找到，故该步骤略。）
	结果	Far less certain,...is [**how**] successfully...（表 + 系 + 主从）本句是倒装句，how 引导的主语从句 [**how**]...experts and bureaucrats can select our peer groups and steer their activities（主 + 谓 1 + 宾 1 + and + 谓 2 + 宾 2）作主语，是主干成分，故还原。该从句中，and 连接并列的谓宾 can select our peer groups 和（can）steer their activities。
理修饰	插入语	插入语 however 为插入语。
	状语	副词 successfully 作状语，修饰主语从句中两个并列的谓语；介词短语 in virtuous directions 作状语。

【结构分析】

句子主干	Far less certain, however, is...（倒装句：表 + 系 + 主从）how 引导的主语从句[**how**] successfully experts and bureaucrats **can select** our peer groupsand 连接并列的谓宾**and (can) steer** their activities
一级修饰	介词短语作状语**in** virtuous directions.

bureaucrat	[ˈbjʊərəkræt] *n.* 官员；官僚
virtuous	[ˈvɜːtʃʊəs] *a.* 品行端正的（文中引申为"良性的"）

【意群训练】

Far less certain, // however, // is how successfully // experts and bureaucrats can select our peer groups // and steer their activities // in virtuous directions.

▶ 实例 2 ▶▶▶▶

"Their capacity for tolerating stress may even be greater than men's," she observes, "it's just that they're dealing with so many more things that they become worn out from it more visibly and sooner." 她还表示"女性可能比男性更能承受压力。只是她们需要应对太多的事情，因而精力被消耗得更快、更明显。"【英语（一）2008 Text 1】

本句中出现了直接引语，且直接引语为两个用双引号括起来的被断开的句子。这时可将两个引号中间分隔直接引语的部分视为插入语，将被插入语分隔的两部分直接引语合成一句理解。具体处理步骤如下：

1. 找插入语标志，并剥离该插入语形式；
2. 找从句标志词，并剥离该从句；
3. 识别并删除非谓语动词结构和其它修饰成分；
4. 识别很像谓语动词的动词。

【难句类型】分隔结构 + 嵌套结构　　　　　　　　难度：★★★★

【难句破解】

找主干	过程	第一步：找插入语标志，并剥离该插入语形式。句中 she observes 将完整的直接引语分隔成两部分，故将其视为插入语，至此将 she observes 剥离。 第二步：找从句标志词，并剥离该从句。❶ 找到第一个标志词 that：距离 that 之后最近的动词是 are dealing with，介词 with 后需跟宾语，故 so many more things 作其宾语，至此将该从句剥离；❷ 找到第二个标志词 that：距离 that 之后最近的动词是系动词 become，worn out 作其表语，至此将该从句剥离。 第三步：识别非谓语动词，同时删除非谓语动词结构及其它修饰成分。本句无非谓语动词结构；删除修饰成分 for tolerating stress，even，than men's，just，from it，more visibly and sooner。

		全句剩下了 Their capacity may be greater 和 it's 这两部分。
	结果	分句一：Their capacity...may...be greater...（主＋系＋表） 副词 even 修饰系动词。 分句二：it's... [that]...（主＋系＋表从） 副词 just 修饰系动词。that 引导的表语从句 [that] they're dealing with so many more things...（主＋谓＋宾）作表语，是主干成分，故还原。
理修饰	定语	介词短语 for tolerating stress 作后置定语，修饰 capacity。
	状语	than men's 作分句一的比较状语。
	插入语	she observes 作插入语。
	状从	第一层：第二个 that 与其前的 so 构成 so...that 结构引导结果状语从句 [that] they become worn out from it more visibly and sooner（主＋系＋表），在 that 引导的表语从句中作结果状语。 第二层：介词短语 from it 作状语；more visibly and sooner 作方式状语。

【结构分析】

for tolerating stress

介词短语作 capacity 的后置定语

一级修饰

than men's"

比较状语

(1) "Their **capacity**...may even be greater...,"（主＋系＋表）

句子主干

并列句

(2) "it's just...（主＋系＋表从）

that 引导的表语从句

[that] they're dealing with **so** many more things

so...that 引导的结果状语从句

[that] they become worn out from it more visibly and sooner."

一级修饰

插入语

she observes,

【词汇注释】

capacity	[kə'pæsəti] *n.* 能力；容量	tolerate	['tɒləreɪt] *vt.* 容忍；忍受

"Their capacity // for tolerating stress // may even be greater // than men's," // she observes, // "it's just // that they're dealing with // so many more things // that they become worn out // from it // more visibly and sooner."

（二） 结构式分隔

对于结构式分隔，考研英语中主要考查状语从句插入所造成的分隔。状语从句在句中的位置非常灵活，有时候为了使句子优美且平衡，会将状语从句置于主句中间，这样就造成了分隔。状语从句虽是修饰成分，但并不像插入语那样可以忽略。对于在判断句子结构方面有困难的考生来说，可将状语从句移至句末，从而将被分隔的主句还原为正常语序，再进行分析。

实例 1

A sacred place of peace, however crude it may be, is a distinctly human need, as opposed to shelter, which is a distinctly animal need. 安宁的圣地体现了人类特有的需求，无论怎样疏于雕琢，都与遮风挡雨之所不同，后者反映了动物特有的需求。【英语（一）2013 翻译】

【难句类型】 分隔结构 + 从句　　　　　　　　　　难度：★★★★☆

【难句破解】

找主干	过程	第一步：找从句标志词，并剥离该从句。❶找到第一个标志词 however：距离 however 之后最近的动词是 may be，至此将该从句剥离；❷找到第二个标志词 which：距离 which 之后最近的动词是 is，短语 a distinctly animal need 作其表语，至此将该从句剥离。 第二步：识别非谓语动词，同时删除非谓语动词结构及其它修饰成分。本句无非谓语动词结构；删除修饰成分 as opposed to shelter。全句剩下了 A sacred place of peace is a distinctly human need，这就是句子的主干部分。 第三步：识别并删除很像谓语动词的动词。（真正的谓语动词已找到，故该步骤略。）
	结果	A sacred place of peace,...., is a distinctly human need...（主 + 系 + 表）
理修饰	状从	however 引导的让步状语从句 [however] crude it may be（表 + 主 + 系）使用了部分倒装，用于强调 crude。该状语从句插入句中，造成了主句中主系的分隔。

补充说明	第一层：as opposed to shelter 用于补充说明 A sacred place of peace。第二层：which 引导非限定性定语从句 **[which]** is a distinctly animal need（主+系+表），补充说明 shelter。
看标点 逗号	根据成对出现的逗号，很容易判断出让步状语从句 however crude it may be 为插入部分，造成主干主系分隔。

【结构分析】

一级修饰	**[however]** crude it may be,

however 引导的让步状语从句，作句子主干的让步状语

句子主干	**A sacred place of peace**,...is a distinctly human need,（主+系+表）

补充说明 a sacred place of peace

一级修饰	as opposed to **shelter**,

which 引导的非限定性定语从句，补充说明 shelter

二级修饰	**[which]** is a distinctly animal need.

【词汇注释】

sacred	['seɪkrɪd] *a.* 神圣的；受尊重的

【意群训练】

A sacred place of peace, // however crude // it may be, // is a distinctly human need, // as opposed to shelter, // which is // a distinctly animal need.

实例 2

Canada's premiers (the leaders of provincial governments), if they have any breath left after complaining about Ottawa at their late July annual meeting, might spare a moment to do something, together, to reduce health-care costs. 在七月下旬的年会上，加拿大各省的省长们（省政府的领导者）对渥太华大发牢骚之后，如果还有力气的话，不妨抽出时间一起去做些实事，以降低医疗保健的费用。【英语（一）2005 新题型】

【难句类型】分隔结构 + 非谓语动词 + 从句   难度：★★★★

【难句破解】

找主干 过程	第一步：找从句标志词，并剥离该从句。找到标志词 if：距离 if 之后最近的动词是及物动词 have，any breath 作其宾语，至此将该从句剥离。

过程		第二步：识别非谓语动词，同时删除非谓语动词结构及其它修饰成分。删除非谓语动词结构 left，to do something 和 to reduce health-care costs。删除修饰成分（the leaders of provincial governments），after complaining about Ottawa，at their late July annual meeting 和 together。全句剩下了 Canada's premiers might spare a moment，这就是句子的主干部分。 第三步：识别并删除很像谓语动词的动词。（真正的谓语动词已找到，故该步骤略。）
结果		<u>Canada's premiers</u>…, <u>might spare</u> <u>a moment</u>…（主＋谓＋宾）
理修饰	状从	第一层：if 引导条件状语从句 **[if]** <u>they</u> <u>have</u> <u>any breath</u> left after complaining about Ottawa at their late July annual meeting（主＋谓＋宾），作主句的条件状语，其插入到句子中间，造成了主句中主谓的分隔。第二层：该从句中，过去分词 left 作后置定语，修饰 breath；介词短语 after complaining about Ottawa 作时间状语。 第三层：介词短语 at their late July annual meeting 作地点状语。
	状语	第一层：动词不定式短语 to do something 作目的状语；副词 together 作状语。第二层：动词不定式短语 to reduce health-care costs 作 to do something 的目的状语。
看标点	括号	括号内的名词短语 the leaders of provincial governments 解释说明 premiers。
	逗号	根据成对出现的逗号，不难判断出条件状语从句 if…meeting 为插入部分，造成主干主谓分隔。

【结构分析】

二级修饰	**to** reduce health-care costs.
	动词不定式短语作目的状语 ↓
一级修饰	**to** do something, together,
	动词不定式短语作句子主干的目的状语
	(the leaders of provincial governments),
	解释说明 premiers ↓
句子主干	Canada's **premiers**…<u>might spare</u> <u>a moment</u>（主＋谓＋宾）
	if 引导的条件状语从句，作句子主干的条件状语
一级修饰	**[if]** they have any breath left
	介词短语作时间状语 ↑
二级修饰	**after** complaining about Ottawa
	介词短语作地点状语 ↑
三级修饰	**at** their late July annual meeting,

34

| premier | ['premɪə(r)] *n.* 总理 *a.* 首要的；最著名的 |
| spare a moment | 抽出一点时间 |

【意群训练】

Canada's premiers // (the leaders of provincial governments), // if they have any breath left // after complaining about Ottawa // at their late July annual meeting, // might spare a moment // to do something, // together, // to reduce health-care costs.

（三）修饰性分隔

1. 主谓分隔

主谓分隔中，插入成分多为定语（从句）、状语（从句）、同位语以及插入语，其中定语和同位语都对主语有修饰作用。该类目下也包含插入式分隔，但因为插入式分隔为重点考查对象，所以将插入式分隔单独列出，作为分隔结构的第一种情况，在前文进行了详细讲解。

实例 1

In the 2006 film version of *The Devil Wears Prada*, Miranda Priestly, played by Meryl Streep, scolds her unattractive assistant for imagining that high fashion doesn't affect her. 在 2006 年电影版《穿普拉达的女王》中，由梅丽尔·斯特里普饰演的米兰达·普瑞斯特利训斥她的助理毫无魅力，认为高端时尚丝毫没有影响到她。【英语（一）2013 Text 1】

【难句类型】分隔结构＋从句＋非谓语动词　　　　　　　　难度：★★★★☆

【难句破解】

找主干	过程	第一步：找从句标志词，并剥离该从句。找到标志词 that：距离 that 之后最近的动词是 doesn't affect，因 affect 是及物动词，故 her 作其宾语，至此将该从句剥离。 第二步：识别非谓语动词，同时删除非谓语动词结构及其它修饰成分。删除非谓语动词结构 played by Meryl Streep。删除修饰成分 In the 2006...*Prada*, for imagining。全句剩下了 Miranda Priestly scolds her unattractive assistant，这就是句子的主干部分。 第三步：识别并删除很像谓语动词的动词。（真正的谓语动词已找到，故该步骤略。）
	结果	...,Miranda Priestly,...,scolds her unattractive assistant... （主＋谓＋宾）

理修饰	状语	第一层：介词短语 In the 2006 film version of *The Devil Wears Prada* 作状语。介词短语 for imagining...作主句的原因状语；其中 that 引导的宾语从句 [that] high fashion doesn't affect her（主＋谓＋宾）作 imagining 的宾语。
	定语	过去分词短语 played by Meryl Streep 作后置定语，修饰主语 Miranda Priestly，并将主句的主语 Miranda Priestly 和谓语 scolds 分隔。

【结构分析】

【词汇注释】

version ['vɜːʃn] *n.* 版本；描述	assistant [ə'sɪstənt] *n.* 助理 *a.* 助理的

【意群训练】

In the 2006 film version of *The Devil Wears Prada*, // Miranda Priestly, // played by Meryl Streep, // scolds her unattractive assistant // for imagining // that high fashion doesn't affect her.

———— 实例 2 ————————————————————————— >>>>

Another urge or need that these gardens appear to respond to, or to arise from, is so intrinsic that we are barely ever conscious of its abiding claims on us. 这些花园似乎还反映着或是源自另一种诉求或需要，这种诉求或需要如此根深蒂固以至于我们几乎意识不到它对人类持久的索求。【英语（一）2013 翻译】

【难句类型】

分隔结构 ＋ 从句 ＋ 否定结构 ＋ 平行结构 ＋ 非谓语动词   难度：★★★★

【难句破解】

找主干	过程	第一步：找从句标志词，并剥离该从句。❶ 找到第一个标志词 that：距离 that 之后最近的动词是 appear，至此将该从句剥离；❷ 找到第二个标志词 that：距离 that 之后最近的动词是 are，conscious 作其表语，至此将该从句剥离。 第二步：识别非谓语动词，同时删除非谓语动词结构及其它修饰成分。删除非谓语动词结构 to respond to 和 to arise from。删除修饰成分 so，of its abiding claims，on us。全句剩下了 Another urge or need is intrinsic，这就是句子的主干部分。 第三步：识别并删除很像谓语动词的动词。（真正的谓语动词已找到，故该步骤略。）
	结果	<u>Another urge or need</u>...is...intrinsic...（主＋系＋表）

理修饰	定从	第一个 that 引导定语从句 [that] <u>these gardens</u> appear to respond to, or to arise from（主＋系＋表1＋or＋表2）修饰主句的主语 Another urge or need，并将主句主语和系动词 is 分隔开。其中，连词 or 连接并列的动词不定式 to respond to 和 to arise from，均在定语从句中作表语。
	状从	第一层：第二个 that 与其前的 so 构成 so...that 结构，引导结果状语从句 [that] <u>we</u> are barely ever conscious（主＋系＋表），作主句的结果状语。第二层：该结果状语从句中，副词 barely 和 ever 作状语，修饰表语 conscious，表否定；介词短语 of its abiding claims 作状语。第三层：介词短语 on us 作 claims 的后置定语。

【结构分析】

一级修饰	[that] these gardens appear to respond to, or to arise from,
	↓ that 引导的定语从句，修饰 Another urge or need
句子主干	**Another urge or need**...is so intrinsic（主＋系＋表）
	so...that 引导的结果状语从句 ↑
一级修饰	[that] we are barely ever conscious
	↑ 介词短语作状语
二级修饰	**of** its abiding **claims**
	↑ 介词短语作后置定语，修饰 claims
三级修饰	**on** us.

| intrinsic | [ɪn'trɪnsɪk] *a.* 固有的；本身的；内在的 |
| abiding | [ə'baɪdɪŋ] *a.* 持久的；长久的；始终不渝的 |

【意群训练】

Another urge or need // that these gardens appear // to respond to, // or to arise from, // is so intrinsic // that we are barely ever conscious // of its abiding claims // on us.

2. 动宾分隔

　　若句中宾语过长，可将修饰成分插入动词和其宾语之间。分析动宾分隔的关键在于区分谓语动词是及物还是不及物。若是及物动词，其后一定要跟宾语，如果后面跟的是介词短语，就说明宾语成分一定是被转移了，分隔结构由此产生。分隔动宾的成分可能是介词短语、补语或从句。出现动宾分隔常常是由于宾语的修饰成分较多，为了保持句子平衡，故将其中一个放在宾语之前。

　　实例 1

On the other hand, he did not accept as well founded the charge made by some of his critics that, while he was a good observer, he had no power of reasoning. 另一方面，一些批评家指责他虽然善于观察，但却不具备推理能力，而他认为这种说法是缺乏依据的。【英语（一）2008 翻译】

【难句类型】分隔结构 + 嵌套结构 + 非谓语动词　　　　　　　　难度：★★★★

【难句破解】

| 找主干 | 过程 | 第一步：找从句标志词，并剥离该从句。❶找到第一个标志词 that 和第二个标志词 while（因二者同时出现，故放在一起分析）：距离 while 之后最近的动词是 was，a good observer 作其表语，至此将 while 引导的从句剥离；❷之后距离 that 后面最近的动词是 had，因 have 是及物动词，故 no power 作其宾语，至此将 that 引导的从句剥离。

第二步：识别非谓语动词，同时删除非谓语动词结构及其它修饰成分。删除非谓语动词结构 made by some of his critics；删除修饰成分 On the other hand, of reasoning。全句剩下了 he did not accept as well founded the charge，这就是句子的主干部分。

第三步：识别并删除很像谓语动词的动词。（真正的谓语动词已找到，故该步骤略。） |

		..., he did not accept as well founded the charge...
	结果	（主 + 谓 + 宾补 + 宾） accept 是及物动词，但是后面没有紧跟宾语，说明动词和宾语被分隔了。由于宾语 the charge 的修饰成分较多，因此将宾补 as well founded 提前，以保持句子平衡。
理修饰	状语	句首的介词短语 On the other hand 作状语。
	定语	过去分词短语 made by some of his critics 作后置定语，修饰 the charge；介词短语 of reasoning 作后置定语，修饰 power。
	同位语从句	第一层：that 引导的同位语从句 [that],...，he had no power of reasoning（主 + 谓 + 宾）解释说明宾语 the charge。第二层：while 引导让步状语从句 [while] he was a good observer（主 + 系 + 表），在同位语从句中作让步状语。

【结构分析】

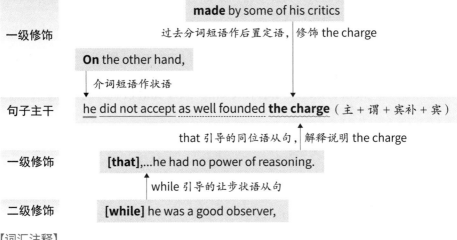

一级修饰   **made** by some of his critics

过去分词短语作后置定语，修饰 the charge

On the other hand,

介词短语作状语

句子主干   he did not accept as well founded **the charge**（主 + 谓 + 宾补 + 宾）

that 引导的同位语从句，解释说明 the charge

一级修饰   **[that]**,...he had no power of reasoning.

while 引导的让步状语从句

二级修饰   **[while]** he was a good observer,

【词汇注释】

well founded	有根据的；有事实依据的
reasoning	['riːzənɪŋ] *n.* 推理；论证

【意群训练】

On the other hand, // he did not accept // as well founded // the charge // made by some of his critics that, // while he was a good observer, // he had no power // of reasoning.

3. 系表分隔

　　系表分隔多为状语或插入语的分隔，要注意半系动词构成的系表结构中也会出现系表分隔。该语法点在考研英语中不作为考查重点，考生了解即可。

·实例 **1** ···▶▶▶▶

Even without knowing what was in the messages, the knowledge of who sent them and to whom was enormously revealing and still could be. 那时即使不知道信息的具体内容，但是信息由谁发送以及发送给谁都被大量泄漏，并且现在可能仍是这种情况。【英语（二）2018 Text 3】

【难句类型】分隔结构＋从句＋平行结构＋省略　　　　　　难度：★★★★
【难句破解】

找主干	过程	**第一步**：找从句标志词，并剥离从句。❶ 找到第一个标志词 what：距离 what 之后最近的动词是 was，in the messages 作其表语，至此将该从句剥离；❷ 找到第二个标志词 who：距离 who 之后最近的动词是 sent，因 send 是及物动词，故 them 作其宾语，至此将该从句剥离。 **第二步**：识别非谓语动词，同时删除非谓语动词结构及其它修饰成分。删除非谓语动词结构 knowing；删除修饰成分 Even without，of，and，to whom，enormously，still。全句剩下了 the knowledge was revealing and could be，这就是句子的主干部分。 **第三步**：识别并删除很像谓语动词的动词。（真正的谓语动词已找到，故该步骤略。）
	结果	the knowledge...was...revealing and...could be (revealing). （主＋系＋表） 为避免重复，could be 之后省略了表语 revealing。
理修饰	状语	**第一层**：介词短语 Even without knowing...messages 作主干的条件状语，其中，what 引导的宾语从句 [what] was in the messages（主＋系＋表）作 knowing 的宾语。**第二层**：副词 enormously 和 still 均作状语，分别修饰 revealing 和 could be，其中 enormously 将系动词 was 和表语 revealing 分隔开。
	定语	**第一层**：介词短语 of who sent them and to whom 作后置定语，修饰 the knowledge。其中，who 引导的宾语从句 [who] sent them（主＋谓＋宾）作 of 的宾语；and 连接并列的宾语从句 to [whom] (the knowledge was sent)（主＋谓）中，to whom 作状语，表对象。

【结构分析】

一级修饰　Even **without** knowing what was in the messages,

介词短语作条件状语

↓

the knowledge...was enormously revealing（主＋系＋表）

句子主干

and 连接并列的系表结构

↑

and still **could be** (revealing).

介词短语作后置定语，修饰 the knowledge

一级修饰　**of** who sent them and to whom

【意群训练】

Even without knowing // what was in the messages, // the knowledge // of who sent them and to whom // was enormously revealing // and still could be.

4. 宾补分隔

宾补分隔是由于宾语有自己的修饰语，或宾语置于句首而造成的分隔。考研英语中出现宾补分隔多是由于宾语有其它修饰成分，但不作为考查重点，了解即可。

实例 1

Studies of both animals and humans have shown that sex hormones somehow affect the stress response, causing females under stress to produce more of the trigger chemicals than do males under the same conditions. 对动物和人类的研究表明：性激素会以某种方式影响两性对压力的反应，在同等压力条件下，它会使雌性比雄性分泌出更多诱发不良反应的化学物质。【英语（一）2008 Text 1】

【难句类型】分隔结构＋非谓语动词＋从句＋倒装　　　　　难度：★★★★

【难句破解】

找主干	过程	第一步：找从句标志词，并剥离该从句。❶ 找到第一个标志词 that：距离 that 之后最近的动词是及物动词 affect，the stress response 作其宾语，至此将该从句剥离；❷ 找到第二个标志词 than：距离 than 之后最近的动词是 do，至此将该从句剥离。第二步：识别非谓语动词，同时删除非谓语动词结构及其它修饰成分。删除非谓语动词结构 causing females...conditions；删除修饰成分 of both animals and humans。全句剩下了 Studies have shown，这就是句子的主谓部分。

	第三步：识别并删除很像谓语动词的动词。（真正的谓语动词已找到，故该步骤略。）
结果	Studies have shown **[that]** sex hormones somehow affect the stress response（主＋谓＋宾从） that 引导的宾语从句 **[that]** <u>sex hormones</u> somehow <u>affect the stress responses</u>（主＋谓＋宾）作 have shown 的宾语，是主干部分，故还原。副词 somehow 修饰谓语 affect。

理修饰	定语	介词短语 of both animals and humans 作后置定语，修饰 Studies。
	状语	第一层：现在分词短语 causing females...the same conditions 作宾语从句的结果状语，其中 females 是 causing 的宾语。第二层：动词不定式短语 to produce more of the trigger chemicals 作结果状语中宾语 females 的补足语，由于 females 由后置定语 under stress 修饰，因此出现了宾补分隔；than 引导比较状语从句 **[than]** <u>do males</u> under the same conditions（谓＋主）修饰结果状语中 than 前面的部分，是主谓倒装结构，其中介词短语 under the same conditions 作后置定语，修饰 males。

【结构分析】

一级修饰	**of** both animals and humans
	↓ 介词短语作后置定语，修饰 Studies
句子主干	**Studies**...have shown **[that]** sex...response,（主＋谓＋宾从）
	现在分词短语作结果状语 ↑
一级修饰	**causing** females under stress to produce...chemicals
	than 引导的比较状语从句 ↑
二级修饰	**[than]** do males under the same conditions.

【词汇注释】

hormone	['hɔ:məʊn] *n.* 激素；荷尔蒙
trigger	['trɪɡə(r)] *n.* 触发；扳机 *vt.* 触发；引起

【意群训练】

Studies// of both animals and humans //have shown // that sex hormones // somehow affect the stress response, // causing females under stress // to produce more of the trigger chemicals // than do males // under the same conditions.

5. 复合谓语分隔

复合谓语分隔主要指：由于某一时态、语态的动词形式中，或情态动词、助动词与其后的实义动词之间加入状语或插入语而出现的分隔。

------ 实例 1 ------ >>>>

Downshifting—also known in America as "voluntary simplicity"—has, ironically, even bred a new area of what might be termed anti-consumerism. 具有讽刺意味的是，"放慢生活节奏"——在美国也称"自愿简单化"——甚至孕育出了一个可称之为反消费主义的崭新领域。【英语（一）2001 Passage 5】

【难句类型】分隔结构 + 从句 + 非谓语动词　　　　　　　难度：★★★☆
【难句破解】

找主干	过程	第一步：找从句标志词，并剥离该从句。找到标志词 what：距离 what 之后最近的动词是 might be termed，因其为被动语态，故 anti-consumerism 作主语补足语，至此将该从句剥离。 第二步：识别非谓语动词，同时删除非谓语动词结构及其它修饰成分。删除非谓语动词结构 known in America as "voluntary simplicity"；删除修饰成分 also, ironically, even, of。全句剩下了 Downshifting has bred a new area，这就是句子的主干部分。 第三步：识别并删除很像谓语动词的动词。（真正的谓语动词已找到，故该步骤略。）
	结果	Downshifting...has...bred a new area...（主 + 谓 + 宾）
理修饰	插入语	两个破折号中间的内容作插入语，解释说明主语 Downshifting。
	状语	副词 ironically 和 even 作状语，修饰谓语，插在 has 和 bred 之间，将谓语分隔开。
	定语	第一层：介词短语 of what... 作后置定语，修饰 a new area。其中，what 引导宾语从句 [what] might be termed anti-consumerism（主 + 谓），作 of 的宾语。第二层：anti-consumerism 作宾从的主语 what 的补足语。
看标点	破折号	破折号将插入语分隔出来，表示解释说明。

【结构分析】

一级修饰　　—also known in America as "voluntary simplicity"—
　　　　　　　　│
　　　　　　插入语，解释说明 Downshifting

句子主干　　**Downshifting**...has, ironically, even bred **a new area**（主 + 谓 + 宾）
　　　　　　　　　　　　　　　　　　　　　　　　　　　　　　　↑
　　　　　　介词短语作后置定语，修饰 a new area

一级修饰　　**of** what might be termed anti-consumerism.

43

【词汇注释】

| ironically | [aɪ'rɒnɪkli] *ad.* 具有讽刺意味地 |
| breed | [bri:d] *v.* 产生；饲养；养育 |

【意群训练】

Downshifting // —also known in America // as "voluntary simplicity" — // has, // ironically, // even bred a new area // of what might be termed // anti-consumerism.

—————— 实例 2 ——————————————————————————————————»»»»

Your outline should smoothly conduct you from one point to the next, but do not permit it to railroad you. 写作提纲应该引导你从一个论点自然地过渡到另一个论点，但是不要让提纲限制你的思维。【英语（一）2008 新题型】

【难句类型】分隔结构＋非谓语动词＋否定结构　　　　　　难度：★★★☆

【难句破解】

<table>
<tr><td rowspan="2">找主干</td><td>过程</td><td>第一步：找从句标志词，并剥离该从句。（本句无从句，故该步骤略。）
第二步：识别非谓语动词，同时删除非谓语动词结构及其它修饰成分。删除非谓语动词结构 to railroad you。删除修饰成分 smoothly, from one point to the next。全句剩下了 Your outline should conduct you, but do not permit it，这就是句子的主干部分。
第三步：识别并删除很像谓语动词的动词。（真正的谓语动词已找到，故该步骤略。）</td></tr>
<tr><td>结果</td><td>Your outline should...conduct you..., but do not permit it to railroad you.（主 1＋谓 1＋宾 1＋but＋谓 2＋宾 2＋宾补）
本句是 but 连接的并列句，but 表转折，其中 but 之后为祈使句。动词不定式短语 to railroad you 作 it（it 指代前面的 outline）的补足语，故还原。</td></tr>
<tr><td>理修饰</td><td>状语</td><td>副词 smoothly 作状语，修饰谓语 1，并将该复合谓语分隔开；介词短语 from one point to the next 作状语。</td></tr>
</table>

【结构分析】

一级修饰	**from** one point **to** the next,
	↓ 介词短语作(1)句的状语
句子主干	(1) Your outline should smoothly conduct you（主＋谓＋宾）
	├ but 连接的并列句，表转折
	(2) **but** do not permit it to railroad you.（祈使句：谓＋宾＋宾补）

railroad	['reɪlrəud] *vt.* 迫使……仓促行事 *n.* 铁路

【意群训练】

Your outline // should smoothly conduct you // from one point to the next, // but do not permit it // to railroad you.

二 嵌套结构

《一千零一夜》这本书经常是一个故事套着另一个故事；"俄罗斯套娃"就是一个小娃娃套着一个小娃娃。嵌套结构与之类似，就是大句子套小句子，大从句套小从句的结构。在长难句中，要找到嵌套，需要先由内向外，再由外向内进行分析。

(一) 主语从句嵌套

结构为：主句 + 从句（"主语从句 + 谓语 + 宾语"或"主语从句 + 系动词 + 表语"）。主语从句嵌套常出现在从句的动词之前，但要注意也有可能出现形式主语 it。考研英语中主语从句出现的频次较低，主语从句嵌套更是少见。它并非考查重点，故这里不作详细讲解。

(二) 宾语从句嵌套

结构为：主句 + 从句（主语 + 谓语 + 宾语从句）。宾语从句嵌套常出现在从句的谓语动词或间接宾语之后。若从句的谓语动词后面是宾语从句，就一定是嵌套宾从，但要注意可能会出现形式宾语 it；若从句的直接宾语为从句，就一定是嵌套宾从。考研英语中常见嵌套出现在宾从、定从中，且有时会省略宾语从句的引导词 that。

实例 1

The Internet—and pressure from funding agencies, who are questioning why commercial publishers are making money from government-funded research by restricting access to it—is making free access to scientific results a reality. 互联网，以及来自资助机构的压力（这些机构质问，商业出版商为什么通过限制科研成果的获取而从政府资助的研究项目中获利），使自由获取科研成果成为现实。【英语（一）2008 Text 2】

【难句类型】嵌套结构 + 分隔结构　　　　　　　　　　　难度：★ ★ ★ ☆

【难句破解】

找主干	过程	第一步：找从句标志词，并剥离该从句。❶ 找到第一个标志词 who：距离 who 之后最近的动词是 are questioning，至此将该从

过程	句剥离；❷ 找到第二个标志词 why：距离 why 之后最近的动词是 are making，因 make 是及物动词，故 money 作其宾语，至此将该从句剥离。 第二步：识别非谓语动词，同时删除非谓语动词结构及其它修饰成分。本句无非谓语动词结构；删除修饰成分 and pressure from funding agencies，from government-funded research，by restricting access to it。全句剩下了 The Internet is making free access to scientific results a reality，这就是句子的主干部分。 第三步：识别并删除很像谓语动词的动词。（真正的谓语动词已找到，故该步骤略。）
结果	The Internet...is making free access to scientific results a reality. （主＋谓＋宾＋宾补）

理修饰	插入语	第一层：两个破折号中间的 and pressure...it 是插入语，对主语进行补充说明。第二层：介词短语 from funding agencies 作后置定语，修饰 pressure。第三层：定语从句 [who] are questioning why...（主＋谓＋宾从）补充说明 funding agencies；其中 why 引导的宾语从句 [why] commercial publishers are making money（主＋谓＋宾）作 are questioning 的宾语。本句的结构为定从＋嵌套宾从。第四层：嵌套宾从中，介词短语 from government-funded research 作状语；介词短语 by restricting access to it 作方式状语。

看标点	破折号	两个破折号分隔出插入语。

【结构分析】

句子主干	The Internet...is making free...results a reality.（主＋谓＋宾＋宾补）
一级修饰	插入语 —and **pressure**
二级修饰	介词短语作后置定语，修饰 pressure **from funding agencies**,
三级修饰	who 引导的非限定性定语从句，补充说明 funding agencies **[who] are questioning** why 引导的宾语从句，作 are questioning 的宾语 **[why]** commercial publishers are making money
四级修饰	介词短语作状语 **from** government-funded research 介词短语作方式状语 **by** restricting access to it—

question	['kwestʃən] *vt.* 质询；怀疑 *n.* 问题；疑问
commercial	[kə'mɜːʃl] *a.* 商业的，贸易的
restrict	[rɪ'strɪkt] *vt.* 限制；约束；限定

【意群训练】

The Internet //—and pressure from funding agencies, // who are questioning // why commercial publishers are making money // from government-funded research // by restricting access to it— // is making free access // to scientific results // a reality.

实例 2

In December 2010 America's Federal Trade Commission (FTC) proposed adding a "do not track" (DNT) option to internet browsers, so that users could tell advertisers that they did not want to be followed. 2010 年 12 月，美国联邦贸易委员会建议在互联网浏览器上添加"禁止追踪"选项，以便用户告知广告商他们不想被追踪。【英语（一）2013 Text 2】

【难句类型】嵌套结构＋非谓语动词　　　　　　　　　　　难度：★★★★

【难句破解】

| 找主干 | 过程 | 第一步：找从句标志词，并剥离该从句。❶找到第一个标志词 so that：距离 so that 之后最近的动词是 could tell，因 tell 是及物动词，故 advertisers 作其宾语，至此将该从句剥离；❷找到第二个标志词 that：距离 that 之后最近的动词是 did not want，至此将该从句剥离。

第二步：识别非谓语动词，同时删除非谓语动词结构及其它修饰成分。删除非谓语动词结构 adding a "do not track" (DNT) option，to be followed；删除修饰成分 In December 2010，to internet browsers。全句剩下了 America's Federal Trade Commission (FTC) proposed，这就是句子的主谓部分。

第三步：识别并删除很像谓语动词的动词。（真正的谓语动词已找到，故该步骤略。） |
| | 结果 | America's Federal Trade Commission (FTC) proposed adding a "do not track" (DNT) option（主＋谓＋宾）
动名词短语作宾语，是主干成分，故还原。 |

理修饰	状语	介词短语 In December 2010 作时间状语；介词短语 to internet browsers 作状语，表对象。
	状从	so that 引导目的状语从句 **[so that]** <u>users</u> <u>could tell</u> <u>advertisers</u> <u>that...</u>（主＋谓＋间宾＋直宾），作主句的目的状语；其中 that 引导宾语从句 **[that]** <u>they</u> <u>did not want</u> <u>to be followed</u>（主＋谓＋宾），作目的状从的直接宾语。本句嵌套结构是状从＋嵌套宾从。
看标点	括号	括号中的内容标明主语的缩写。

【结构分析】

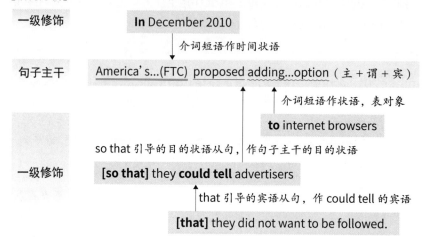

一级修饰　　In December 2010
　　　　　　介词短语作时间状语
句子主干　　America's...(FTC) proposed adding...option（主＋谓＋宾）
　　　　　　　　　　介词短语作状语，表对象
　　　　　　　　　　to internet browsers
　　　so that 引导的目的状语从句，作句子主干的目的状语
一级修饰　　[so that] they could tell advertisers
　　　　　　that 引导的宾语从句，作 could tell 的宾语
　　　　　　[that] they did not want to be followed.

【词汇注释】

propose	[prə'pəʊz] *vt.* 建议；打算 *v.* 求婚
browser	['braʊzə(r)] *n.* 浏览程序，浏览器（用于在互联网上查阅信息）

【意群训练】

In December 2010 // America's Federal Trade Commission (FTC) // proposed adding a "do not track" (DNT) option // to internet browsers, // so that users could tell advertisers // that they did not want // to be followed.

（三）　表语从句嵌套

　　　结构为：主句＋从句（主语＋系动词＋表语从句）。表语从句嵌套常出现在从句系动词之后，若从句动词为系动词，且后面有表语从句，就一定是嵌套表从。考研英语中常见嵌套在宾从、定从中，嵌套表从不是考查重点。

The Federal Circuit issued an unusual order stating that the case would be heard by all 12 of the court's judges, rather than a typical panel of three, and that one issue it wants to evaluate is whether it should "reconsider" its State Street Bank ruling. 联邦巡回法院发布了一条不同寻常的法令：要求此案由全院 12 名法官联席审理，而不是常规的 3 人法官组审理。同时法院还将评估一个议题——是否应该"重新考虑"对美国道富银行案的裁决。【英语（一）2010 Text 2】

【难句类型】嵌套结构＋平行结构＋非谓语动词＋省略   难度：★★★★☆

【难句破解】

找主干	过程	第一步：找从句标志词，并剥离该从句。❶ 找到第一个标志词 that：距离 that 之后最近的动词是 would be heard，至此将该从句剥离；❷ 找到第二个标志词 that：that 之后有两个动词 wants 和 is，因此在第三步分析；❸ 找到第三个标志词 whether：距离 whether 之后最近的动词是 should "reconsider"，因 reconsider 是及物词，故 its State Street Bank ruling 作其宾语，至此将该从句剥离。
		第二步：识别非谓语动词，同时删除非谓语动词结构及其它修饰成分。删除非谓语动词结构 stating, to evaluate。删除修饰成分 by all 12 of...of three。全句剩下了 The Federal Circuit issued an unusual order, and that one issue it wants is。
		第三步：识别并删除很像谓语动词的动词。根据辨析真假谓语动词的方法，全句剩下了三个动词 issued，wants 和 is，由第一步中的❷ 可知，wants 和 is 为第二个标志词 that 之后的动词，其中 wants 的宾语是 to evaluate，而 evaluate 后缺失宾语，因此 it wants to evaluate 是省略关系词 that/which 的定语从句，修饰 one issue，故将该从句剥离；则 is 是第二个 that 引导的从句的谓语动词，至此将该从句剥离。全句剩下了 The Federal Circuit issued an unusual order，这就是句子的主干部分。
	结果	The Federal Circuit issued an unusual order...（主＋谓＋宾）
理修饰	定语	第一层：stating 作后置定语，修饰宾语 an unusual order；其中两个并列的宾语从句 [that] the case would be heard（主＋谓）和 [that] one issue it wants to evaluate is whether...（主＋系＋表从）作 stating 的宾语。第二层：在第一个宾语从句中，介词短语 by all 12 of the court's judges 作状语，引出动作的执行者，rather than 将 all 12 of the court's judges 与其后的 a typical

panel of three 并列，肯定前者，否定后者。在第二个宾语从句中，省略关系词 that/which 的定语从句 **(that/which)** <u>it</u> wants to evaluate（主＋谓＋宾）修饰 one issue，嵌套结构为宾从＋嵌套定从；whether 引导的表语从句 **[whether]** <u>it</u> should "reconsider" its State Street Bank ruling（主＋谓＋宾）在第二个宾语从句中作表语，嵌套结构为宾从＋嵌套表从。

【结构分析】

句子主干	The Federal Circuit issued **an unusual order**（主＋谓＋宾）

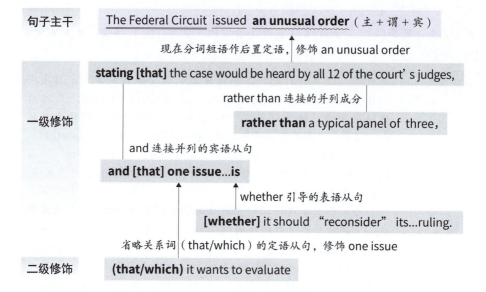

一级修饰	现在分词短语作后置定语，修饰 an unusual order **stating [that]** the case would be heard by all 12 of the court's judges, rather than 连接的并列成分 **rather than** a typical panel of three, and 连接并列的宾语从句 **and [that] one issue**...is whether 引导的表语从句 **[whether]** it should "reconsider" its...ruling.
二级修饰	省略关系词（that/which）的定语从句，修饰 one issue **(that/which)** it wants to evaluate

【词汇注释】

reconsider [ˌriːkənˈsɪdə(r)] *vt.* 重新考虑；重新审议

【意群训练】

The Federal Circuit // issued an unusual order // stating // that the case would be heard // by all 12 of the court's judges, // rather than a typical panel of three, // and that one issue // it wants to evaluate // is whether it should "reconsider" // its State Street Bank ruling.

(四) 同位语从句嵌套

结构为：主句＋从句，而从句中的某一成分又包含一个同位语从句。同位语从句嵌套常出现在从句的主语、宾语或表语之后，考研英语中出现较少，了解即可，故这里不作详细讲解。

结构为：主句＋从句，而从句中的某一成分又被一个定语从句所修饰。定语从句嵌套在考研英语中很常见，且嵌套位置很灵活，常见的是嵌套在宾从或状从中。有时嵌套定从的先行词可能会被其它修饰词隔开，这时要注意判断先行词。要注意，在考研英语中，定语从句嵌套可能会出现关系词 that/which 被省略的情况。

实例 1

A further concern is that the use of electronic means of payment leaves an electronic trail that contains a large amount of personal data. 更令人担忧的是，在使用电子方式进行支付时会留下含有大量个人数据的电子痕迹。

【英语（二）2013 完形】

【难句类型】嵌套结构　　　　　　　　　　　　　　　　难度：★★★

【难句破解】

找主干	过程	第一步：找从句标志词，并剥离从句。❶找到第一个标志词 that：距离 that 之后最近的动词是 leaves，an electronic trail 作其宾语，至此将该从句剥离；❷找到第二个标志词 that：距离 that 之后最近的动词是 contains，因 contain 是及物动词，故 a large amount of personal data 作其宾语，至此将该从句剥离。 第二步：识别非谓语动词，同时删除非谓语动词结构及其它修饰成分。本句无非谓语动词结构及其它修饰成分。全句剩下了 A further concern is，这就是句子的主系部分。 第三步：识别并删除很像谓语动词的动词。（真正的谓语动词已找到，故该步骤略。）
	结果	A further concern is [that]...（主＋系＋表从） that 引导的表语从句 [that] the use...leaves an electronic trail（主＋谓＋宾）作表语，是主干成分，故还原。
理修饰	定语	第一层：介词短语 of electronic means 作后置定语，修饰表语从句的主语 the use。第二层：介词短语 of payment 作后置定语，修饰 means。
	定从	that 引导的定语从句 [that] contains a large amount of personal data（主＋谓＋宾）修饰表语从句的宾语 an electronic trail。本句嵌套结构为表从＋嵌套定从。

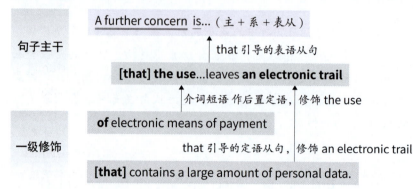

句子主干　A further concern is... (主 + 系 + 表从)

that 引导的表语从句

[that] the use...leaves an electronic trail

介词短语 作后置定语, 修饰 the use

一级修饰

of electronic means of payment

that 引导的定语从句, 修饰 an electronic trail

[that] contains a large amount of personal data.

【意群训练】

A further concern is // that the use // of electronic means of payment // leaves an electronic trail // that contains // a large amount of personal data.

实例 2

But almost all have ignored the big, profitable opportunity in their own backyard: the wholesale food and drink trade, which appears to be just the kind of market retailers need. 但是，几乎所有的食品零售商都忽视了自家后院的一个巨大盈利机会，即食品和饮料的批发生意，而这似乎正是零售商需要的市场。【英语（一）2010 新题型】

【难句类型】嵌套结构 + 省略　　　　　　　　　难度：★ ★ ★ ★

【难句破解】

找主干　过程	第一步：找从句标志词，并剥离该从句。找到标志词 which：距离 which 之后最近的动词是 appears to be，just the kind of market 作其表语，至此将该从句剥离。 第二步：识别非谓语动词，同时删除非谓语动词结构及其它修饰成分。本句无非谓语动词结构；删除修饰成分 in their own backyard，the wholesale food and drink trade。全句剩下了 But almost all have ignored the big, profitable opportunity retailers need。 第三步：识别并删除很像谓语动词的动词。根据辨析真假谓语动词的方法，及物动词 need 后缺失宾语，因此 retailers need 是省略关系词 that/which 的定语从句，need 是该从句的谓语动词，至此将该从句剥离。全句剩下了 But almost all have ignored the big, profitable opportunity，这就是句子的主干部分。

结果		But almost all have ignored the big, profitable opportunity
		（主＋谓＋宾）
		But 是表转折的连词，表示与上文的转折关系。

	定语	介词短语 in their own backyard 作后置定语，修饰 opportunity。
理修饰	解释说明	第一层：冒号后的内容对宾语 the big, profitable opportunity 进行解释说明。第二层：which 引导非限定性定语从句 [which] appears to be just the kind of market（主＋系＋表），补充说明 the wholesale food and drink trade。第三层：(that/which) retailers need（宾＋主＋谓）是省略关系词 that/which 的定语从句，修饰 market。本句的嵌套结构为定从＋嵌套定从。

看标点	冒号	冒号表示对前文内容进行解释说明。

【结构分析】

句子主干　　But almost all have ignored **the...opportunity**（主＋谓＋宾）

介词短语作后置定语，修饰 opportunity

in their own backyard:

一级修饰　　解释说明 the big, profitable opportunity

the wholesale food and drink trade,

which 引导的非限定性定语从句，补充说明 the wholesale food and drink trade

二级修饰　　**[which]** appears to be just the kind of **market**

省略关系词 (that/which) 的定语从句，修饰 market

三级修饰　　**(that/which)** retailers need.

【词汇注释】

ignore	[ɪg'nɔː(r)] *vt.* 忽视；对……不予理会；不予理睬
backyard	[ˌbæk'jɑːd] *n.* 后院
wholesale	['həʊlseɪl] *a.* 批发的；大规模的

【意群训练】

But almost all have ignored // the big, profitable opportunity // in their own backyard: // the wholesale food and drink trade, // which appears to be // just the kind of market // retailers need.

Instead of including that paragraph, she added one that described Lengel's crabbed response to the girls so that she could lead up to the A&P "policy" he enforces. 这位学生没有保留这一段，而是添加了一段话，描写兰格尔对那几个女孩的恶劣态度，这样就可以把内容导向兰格尔所推行的 A&P "政策"。【英语（一）2008 新题型】

【难句类型】嵌套结构＋省略　　　　　　　　　　　　　难度：★★★★
【难句破解】

| 找主干 | 过程 | 第一步：找从句标志词，并剥离该从句。❶找到第一个标志词 that：距离 that 之后最近的动词是 described，因 describe 是及物动词，故 Lengel's crabbed response 作其宾语，至此将该从句剥离；❷找到第二个标志词 so that：距离 so that 之后最近的动词是 could lead up to，介词 to 之后需要宾语，故 the A&P "policy" 作其宾语，至此将该从句剥离。

第二步：识别非谓语动词，同时删除非谓语动词结构及其它修饰成分。本句无非谓语动词结构；删除修饰成分 Instead of including that paragraph, to the girls。全句剩下了 she added one he enforces。

第三步：识别并删除很像谓语动词的动词。根据辨析真假谓语动词的方法，及物动词 enforces 后缺失宾语，因此 he enforces 是省略关系词 that/which 的定语从句，enforces 是该从句的谓语动词，至此将该从句剥离。全句剩下了 she added one，这就是句子的主干部分。 |
| | 结果 | she added one...（主＋谓＋宾） |

理修饰	状语	介词短语 Instead of including that paragraph 作状语。
	定从	第一层：that 引导的定语从句 **[that]** described Lengel's crabbed response to the girls（主＋谓＋宾）修饰宾语 one。第二层：介词短语 to the girls 作后置定语，修饰 response。
	状从	第一层：so that 引导目的状语从句 **[so that]** she could lead up to the A&P "policy" he enforces（主＋谓＋宾），作主句的目的状语。第二层：省略关系词 that/which 的定语从句 **(that/which)** he enforces（宾＋主＋谓）修饰 the A&P "policy"，that/which 作 enforces 的宾语。本句的嵌套结构为状从＋嵌套定从。

【结构分析】

一级修饰	**Instead of** including that paragraph,

介词短语作状语

句子主干　　she added **one**（主＋谓＋宾）

that 引导的定语从句，修饰 one

[that] described Lengel's crabbed response to the girls

一级修饰　　so that 引导的目的状语从句，作句子主干的目的状语

[so that] she could lead up to **the A&P "policy"**

省略关系词（that/which）的定语从句，修饰 the A&P "policy"

二级修饰　　**(that/which)** he enforces.

【词汇注释】

crabbed	['kræbɪd] *a.* 暴躁的；难懂的；潦草的	lead up to	导向；导致

【意群训练】

Instead of including that paragraph, //she added one // that described Lengel's crabbed response // to the girls // so that she could lead up to // the A&P "policy" // he enforces.

(六)　状语从句嵌套

结构为：主句＋从句，而从句中的某一成分或整个从句又被一个状语从句修饰。状语从句嵌套在考研英语中很常见，尤其是时间、条件、让步、比较状从，它的位置很灵活，可以嵌套在各种从句中，是考研长难句的一个重点。要注意区分状从修饰的是主句还是从句，修饰从句时才是嵌套状从。

---- 实例 1 ----

Research on animal intelligence also makes us wonder what experiments animals would perform on humans if they had the chance.
对动物智力的研究也使我们想弄明白：如果动物有机会的话，它们会对人类做什么样的实验。【英语（一）2009 完形】

【难句类型】嵌套结构　　　　　　　　　　　　　　　难度：★★★☆

【难句破解】

找主干	过程	第一步：找从句标志词，并剥离该从句。❶找到第一个标志词 what：距离 what 之后最近的动词是 would perform，至此将该从

	句剥离；❷找到第二个标志词 if：距离 if 之后最近的动词是 had，因 have 是及物动词，故 the chance 作其宾语，至此将该从句剥离。第二步：识别非谓语动词，同时删除非谓语动词结构及其它修饰成分。本句无非谓语动词结构；删除修饰成分 on animal intelligence, also, on humans。全句剩下了 Research makes us wonder，这就是句子的主干部分。第三步：识别并删除很像谓语动词的动词。（真正的谓语动词已找到，故该步骤略。）
过程	
结果	Research...makes us wonder...（主＋谓＋宾＋宾补） 省略 to 的动词不定式短语 wonder... 作宾语 us 的补足语。

	定语	介词短语 on animal intelligence 作后置定语，修饰主语 Research。
理修饰	宾从	what 引导的宾语从句 [what] experiments animals would perform on humans（宾＋主＋谓）作 wonder 的宾语。第一层：介词短语 on humans 作状语，表对象；if 引导条件状语从句 [if] they had the chance（主＋谓＋宾），在宾语从句中作条件状语。本句嵌套结构为宾从＋嵌套状从。

【结构分析】

| 一级修饰 | **on** animal intelligence |

↓ 介词短语作后置定语，修饰 Research

Research...also makes us **wonder**（主＋谓＋宾＋宾补）

| 句子主干 | what 引导的宾语从句，作 wonder 的宾语 |

[what] experiments animals would perform on humans

↑ if 引导的条件状语从句

| 一级修饰 | [if] they had the chance. |

【词汇注释】

| perform | [pə'fɔ:m] *vt.* 做；履行；执行 |

【意群训练】

Research on animal intelligence // also makes us wonder // what experiments // animals would perform // on humans // if they had the chance.

I have excluded him because, while his accomplishments may contribute to the solution of moral problems, he has not been charged with the task of approaching any but the factual aspects of those problems. 我之所以将普通科学家排除在外，是因为尽管他的成果可能有助于解决道德问题，但他承担的任务只不过是研究这些问题的事实层面。【英语（一）2006 翻译】

【难句类型】嵌套结构　　　　　　　　　　　　　　难度：★★★★
【难句破解】

找主干	过程	第一步：找从句标志词，并剥离该从句。❶找到第一个标志词 because 和第二个标志词 while（因二者同时出现，故放在一起分析）：距离 while 之后最近的动词是 may contribute to，介词 to 之后需要宾语，故 the solution 作其宾语，至此将 while 引导的从句剥离；❷至此距离 because 后面最近的动词剩下 has not been charged with，介词 with 之后需跟宾语，故 the task 作其宾语，至此将 because 引导的从句剥离。 第二步：识别非谓语动词，同时删除非谓语动词结构及其它修饰成分。本句无非谓语动词结构；删除修饰成分 of moral problems，of approaching...aspects，of those problems。全句剩下了 I have excluded him，这就是句子的主干部分。 第三步：识别并删除很像谓语动词的动词。（真正的谓语动词已找到，故该步骤略。）
	结果	I have excluded him...（主＋谓＋宾）
理修饰	状从	第一层：because 引导原因状语从句 [because]..., he has not been charged with the task（主＋谓＋宾）。第二层：介词短语 of approaching...aspects 作后置定语，修饰 the task，而介词短语 of those problems 作后置定语，修饰 the factual aspects；while 引导让步状语从句 [while] his accomplishments may contribute to the solution（主＋谓＋宾）在原因状语从句中作让步状语。第三层：介词短语 of moral problems 作后置定语，修饰 the solution。本句嵌套结构为状从＋嵌套状从。

句子主干　　I have excluded him　（主＋谓＋宾）

　　　　　　　　because 引导的原因状语从句，作句子主干的原因状语

一级修饰　　[because],...he has not been charged with **the task**

　　　　　　　　　　　　介词短语作后置定语，修饰 the task

　　　　　　of approaching any but the factual aspects of those problems.

二级修饰　　while 引导的让步状语从句

　　　　　　[while] his accomplishments may contribute to **the solution**

　　　　　　　　介词短语作后置定语，修饰 the solution

三级修饰　　　　　　　　　　　　**of** moral problems,

【词汇注释】

accomplishment	[əˈkʌmplɪʃmənt] n. 成就；才艺；完成
be charged with	承担；被控告
approach	[əˈprəʊtʃ] v. 靠近；接近；接洽 vt. 建议 n. 方法

【意群训练】

I have excluded him // because, // while his accomplishments // may contribute to // the solution of moral problems, // he has not been charged // with the task of // approaching any but the factual aspects // of those problems.

（七）　多个从句嵌套

　　考研英语中有时会出现多个从句嵌套的结构，即从句中还嵌套从句的现象。分析这种句子时，要准确抓住主干，理清各个句子之间的主从关系。

　　　实例 **1**

Boston Globe reporter Chris Reidy notes that the situation will improve only when there are comprehensive programs that address the many needs of the homeless. 《波士顿环球报》记者克里斯·雷迪认为，只有通过全面的规划来解决这些无家可归者的各种需求，这种局面才能有所改善。【英语（一）2006 完形】

【难句类型】嵌套结构＋强调　　　　　　　　　　难度：★★★★☆

【难句破解】

找主干	过程	第一步：找从句标志词，并剥离该从句。❶找到第一个标志词that：距离that之后最近的动词是will improve，至此将该从句剥离；❷找到第二个标志词when：距离when之后最近的动词是are，与前面的there构成there be结构，comprehensive programs作主语，至此将该从句剥离；❸找到第三个标志词that：距离that之后最近的动词是及物动词address，the many needs作其宾语，至此将该从句剥离。 第二步：识别非谓语动词，同时删除非谓语动词结构及其它修饰成分。本句无非谓语动词结构；删除修饰成分*Boston Globe* reporter和of the homeless。全句剩下了Chris Reidy notes，这就是句子的主谓部分。 第三步：识别并删除很像谓语动词的动词。（真正的谓语动词已找到，故该步骤略。）
	结果	...Chris Reidy notes [that] the situation will improve...（主＋谓＋宾从） that引导的宾语从句 [that] the situation will improve...（主＋谓）作notes的宾语，是句子的主干成分，故还原。
理修饰	同位语	*Boston Globe* reporter是主语Chris Reidy的同位语，用于说明主语的身份。
	状从	第一层：when引导的条件状语从句中，there are comprehensive programs是一个there be句型，该从句作宾语从句的条件状语，only表强调。第二层：that引导的定语从句 [that] address the many needs of the homeless（主＋谓＋宾），修饰programs。其中，that代替先行词programs作从句的主语；本句嵌套结构为宾从＋嵌套状从＋嵌套定从。第三层：介词短语of the homeless作后置定语，修饰needs。

【结构分析】

一级修饰　　*Boston Globe* reporter
　　　　　　　↓ Chris Reidy 的同位语
句子主干　　**Chris Reidy** notes [that] the...improve（主＋谓＋宾从）
　　　　　　　↑ when 引导的条件状语从句
一级修饰　　only [when] there are comprehensive **programs**
　　　　　　　　　　↑ that 引导的定语从句，修饰 programs
二级修饰　　[that] address the many **needs**
　　　　　　　　　　↑ 介词短语作后置定语，修饰 needs
三级修饰　　**of** the homeless.

59

comprehensive	[ˌkɒmprɪˈhensɪv] *a.* 全面的；详尽的；所有的；综合性的

【意群训练】

Boston Globe reporter // Chris Reidy // notes // that the situation will improve // only when there are // comprehensive programs // that address the many needs // of the homeless.

---- 实例 2 --->>>>

That matters because theory suggests that the maximum sustainable yield that can be cropped from a fishery comes when the biomass of a target species is about 50% of its original levels. 这很重要，因为"动态基准"理论指出：当目标物种的生物量大约是初始水平的 50% 时，渔场能够获得最大持续渔获量。【英语（一）2006 Text 3】

【难句类型】嵌套结构　　　　　　　　　　　　难度：★★★★★
【难句破解】

找主干	过程	第一步：找从句标志词，并剥离该从句。❶找到第一个标志词 because：距离 because 之后最近的动词是 suggests，至此将该从句剥离；❷找到第二个标志词 that：距离 that 之后最近的动词是 can be cropped，但该动词距离第三个标志词 that 更近，因此其应是第三个标志词 that 引导的从句的动词，故可将第三个标志词 that 引导的从句 that can be cropped 剥离；❸之后可找到第二个标志词 that 引导的从句真正的谓语 comes，至此将该从句剥离；❹找到第四个标志词 when：距离 when 之后最近的动词是 is，about 50% 作其表语，至此将该从句剥离。第二步：识别非谓语动词，同时删除非谓语动词结构及其它修饰成分。本句无非谓语动词结构；删除修饰成分 from a fishery，of its original levels。全句剩下了 That matters，这就是句子的主谓部分。第三步：识别并删除很像谓语动词的动词。（真正的谓语动词已找到，故该步骤略。）
	结果	That matters...（主 + 谓）
理修饰	状从	第一层：because 引导的原因状语从句 **[because]** theory suggests **[that]**...（主 + 谓 + 宾从）作主句的原因状语，其中第一个 that 引导的宾语从句 **[that]** the maximum sustainable yield...comes（主 + 谓）作 suggests 的宾语。第二层：第二个 that 引导的定语从句 **[that]** can be cropped from a fishery（主 + 谓）修饰 yield，其中介词短语 from a fishery 作状语；when 引导

的时间状语从句 **[when]** the biomass of a target species is about 50% of its original levels（主＋系＋表），作宾从的时间状语，本句嵌套结构为状从＋嵌套宾从＋嵌套定从/嵌套状从。第三层：该状语从句中，介词短语 of a target species 作后置定语，修饰主语 the biomass，介词短语 of its original levels 作后置定语，修饰表语 about 50%。

【结构分析】

句子主干　　That matters（主＋谓）

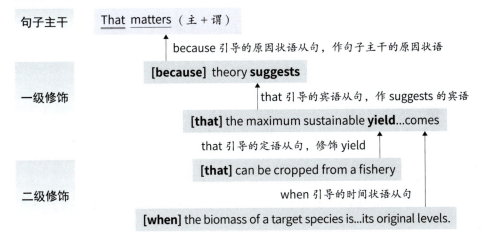

一级修饰

because 引导的原因状语从句，作句子主干的原因状语

[because] theory **suggests**

that 引导的宾语从句，作 suggests 的宾语

[that] the maximum sustainable **yield**...comes

that 引导的定语从句，修饰 yield

[that] can be cropped from a fishery

二级修饰

when 引导的时间状语从句

[when] the biomass of a target species is...its original levels.

【词汇注释】

yield	[ji:ld] *n.* 产量；产出；利润 *v.* 出产；屈服
crop	[krɒp] *vt.* 收获；收割 *n.* 庄稼；收成
sustainable	[sə'steɪnəbl] *a.* 可持续的；不破坏生态平衡的

【意群训练】

That matters // because theory suggests // that the maximum sustainable yield // that can be cropped // from a fishery // comes // when the biomass // of a target species // is about 50% // of its original levels.

（三）平行结构（并列结构）

　　平行结构，即并列结构，指两个或两个以上意义相关、层次相同、语法功能相同的词、词组或句子并列在一起，在句子中作同一个成分。平行的多个成分可以很简单（单个的词或词组平行），也可以很复杂（句子平行），平行的各个成分通常用并列连词连接。连接平行结构的连词主要有：

and, but, or, or else, as well as, both...and, either...or, neither...nor, not only...but (also), rather than 等。有趣的是，英语中的平行结构实际上涵盖了汉语中的排比、对偶以及反复等修辞手段，因此在备考考研英语的过程中，一定要掌握常见的平行结构。

（一）单词（词组）平行

1. 名词（词组）平行

这类平行结构形式一致，很容易区分。在考研英语中较为常见，但不作为考查重点。

— 实例 1

Nevertheless, as any biographer knows, a person's early life and its conditions are often the greatest gift to an individual. 不过，正如任何一位传记作家所知道的那样，一个人的早期生活和那时的环境往往是他得到的最珍贵的礼物。【英语（一）2011 翻译】

【难句类型】平行结构＋从句　　　　　　　　　　　　　　难度：★★★
【难句破解】

找主干	过程	第一步：找从句标志词，并剥离该从句。找到标志词 as：距离 as 之后最近的动词是 knows，至此将该从句剥离。 第二步：识别非谓语动词，同时删除非谓语动词结构及其它修饰成分。本句无非谓语动词结构；删除修饰成分 Nevertheless, often, to an individual。全句剩下了 a person's early life and its conditions are the greatest gift，这就是句子的主干部分。 第三步：识别并删除很像谓语动词的动词。（真正的谓语动词已找到，故该步骤略。）
	结果	..., a person's early life and its conditions are the greatest gift...（主＋系＋表）
理修饰	状语	句首的副词 Nevertheless 作状语；副词 often 作状语修饰 are。
	定从	as 引导的非限定性定语从句 [as] any biographer knows（宾＋主＋谓）修饰主句，as 代替主句的内容，在从句中作 knows 的宾语。
	定语	介词短语 to an individual 作后置定语，修饰 gift。
看标点	逗号	根据成对出现的逗号，不难判断出 as...knows 为插入部分，即非限定性定语从句作插入语。

【结构分析】

一级修饰	Nevertheless，**[as]** any biographer knows，

as 引导的非限定性定语从句

句子主干	a person's...conditions <u>are often the greatest **gift**</u> (主 + 系 + 表)

介词短语作后置定语，修饰 gift

一级修饰	**to** an individual.

【词汇注释】

individual	[ˌɪndɪˈvɪdʒuəl] *n.* 个人 *adj.* 单独的；个别的

【意群训练】

Nevertheless, // as any biographer knows, // a person's early life and its conditions // are often the greatest gift // to an individual.

2. 形容词、副词平行

形式一致，容易区分。此类平行在考研英语中不作为考查重点。

------ 实例 1 ------

The theory also seems to explain the sudden and unexpected popularity of certain looks, brands, or neighborhoods. 这个理论似乎也解释了为什么某些样式、品牌或者地段会突然受到意想不到的欢迎。【英语（一）2010 Text 3】

【难句类型】平行结构 + 非谓语动词   难度：★★★

【难句破解】

找主干	过程	第一步：找从句标志词，并剥离该从句。(本句中无从句，故该步骤略。) 第二步：识别非谓语动词，同时删除非谓语动词结构及其它修饰成分。删除非谓语动词结构 to explain...popularity。删除修饰成分 also，sudden and unexpected，of certain looks, brands, or neighborhoods。全句剩下了 The theory seems，这就是句子的主系部分。 第三步：识别并删除很像谓语动词的动词。（真正的谓语动词已找到，故该步骤略。）
	结果	<u>The theory</u>...<u>seems to explain the...popularity</u>... (主 + 系 + 表) 动词不定式短语 to explain the...popularity 作表语，是句子的主干成分，故还原。副词 also 作状语，修饰 seems。

理修饰	定语	sudden 和 unexpected 为两个并列的形容词作前置定语修饰表语 popularity；介词短语 of certain looks, brands, or neighborhoods 作后置定语，同样修饰 popularity，且该后置定语中出现了三个并列的名词。

【结构分析】

句子主干	The theory also seems to explain the…and unexpected **popularity**

介词短语作后置定语，修饰 popularity

一级修饰	**of** certain looks, brands, or neighborhoods.

【词汇注释】

popularity	[ˌpɒpjuˈlærəti] *n.* 受欢迎；普及；流行

【意群训练】

The theory also seems // to explain the sudden and unexpected popularity // of certain looks, brands, or neighborhoods.

3. 动词（谓语动词和非谓语动词）平行

形式一致，容易区分。考研英语中，经常出现谓语和其后的宾语一起并列的情况。需要注意的是，除了谓语动词，非谓语动词也会出现平行结构。

---- 实例 1 ---->>>>>

For H&M to offer a \$5.95 knit miniskirt in all its 2,300-plus stores around the world, it must rely on low-wage overseas labor, order in volumes that strain natural resources, and use massive amounts of harmful chemicals. 对于 H&M 公司来说，如果要在其全球 2300 多家门店出售一款 5.95 美元的针织迷你裙，它就必须依赖廉价的海外劳动力，以及造成自然资源过度消耗的批量订单，并使用大量有害化学物质。【英语（一）2013 Text 1】

【难句类型】平行结构 + 从句   难度：★ ★ ★ ★
【难句破解】

找主干	过程	第一步：找从句标志词，并剥离该从句。找到标志词 that：距离 that 之后最近的动词是及物动词 strain，natural resources 作其宾语，至此将该从句剥离。 第二步：识别非谓语动词，同时删除非谓语动词结构及其它修饰成分。删除非谓语动词结构 to offer a \$5.95 knit miniskirt；删除修

找主干	过程	饰成分 For H&M，in all its 2,300-plus stores around the world，in volumes。全句剩下了 it must rely on low-wage overseas labor, order and use massive amounts of harmful chemicals，这就是句子的主干部分。 第三步：识别并删除很像谓语动词的动词。（真正的谓语动词已找到，故该步骤略。）
	结果	..., it must rely on low-wage overseas labor, order...and use massive amounts of harmful chemicals.（主＋谓1＋宾1＋and＋谓2＋宾2） 该句中，and 连接的两个并列谓语动词之后都有宾语，构成平行的谓宾结构。
理修饰	状语	第一层：介词短语 For H&M 作状语，引出动作的执行者；动词不定式短语 to offer a $5.95 knit miniskirt 作目的状语。第二层：介词短语 in all its 2,300-plus stores around the world 作地点状语。
	定语	第一层：介词短语 in volumes 作后置定语，修饰 order；定语从句 **[that]** strain natural resources（主＋谓＋宾）修饰 order。

【结构分析】

二级修饰　in all its 2,300-plus stores around the world,

介词短语作地点状语

二级修饰　For H&M **to** offer a $5.95 knit miniskirt

[that] strain natural resources,

that 引导的定语从句，修饰 order

动词不定式短语作目的状语

句子主干　it **must rely on** low-wage...labor，**order** in volumes（主＋谓＋宾）

and 连接的并列谓宾

and use massive amounts of harmful chemicals.

【词汇注释】

knit	[nɪt] *n.* 针织衫 *vt.&vi.* 编织；使紧密结合
strain	[streɪn] *vt.* 过度使用；拉紧；过滤 *n.* 压力；拉力

【意群训练】

For H&M // to offer a $5.95 knit miniskirt // in all its 2,300-plus stores // around the world, // it must rely on // low-wage overseas labor, // order in volumes // that strain natural resources, // and use massive amounts of // harmful chemicals.

---- 实例 2 --->>>

In many such cases, a cursory search for causes finds that some small group of people was wearing, promoting, or developing whatever it is before anyone else paid attention. 在诸多此类情形中，粗略调查其原因发现，在其他人留意之前，一小部分人已经在穿戴、宣传或开发各类东西了。
【英语（一）2010 Text 3】

【难句类型】平行结构 + 嵌套结构　　　　　　　　　　　难度：★★★★
【难句破解】

找主干	过程	第一步：找从句标志词，并剥离该从句。❶找到第一个标志词 that：距离 that 之后最近的动词是 was wearing, promoting, or developing，至此将该从句剥离；❷找到第二个标志词 whatever：距离 whatever 之后最近的动词是 is，至此将该从句剥离；❸找到第三个标志词 before：距离 before 之后最近的动词是及物动词 pay 的过去式 paid，attention 作其宾语，至此将该从句剥离。 第二步：识别非谓语动词，同时删除非谓语动词结构及其它修饰成分。本句无非谓语动词结构；删除修饰成分 In many such cases 和 for causes。全句剩下了 a cursory search finds，这就是句子的主谓部分。 第三步：识别并删除很像谓语动词的动词。（真正的谓语动词已找到，故该步骤略。）
	结果	..., a cursory search...finds [that]...（主 + 谓 + 宾从） that 引导的宾语从句 [that] some small group of people was wearing, promoting, or developing [whatever]...（主 + 谓 + 宾从）作 finds 的宾语，是主干成分，故还原。该宾从的谓语中包含三个并列的谓语动词。
理修饰	状语	介词短语 In many such cases 作主句的状语，表范围。
	定语	介词短语 for causes 作后置定语，修饰主语 a cursory search。
	宾从 的修饰	主句宾从的宾语是 whatever 引导的嵌套宾从 [whatever] it is（表 + 主 + 系）。第一层：before 引导的时间状语从句 [before] anyone else paid attention（主 + 谓 + 宾）作 that 引导的宾从的时间状语，本句的嵌套结构是宾从 + 嵌套宾从 / 嵌套状从。

66

【结构分析】

一级修饰   **In** many such cases,

介词短语作状语

a cursory search for causes **finds**（主＋谓＋宾从）

that 引导的宾语从句，作 finds 的宾语

句子主干   **[that]** some small group…**was wearing, promoting, or developing**

whatever 引导的宾语从句，作三个并列谓语的宾语

[whatever] it is

before 引导的时间状语从句

一级修饰   **[before]** anyone else paid attention.

【词汇注释】

cursory	['kɜːsəri] *a.* 粗略的；仓促的

【意群训练】

In many such cases, // a cursory search for causes finds // that some small group of people was wearing, promoting, or developing // whatever it is // before anyone else paid attention.

（二）　短语平行

1. 介词短语平行

　　介词短语平行常见的有 of 介词短语的平行和 with、over 介词短语的平行。该结构是考研英语中的常考点，而且有时会出现不同介词构成的介词短语平行的情况。

--------- 实例 1

In those far-off days, it was taken for granted that the critics of major papers would write in detail and at length about the events they covered. 在那些遥远的岁月里，人们理所当然地认为：主流报纸的评论家们会把他们所报道的事件充分详细地记录下来。【英语（一）2010 Text 1】

【难句类型】平行结构＋省略＋嵌套结构   难度：★★★★

【难句破解】

找主干	过程	第一步：找从句标志词，并剥离该从句。找到标志词 that：距离 that 之后最近的动词是 would write，至此将该从句剥离。

找主干	过程	第二步：识别非谓语动词，同时删除非谓语动词结构及其它修饰成分。本句无非谓语动词结构；删除修饰成分 In those far-off days，for granted，in detail and at length，about the events。全句还剩下 it was taken they covered。 第三步：识别并删除很像谓语动词的动词。根据辨析真假谓语动词的方法，及物动词 covered 后缺失宾语，因此 they covered 是省略 that/which 的定语从句，covered 是该从句的谓语动词，至此将该从句剥离。全句剩下了 it was taken，这就是句子的主谓部分。
	结果	...it was taken for granted [that]...（主＋谓＋主补） it 为形式主语，for granted 为主语补足语，与主语联系紧密；that 引导的主语从句为真正的主语，是主干成分，故二者均还原。
理修饰	状语	介词短语 In those far-off days 作时间状语。
	主从	that 引导主语从句 **[that]** the critics...would write...about the events（主＋谓＋宾），作句子主干的真正主语。第一层：介词短语 of major papers 作后置定语，修饰主从的主语 the critics；主从的谓语 would write about 被 and 连接的两个并列的介词短语 in detail 和 at length 修饰；省略关系词的定语从句 **(that/which)** they covered（宾＋主＋谓）修饰其先行词 the events，that / which 代替先行词作定从的宾语。

【结构分析】

一级修饰　　**In** those far-off days,

　　　　　　　介词短语作时间状语

句子主干　　**it** was taken for granted （主＋谓）

　　　　　it 作形式主语，that 引导的主语从句作真正的主语

　　　　　[that] the critics...would write...about **the events**

　　介词短语作后置定语，修饰 the critics

　　　　　　of major papers

　　　　　　　　　　　　　　　　省略关系词（that/which）的
　　　　　　　　　　　　　　　　定语从句，修饰 the events

一级修饰　　　　　　　　　　**(that/which)** they covered.

　　　　　　　　　and 连接的并列介词短语作状语

　　　　　　　　in detail **and at** length

【词汇注释】

far-off	['fɑː(r)ɒf] *a.* 遥远的

in detail and at length	充分而详细地
take it for granted	视为当然；把……当成理所当然

【意群训练】

In those far-off days, // it was taken for granted // that the critics // of major papers // would write // in detail and at length // about the events // they covered.

2. 分词短语平行

分词短语平行即现在分词短语或过去分词短语的平行,形式一致,容易区分。

------ 实例 1 ------ >>>>>

Politicians have repeatedly "backloaded" public-sector pay deals, keeping the pay increases modest but adding to holidays and especially pensions that are already generous. 政治家们一再"变相上调"公共部门的薪酬待遇, 使薪酬保持低幅增长, 但却增加了节假日, 尤其是增加了原本就已经丰厚的养老金。【英语（一）2012 Text 4】

【难句类型】平行结构 + 非谓语动词 + 从句   难度：★★★☆

【难句破解】

找主干	过程	第一步：找从句标志词, 并剥离该从句。找到标志词 that：距离 that 之后最近的动词是 are, generous 作其表语, 至此将该从句剥离。第二步：识别非谓语动词, 同时删除非谓语动词结构及其它修饰成分。删除非谓语动词结构 keeping the pay increases modest 和 adding to...pensions。删除修饰成分 repeatedly。因 but 在两个非谓语动词结构之间, 表并列, 故也删除。全句剩下了 Politicians have "backloaded" public-sector pay deals, 这就是句子的主干部分。第三步：识别并删除很像谓语动词的动词。（真正的谓语动词已找到, 故该步骤略。）
	结果	Politicians have..."backloaded" public-sector pay deals...（主 + 谓 + 宾）副词 repeatedly 作状语, 修饰谓语 have "backloaded"。
理修饰	状语	第一层：but 连接两个并列的现在分词短语 keeping the pay increases modest 和 adding to...pensions, 作主句的伴随状语。第二层：that 引导的定语从句 [that] are already generous（主 + 系 + 表）, 修饰 pensions, 其中副词 already 作状语。

句子主干　Politicians have repeatedly "backloaded" public...deals

↑ 现在分词短语作伴随状语

一级修饰

keeping the pay increases modest

but 连接的并列现在分词短语，作伴随状语

but adding to holidays and especially **pensions**

that 引导的定语从句，修饰 pensions

二级修饰　[that] are already generous.

【词汇注释】

modest	['mɒdɪst] *a.* 些许的；谦虚的；庄重的
pension	['penʃn] *n.* 养老金；退休金；抚恤金

【意群训练】

Politicians have repeatedly "backloaded" // public-sector pay deals, // keeping the pay increases modest // but adding to holidays and especially pensions // that are already generous.

3. 动名词短语平行

平行的动名词短语形式一致，容易区分，但要注意区分动名词和现在分词：若在句中作宾语或主语，或有名词性质，则是动名词；若作状语，则是现在分词；若作表语或定语，则需要进行判断。

------ 实例 1 ------

Parts of the ceremony involve ritual hair cutting, tying cotton threads soaked in holy water around the bride's and groom's wrists, and passing a candle around a circle of happily married and respected couples to bless the union. 典礼包含剪发仪式，将浸过圣水的棉线系在新娘和新郎的手腕上，把一只蜡烛在婚姻幸福且受人尊敬的夫妻中传递一圈以祝福这场婚姻等环节。【英语（一）2016 完形】

【难句类型】平行结构＋非谓语动词　　　　　　　难度：★★★★

【难句破解】

找主干	过程	第一步：找从句标志词，并剥离该从句。(本句中无从句，故该步骤略。)

找主干	过程	第二步：识别非谓语动词，同时删除非谓语动词结构及其它修饰成分。删除非谓语动词结构 tying cotton threads，soaked in holy water，passing a candle 和 to bless the union。删除修饰成分 around the bride's and groom's wrists，around a circle，of happily married and respected couples。全句剩下了 Parts of the ceremony involve ritual hair cutting，这就是句子主干的一部分。 第三步：识别并删除很像谓语动词的动词。（真正的谓语动词已找到，故该步骤略。）
	结果	Parts of the ceremony involve ritual hair cutting, tying cotton threads...and passing a candle...（主＋谓＋宾1＋宾2＋and＋宾3）and 连接的两个并列的动名词短语亦作宾语，是句子主干成分，故还原，这才是完整的句子主干部分。
理修饰	定语	过去分词短语 soaked in holy water 作后置定语，修饰 cotton threads。
	状语	第一层：介词短语 around a circle 作方式状语；动词不定式短语 to bless the union 作目的状语。第二层：介词短语 of happily married and respected couples 作后置定语，修饰 a circle。

【结构分析】

一级修饰	**to** bless the union.	
	↓ 动词不定式短语作目的状语	
句子主干	**Parts of the ceremony** involve ritual hair cutting （主＋谓＋宾）	
	┃ 并列宾语	
	tying cotton threads...around the bride's and groom's wrists,	
	┃ 过去分词短语作后置定语，修饰 cotton threads	
一级修饰	**soaked** in holy water	
	┃ and 连接的并列动名词短语，作宾语	
句子主干	**and passing** a candle	
	↑ 介词短语作方式状语	
一级修饰	**around a circle**	
	↑ 介词短语作后置定语，修饰 a acircle	
二级修饰	**of** happily married and respected couples	

71

ritual	['rɪtʃuəl] *a.* 仪式上的；习惯的 *n.* 仪规；习惯
soak	[səuk] *vi.* 浸泡；渗透 *vt.* 使湿透

【意群训练】

Parts of the ceremony involve // ritual hair cutting, // tying cotton threads // soaked in holy water // around the bride's and groom's wrists, // and passing a candle // around a circle // of happily married and respected couples // to bless the union.

4. 动词不定式短语平行

平行的动词不定式短语形式一致，容易区分。动词不定式短语常平行作状语、主语、宾语或表语。分词短语平行、动名词短语平行和不定式短语平行都属于非谓语动词短语的平行结构。

实例 1

And in Europe, some are up in arms over a proposal to drop a specific funding category for social-science research and to integrate it within cross-cutting topics of sustainable development. 在欧洲，有些人竭力反对一项"终止专用于社会科学研究的资金，转而将其融入可持续发展的跨领域课题"的提案。【英语（一）2013 新题型】

【难句类型】平行结构 + 非谓语动词　　　　　　　　　　难度：★★★

【难句破解】

找主干	过程	第一步：找从句标志词，并剥离该从句。（本句中无从句，故该步骤略。） 第二步：识别非谓语动词，同时删除非谓语动词结构及其它修饰成分。删除非谓语动词结构 to drop a specific funding category，to integrate it。删除修饰成分 in Europe, for social-science research, within cross-cutting topics, of sustainable development。and 在这些被删除的成分之间，起连接作用，故也删除。全句剩下了 some are up in arms over a proposal，这就是句子的主干部分。 第三步：识别并删除很像谓语动词的动词。（真正的谓语动词已找到，故该步骤略。）

	结果	And..., some are up in arms over a proposal...（主＋谓＋宾） 句首的连词 And 表顺接。
理修饰	状语	介词短语 in Europe 作地点状语。
	定语	第一层：and 连接并列的动词不定式短语 to drop a specific funding category 和 to integrate it 作后置定语，修饰 a proposal。 第二层：介词短语 for social-science research 作后置定语，修饰 category；介词短语 within cross-cutting topics 作第二个动词不定式短语的状语。第三层：介词短语 of sustainable development 作后置定语，修饰 topics。

【结构分析】

句子主干　And in Europe, some are up in arms over **a proposal**（主＋谓＋宾）

动词不定式短语作后置定语，修饰 a proposal

to drop a specific funding category for social-science research

一级修饰　and 连接的并列动词不定式短语

and to integrate it

介词短语作状语

二级修饰　**within** cross-cutting **topics**

介词短语作后置定语，修饰 topics

三级修饰　**of** sustainable development.

【词汇注释】

be up in arms over	竭力反对；强烈抗议
integrate	['ɪntɪɡreɪt] v. 使合并；使加入

【意群训练】

And in Europe, // some are up in arms over // a proposal // to drop a specific funding category // for social-science research // and to integrate it // within cross-cutting topics // of sustainable development.

（三）句子平行

1. 从句平行

　　从句平行由同类型的从句并列而成，一个句子中可能出现不止一处平行，考研英语中常见状从和宾从的平行结构。注意要将从句的平行结构与嵌套结构区分开。

实例 1

Unable to tell whether someone really objects to behavioural ads or whether they are sticking with Microsoft's default, some may ignore a DNT signal and press on anyway. 由于无法辨别用户是真的反对行为广告，还是坚持使用微软的默认设置，一些公司可能会忽略"禁止追踪"信号，继续追踪用户信息。【英语（一）2013 Text 2】

【难句类型】平行结构＋从句   难度：★★★
【难句破解】

找主干	过程	第一步：找从句标志词，并剥离该从句。❶找到第一个标志词 whether：距离 whether 之后最近的动词是 objects to，介词 to 后需跟宾语，故 behavioural ads 作其宾语，至此将该从句剥离；❷找到第二个标志词 whether：距离 whether 之后最近的动词是 are sticking with，介词 with 后需跟宾语，故 Microsoft's default 作其宾语，至此将该从句剥离。 第二步：识别非谓语动词，同时删除非谓语动词结构及其它修饰成分。本句无非谓语动词结构；删除修饰成分 Unable to tell...or...，anyway。全句剩下了 some may ignore a DNT signal and press on，这就是句子的主干部分。 第三步：识别并删除很像谓语动词的动词。（真正的谓语动词已找到，故该步骤略。）
	结果	..., some <u>may ignore</u> a <u>DNT signal</u> and <u>press on</u>...（主＋谓 1＋宾＋and＋谓 2）
理修饰	状语	第一层：形容词短语 Unable to tell... 作原因状语；anyway 作状语，修饰 press on。在原因状语中，or 连接两个并列的宾语从句 **[whether]** someone really <u>objects to</u> behavioural ads（主＋谓＋宾）和 **[whether]** they <u>are sticking with</u> Microsoft's default（主＋谓＋宾），共同作 tell 的宾语；第一个宾从中，副词 really 作状语，修饰谓语 objects to。

Unable to **tell**

　　　　　whether 引导的宾语从句，作 tell 的宾语

一级修饰　　**[whether]** someone really objects to behavioural ads

　　　　　or 连接的并列宾语从句

　　　　　or [whether] they are sticking with Microsoft's default,

　　　　　形容词短语作原因状语

句子主干　　some may ignore a DNT signal and press on anyway.（主＋谓＋宾）

【词汇注释】

object to	反对……；抗议……
stick with	坚持……；紧跟
press on	决心继续；向前推进；压

【意群训练】

Unable to tell // whether someone really objects to // behavioural ads // or whether they are sticking with // Microsoft's default, // some may ignore // a DNT signal // and press on anyway.

─── 实例 2 ────────────────────────────────>>>>

According to accounts of the experiments, their hourly output rose when lighting was increased, but also when it was dimmed. 根据实验描述，当照明灯光变亮时，女工每小时的产量就会增加，而当照明灯光变暗时，她们每小时的产量也会增加。　【英语（一）2010 完形】

【难句类型】平行结构＋从句　　　　　　　　　　　难度：★★★

【难句破解】

找主干	过程	第一步：找从句标志词，并剥离该从句。❶找到第一个标志词 when：距离 when 之后最近的动词是 was increased，至此将该从句剥离；❷找到第二个标志词 when：距离 when 之后最近的动词是 was dimmed，至此将该从句剥离。 第二步：识别非谓语动词，同时删除非谓语动词结构及其它修饰成分。本句无非谓语动词结构；删除修饰成分 According to accounts of the experiments, also。因 but 在两个从句之间，起连接作用，故也删除。全句剩下了 their hourly output rose，这就是句子的主谓部分。

找主干		第三步：识别并删除很像谓语动词的动词。（真正的谓语动词已找到，故该步骤略。）
	结果	..., their hourly output rose...（主＋谓）
理修饰	状语	介词短语 According to accounts of the experiments 作状语。
	状从	but 连接两个并列的 when 引导的时间状语从句 [when] lighting was increased（主＋谓）和 [when] it was dimmed（主＋谓），二者都是被动语态，作主句的时间状语；副词 also 修饰第二个状从。

【结构分析】

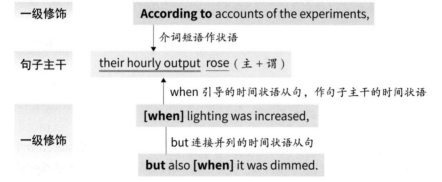

【意群训练】

According to accounts of the experiments, // their hourly output rose // when lighting was increased, // but also when it was dimmed.

2. 整句平行

　　整句平行由几个句子并列而成。可能是简单句的平行，简单句与复合句的平行，或复合句的平行。有时，一个句子中会出现不止一处平行。在整句平行中，几个分句的连接方式可能为逗号＋并列连词，并列连词或分号。

　　要注意辨别谓宾平行和整句平行，如果几个平行结构只有一个主语，那么这是谓宾平行；如果每个平行结构都有自己的主语，这就是整句平行。

Children will play with dolls equipped with personality chips, computers with in-built personalities will be regarded as workmates rather than tools, relaxation will be in front of smell-television, and digital age will have arrived. 儿童将与装有个性化芯片的玩具娃娃玩耍，具有个性内置的计算机将被视为工作伙伴而不是工具，人们将在气味电视机前消遣自娱，届时数字化时代就到来了。【英语（一）2001 翻译】

【难句类型】平行结构 + 非谓语动词 + 省略　　　　　　　难度：★★★☆

【难句破解】

找主干	过程	第一步：找从句标志词，并剥离该从句。（本句中无从句，故该步骤略。） 第二步：识别非谓语动词，同时删除非谓语动词结构及其它修饰成分。删除非谓语动词结构 equipped with personality chips；删除修饰成分 with dolls，with in-built personalities，as workmates rather than tools，in front of smell-television。全句剩下了 Children will play, computers will be regarded , relaxation will be, and digital age will have arrived，这就是句子主干的一部分。 第三步：识别并删除很像谓语动词的动词。（真正的谓语动词已找到，故该步骤略。）
	结果	Children will play…, computers…will be regarded as workmates rather than (as) tools, relaxation will be in front of smell-television, and digital age will have arrived.（主 1 + 谓 1 + 主 2 + 谓 2 + 主补 + 主 3 + 系 + 表 + and + 主 4 + 谓 4） 该主干中包含了四个并列的简单句。其中介词短语 as workmates rather than tools 作主语补足语，与主语联系紧密；介词短语 in front of smell-television 作表语，是主干成分，故二者均还原。
理修饰	状语	第一层：介词短语 with dolls 作状语，修饰 will play。第二层：过去分词短语 equipped with personality chips 作后置定语，修饰 dolls。
	定语	介词短语 with in-built personalities 作后置定语，修饰 computers。
	补语	rather than 连接并列的主语补足语 as workmates 和（as）tools，肯定前者，否定后者，属于介词短语平行。为避免重复，tools 前的 as 被省略了。

【结构分析】

二级修饰　　**equipped** with personality chips,
　　　　　　　　　　　过去分词短语作后置定语，修饰 dolls

一级修饰　　　　　　**with dolls**
　　　　　介词短语作状语，修饰 will plays
　　　　　Children **will play**（主＋谓）
　　　　　　　　　　并列句
　　computers... will be regarded（主＋谓）
　　　　　　　　　并列句
　　　　　relaxation　will be　in front of smell-television
　　　　　　　　　and 连接的并列句
　　　　　　and digital age　will have arrived（主＋谓）
句子主干　　　　介词短语作后置定语，修饰 computers
　　　　　with in-built personalities
　　　　rather than 连接并列的介词 短语，作 computers 的补足语
一级修饰　**as** workmates **rather than**（**as**）tools,

【词汇注释】

equip	[ɪ'kwɪp] *vt.* 配备，装备；使有所准备；使有能力
personality	[ˌpɜ:sə'næləti] *n.* 个性；气质；名人
be regarded as	被认为是……，被看作是……

【意群训练】

Children will play with dolls // equipped with personality chips, // computers with in-built personalities // will be regarded // as workmates rather than tools, // relaxation will be // in front of smell-television, // and digital age // will have arrived.

---- 实例 2 ----

In theory, the success of an applicant should not depend on the few others chosen randomly for interview during the same day, but Dr. Simonsohn suspected the truth was otherwise. 理论上，某个申请者的成功不应取决于同一天被随机抽选参加面试的其他几名申请者，但是，西蒙逊博士怀疑事实并非如此。【英语（一）2013 完形】

【难句类型】平行结构＋省略＋从句　　　　　　　　　　　　难度：★★★☆

【难句破解】

<table>
<tr><td rowspan="2">找主干</td><td rowspan="2">过程</td><td>第一步：找从句标志词，并剥离该从句。（本句中无从句标志词，故该步骤略。）
第二步：识别非谓语动词，同时删除非谓语动词结构及其它修饰成分。删除非谓语动词结构 chosen randomly for interview。删除修饰成分 In theory，of an applicant，during the same day。全句还剩下 the success should not depend on the few others, but Dr. Simonsohn suspected the truth was otherwise。
第三步：识别并删除很像谓语动词的动词。根据辨析真假谓语动词的方法，句中剩下三个动词 should not depend on，suspected 和 was。其中前两个动词由 but 连接，且后均跟有宾语，说明它们是并列关系。则前面这两个并列的动词是主干的谓语动词，后面的 was 是省略 that 的宾语从句 the truth was otherwise 的动词，故将该从句剥离。全句剩下了 the success should not depend on the few others, but Dr. Simonsohn suspected，这就是句子的主干部分。</td></tr>
<tr></tr>
<tr><td></td><td>结果</td><td>…, the success…should not depend on the few others…, but Dr. Simonsohn suspected (that) the truth was otherwise.（主 1 ＋谓 1 ＋宾＋ but ＋主 2 ＋谓 2 ＋宾从）
本句是简单句和复合句的平行结构。其中省略 that 的宾语从句 (that) the truth was otherwise（主＋系＋表）作 suspected 的宾语，是主干成分，故还原。</td></tr>
<tr><td rowspan="2">理修饰</td><td>状语</td><td>句首的 In theory 作状语。</td></tr>
<tr><td>定语</td><td>第一层：介词短语 of an applicant 作 the success 的后置定语；过去分词短语 chosen randomly…day 作后置定语，修饰 the few others。
第二层：介词短语 during the same day 作 chosen 的时间状语。</td></tr>
</table>

【结构分析】

二级修饰　　　　　　　　　　　**during** the same day,

　　　　　　　　　　　　　　　　│　介词短语作 chosen 的时间状语
　　　　　　　　　　　　　　　　↑

一级修饰　　　　　　　　　**chosen** randomly for interview

　　　　　　　　过去分词短语作后置定语，修饰 the few others │

In theory, the success of an applicant should…on **the few others**

句子主干　　│ but 连接的并列句

but Dr. Simonsohn suspected **(that)** the…otherwise.（主＋谓＋宾从）

【词汇注释】

applicant	['æplɪkənt] *n.* 申请人
randomly	['rændəmli] *ad.* 随机地；随便地；任意地

【意群训练】

In theory, // the success of an applicant // should not depend on // the few others // chosen randomly // for interview during the same day, // but Dr. Simonsohn suspected // the truth was otherwise.

（四） 特殊的平行结构

1. 词（词组）后的平行

这种情况即指固定词组的平行。常见的有 prefer A to B, prefer doing A to doing B, prefer to do A rather than do B, A rather than B 等。

实例 1

Firms seem to invest more in places where most people are relatively happy, rather than in places with happiness inequality. 公司似乎会在大多数人相对幸福的地区投资更多，而非人们的幸福感不均衡的地方。【英语（二）2016 完形】

【难句类型】平行结构 + 从句 + 非谓语动词　　　　　　　　　难度：★★★

【难句破解】

找主干	过程	第一步：找从句标志词，并剥离从句。找到标志词 where：距离 where 之后最近的动词是 are, happy 作其表语，至此将该从句剥离。第二步：识别非谓语动词，同时删除非谓语动词结构及其它修饰成分。删除非谓语动词结构 to invest more；删除修饰成分 in places，rather than in places，with happiness inequality。全句剩下了 Firms seem，这就是句子的主系部分。第三步：识别并删除很像谓语动词的动词。（真正的谓语动词已找到，故该步骤略。）
	结果	Firms seem to invest more...（主 + 系 + 表）动词不定式 to invest more 作表语，是主干成分，故还原。
理修饰	状语一	第一层：介词短语 in places 作地点状语。第二层：where 引导的定语从句 where most people are relatively happy（主 + 系 + 表）修饰 places，其中副词 relatively 作状语，修饰 happy。
	状语二	第一层：rather than 连接并列的介词短语 in places，作地点状语，肯定前者，否定后者。第二层：介词短语 with happiness inequality 作后置定语，修饰 places。

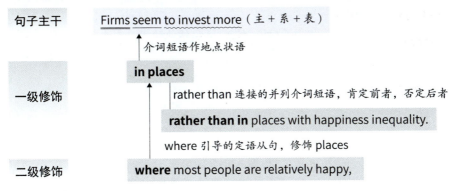

Firms seem to invest more // in places // where most people are relatively happy, rather than in places // with happiness inequality.

2. 结构后的平行

结构后的平行即指固定句式中的平行。考研中的结构平行一般较明显，找标志词即可。常见的有 would rather/sooner do A than do B，had rather/sooner do A than do B，would/had as soon as do A than do B，either...or, neither...nor, not only...but also 等。

········ 实例 1 ········>>>>>>

For the time, attention, and money of the art-loving public, classical instrumentalists must compete not only with opera houses, dance troupes, theater companies, and museums, but also with the recorded performances of the great classical musicians of the 20th century. 为了赢得艺术爱好者的时间、关注以及金钱，古典音乐的演奏家不仅必须要和剧院、舞蹈团、剧团及博物馆竞争，还要和 20 世纪伟大的古典音乐家们的录制品竞争。【英语（一）2011 Text 1】

【难句类型】平行结构　　　　　　　　　　　　难度：★★★☆

【难句破解】

| 找主干 | 过程 | 第一步：找从句标志词，并剥离该从句。（本句中无从句，故该步骤略。）第二步：识别非谓语动词，同时删除非谓语动词结构及其它修饰成分。本句无非谓语动词结构；删除修饰成分 For the time...public；not only with...recorded performances；of the great classical musicians，of the 20th century。全句剩下了 |

		classical instrumentalists must compete，这就是句子的主干部分。 第三步：识别并删除很像谓语动词的动词。（真正的谓语动词已找到，故该步骤略。）
	结果	..., classical instrumentalists <u>must compete</u>...（主＋谓）
理修饰	状语一	第一层：介词短语 For the time, attention, and money 作目的状语，其中 and 连接三个并列的名词。第二层：介词短语 of the art-loving public 作后置定语，修饰第一层中三个并列的名词。
	状语二	第一层：not only...but also 连接并列的介词短语 with opera houses,...and museums 和 with the recorded performances 作状语，表对象。第二层：介词短语 of the great classical musicians 作后置定语，修饰 performances。第三层：介词短语 of the 20th century 作后置定语，修饰 musicians。

【结构分析】

一级修饰　　**For** the time, attention, and money of the art-loving public,

　　　　　　↓　介词短语作目的状语

句子主干　　classical instrumentalists <u>must compete</u>（主＋谓）

　　　　　　↑　并列的介词短语作状语，表对象

一级修饰　　**not only with** opera houses,...and museums,

　　　　　　　　　　not only...but also 连接的并列介词短语

　　　　　　but also with the recorded **performances**

　　　　　　　介词短语作后置定语，修饰 performances

二级修饰　　**of** the great classical **musicians**

　　　　　　介词短语作后置定语，修饰 musicians

三级修饰　　　　　**of** the 20th century.

【词汇注释】

instrumentalist	[ˌɪnstrə'mentəlɪst] *n.* 乐器演奏者
troupe	[tru:p] *n.* 表演团，班子

【意群训练】

For the time, attention, and money // of the art-loving public, // classical instrumentalists must compete // not only with opera houses, dance

82

troupes, theater companies, and museums, // but also with the recorded performances // of the great classical musicians // of the 20th century.

（五）　重要说明

1. 平行结构的各平行部分，要么结构一致，要么词性相同。

2. 有时也会不出现并列连词：并列连词用分号代替，或替换成 not, rather than, instead of 等表示并列关系的词语。

3. 多个成分平行，只保留最后一个成分前的连词，其余成分间不需要连词。

四　否定结构

含有否定结构的句子即有否定意义。句子的否定意义可以通过句中的否定词体现，也可以通过句子结构体现。在表达否定概念时，英语和汉语存在着词汇和逻辑上的差异。因此，在考研英语中，正确理解否定结构的意义非常重要。常见的否定结构有：全部否定、部分否定、双重否定、转移否定、转换否定和重复否定。

（一）　全部否定

全部否定表示对事实的全部否定，意为"都不……"。常用于全部否定的词有：no, not, nor, never, neither, none, nothing, nobody, nowhere, by no means, in no way 等。表示全部否定的词比较多，且都为常见词汇，在考研中出现频率较高，一般比较容易判断。

实例 1

Neither of these patterns is borne out by the analysis, suggesting that the structures of the languages are lineage-specific and not governed by universals. 这两种模式均未通过此次分析得以证实，这表明语言结构具有种系特异性，而不受普遍规律支配。【英语（一）2012 翻译】

【难句类型】否定结构＋非谓语动词＋从句　　　　　　　　难度：★★★
【难句破解】

找主干	过程	第一步：找从句标志词，并剥离该从句。找到标志词 that：距离 that 之后最近的动词是 are，and 连接并列的谓语动词 are lineage-specific 和（are）not governed，至此将该从句剥离。第二步：识别非谓语动词，同时删除非谓语动词结构及其它修饰成分。删除非谓语动词 suggesting。删除修饰成分 by the analysis,

	by universals。全句剩下了 Neither of these patterns is borne out，这就是句子的主干部分。 第三步：识别并删除很像谓语动词的动词。（真正的谓语动词已找到，故该步骤略。）
结果	Neither of these patterns is borne out...（主＋谓） 本句的谓语 is borne out 使用了被动语态，其后的介词 by 引出动作的发出者 the analysis。句首的 Neither 表示全部否定。
理修饰　状语	第一层：现在分词短语 suggesting... 作伴随状语；that 引导的宾语从句 [that] the structures of the languages are lineage-specific and not governed by universals（主＋系＋表＋and＋谓）作 suggesting 的宾语，其中介词短语 of the languages 作后置定语，修饰 the structures；and 连接并列的谓语：谓语一是系表结构，谓语二使用了被动语态，其中的 not 表示全部否定；介词 by 引出动作的发出者 universals。

【结构分析】

句子主干	Neither...patterns is borne out by the analysis,（主＋谓）

现在分词短语作伴随状语

suggesting [that] the...languages **are** lineage-specific

and 连接的并列谓语

一级修饰　**and (are) not governed** by universals.

【词汇注释】

be borne out	被证实，被印证
lineage	['lɪnɪɪdʒ] *n.* 世系；宗系；家系；血统
govern	['gʌvn] *vt.* 支配；管理

【意群训练】

Neither of these patterns // is borne out // by the analysis, // suggesting that // the structures of the languages are // lineage-specific // and not governed // by universals.

（二）　部分否定

在部分否定中，否定词 not 不否定全句，而是否定句中的一部分，意为"不都……"。常见结构有：not ＋ all/both/everybody/everything/always/

often/many/much 等。部分否定在考研英语中不常考查，但一旦该结构出现，注意一定不要误解其意思。

------ 实例 1 ------

But not all parts of the brain are equally involved; the limbic system (the "emotional brain") is especially active, while the prefrontal cortex (the center of intellect and reasoning) is relatively quiet. 但并不是大脑的所有区域都同等程度地参与做梦；大脑边缘系统（大脑控制情绪的区域）最为活跃，而前额皮层（大脑控制思维和推理的中心）就相对平静。【英语（一）2005 Text 3】

【难句类型】否定结构 + 平行结构   难度：★★★★
【难句破解】

找主干	过程	第一步：找从句标志词，并剥离该从句。(本句中无从句，故该步骤略。连词 while 在句中并非从句标志词，它连接并列分句，表对比。) 第二步：识别非谓语动词，同时删除非谓语动词结构及其它修饰成分。本句无非谓语动词结构；删除修饰成分 equally，(the "emotional brain")，especially，(the center of intellect and reasoning)，relatively。全句剩下了 But not all parts of the brain are involved; the limbic system is active, while the prefrontal cortex is quiet，这就是句子的主干部分。 第三步：识别并删除很像谓语动词的动词。(真正的谓语动词已找到，故该步骤略。)
	结果	But not all parts of the brain are...involved; the limbic system...is...active, while the prefrontal cortex...is...quiet.（主 1 + 系 1 + 表 1 + 主 2 + 系 2 + 表 2 + while + 主 3 + 系 3 + 表 3） 句首的 But 是表转折的连词；连词 while 连接并列分句，表对比；not all 是部分否定结构，意为"并不是所有"。
理修饰	状语	副词 equally 作状语，修饰 involved；副词 especially 作状语，修饰 active；副词 relatively 作状语，修饰 quiet。
	同位语	(the "emotional brain") 作 the limbic system 的同位语，对其进行解释说明；(the center of intellect and reasoning) 作 the prefrontal cortex 的同位语，对其进行解释说明。
看标点	分号	句中分号表并列，连接前后两个并列分句。
	括号	括号中内容是其前名词短语的同位语，起解释说明的作用。

| 句子主干 | But <u>not all parts of the brain</u> <u>are</u> equally <u>involved</u>;（主＋系＋表） |

分号连接的并列句

<u>the limbic system</u>...<u>is</u> especially <u>active</u>,（主＋系＋表）

the limbic system 的同位语

| 一级修饰 | （the "emotional brain"） |

while 连接的并列句，表对比

| 句子主干 | [while] **<u>the prefrontal cortex</u>**...<u>is</u> relatively <u>quiet</u>.（主＋系＋表） |

the prefrontal cortex 的同位语

| 一级修饰 | (the center of intellect and reasoning) |

【词汇注释】

limbic	['lɪmbɪk] *a.* 脑边缘系统的；边的
prefrontal	[pri:'frʌntl] *a.* 前额叶的；锋前的
cortex	['kɔ:teks] *n.* 皮层，皮质；大脑皮层

【意群训练】

But // not all parts of the brain // are equally involved; // the limbic system // (the "emotional brain") // is especially active, // while the prefrontal cortex // (the center // of intellect and reasoning) // is relatively quiet.

（三） 双重否定

　　双重否定即"否定＋否定＝肯定"，意为"没有……，就不……"，双重否定往往强调说话者的强烈语气，或表示委婉的陈述。常见结构为 no/without...not...，no/not 等＋表示否定意义的形容词，no/not/never/few ＋ without...，no/not/never/few 等＋表示否定意义的动词或短语。双重否定在考研英语中不常考查，但要注意将双重否定与重复否定区分开。

──── 实例 1 ──▶▶▶

Certainly people do not seem less interested in success and its signs now than formerly. 当然，现在人们对成功及其标志的兴趣与以前相比似乎丝毫未减。【英语（一）2000 Passage 5】

【难句类型】否定结构＋比较结构　　　　　　　　　　　难度：★★★

【难句破解】

找主干	过程	第一步: 找从句标志词,并剥离从句。(本句中无从句,故该步骤略。) 第二步: 识别非谓语动词,同时删除非谓语动词结构及其它修饰成分。本句无非谓语动词结构;删除修饰成分 Certainly, in success and its signs, now, than formerly。本句剩下了 people do not seem less interested,这就是句子的主干部分。 第三步: 识别并删除很像谓语动词的动词。(真正的谓语动词已找到,故该步骤略。)
	结果	...people do not seem less interested...(主 + 系 + 表) not 和 less 均表否定,但在本句中,这两个词连用,表肯定,意为"并没有减少",即"仍然很多"。
理修饰	状语	句首的副词 Certainly 作状语,修饰整个句子;副词 now 作时间状语;介词短语 in success and its signs 作 interested 的状语;介词短语 than formerly 作比较状语。

【结构分析】

句子主干　　Certainly people do not seem less **interested**(主 + 系 + 表)

介词短语作 interested 的状语 ↑

一级修饰　　**in** success and its signs now than formerly.

【意群训练】

Certainly people do not seem // less interested in success // and its signs // now // than formerly.

------ 实例 2 ------ >>>>

Certainly, no homework should be assigned that students cannot complete on their own or that they cannot do without expensive equipment. 当然,学生不能独立完成的家庭作业,或者需要昂贵的设备才能完成的家庭作业是不该布置的。【英语(二)2012 Text 1】

【难句类型】否定结构 + 平行结构 + 从句　　　　　　难度: ★ ★ ★

【难句破解】

找主干	过程	第一步: 找从句标志词,并剥离从句。❶ 找到第一个标志词 that: 距离 that 之后最近的动词是 cannot complete,至此将该从句剥离; ❷ 找到第二个标志词 that: 距离 that 之后最近的动词是 cannot do,至此将该从句剥离。

		第二步：识别非谓语动词，同时删除非谓语动词结构及其它修饰成分。本句无非谓语动词结构；删除修饰成分 Certainly, on their own, without expensive equipment。全句剩下了 no homework should be assigned，这就是句子的主干部分。 第三步：识别并删除很像谓语动词的动词。（真正的谓语动词已找到，故该步骤略。）
	结果	Certainly, <u>no homework should be assigned</u>…（主＋谓） 句首的副词 Certainly 作状语。
理修饰	定从	第一层：第一个 that 引导的定语从句修饰 homework；从句中，主语为 students，谓语为 cannot complete，that 代替先行词 homework 作宾语。or 连接第二个 that 引导的并列定语从句，修饰 homework；从句中，主语为 they，谓语为 cannot do，that 代替 homework 作宾语。第二层：第一个 that 引导的定语从句中，介词短语 on their own 作方式状语。第二个 that 引导的定语从句中，介词短语 without expensive equipment 作条件状语；cannot 和 without 构成双重否定，表示肯定含义"需要……才能……"。

【结构分析】

句子主干　　Certainly, <u>no **homework** should be assigned</u>（主＋谓）

↑ that 引导的定语从句，修饰 homework

that students cannot complete on their own

　　or 连接并列的定语从句

一级修饰　　**or that** they cannot do

↑ 介词短语作条件状语

二级修饰　　**without** expensive equipment.

【意群训练】

Certainly, // no homework should be assigned // that students cannot complete // on their own // or that they cannot do // without expensive equipment.

━━ 实例 3 ━━━━━━━━━━━━━━━━━━━━━━━━>>>>

All the same, no thinking man can refuse to accept their first proposition: that a great change in our emotional life calls for a change of expression. 尽管如此，善于思考的人肯定会接受他们的基本主张：情感生活的巨大变化要求表达方式随之变化。【英语（一）2000 Passage 3】

【难句破解】

找主干	过程	第一步：找从句标志词，并剥离该从句。找到标志词 that：距离 that 之后最近的动词是 calls for，介词 for 后需跟宾语，故 a change 作其宾语，至此将该从句剥离。第二步：识别非谓语动词，同时删除非谓语动词结构及其它修饰成分。删除非谓语动词结构 to accept their first proposition；删除修饰成分 All the same 和 of expression。全句剩下了 no thinking man can refuse，这就是句子的主谓部分。第三步：识别并删除很像谓语动词的动词。（真正的谓语动词已找到，故该步骤略去。）
	结果	..., no thinking man can refuse to accept their first proposition: ...（主＋谓＋宾）动词不定式短语 to accept their first proposition 作宾语，是主干成分，故还原。句中的 no 和具有否定意义的动词 refuse 构成双重否定结构，意为"没有……能拒绝"，即"……都能接受"。
理修饰	插入语	句首的 All the same 作插入语。
	同位语从句	第一层：冒号后的 that 引导同位语从句 [that] a great change in our emotional life calls for a change of expression，对 their first proposition 进行解释说明。第二层：介词短语 in our emotional life 作后置定语，修饰第一个 change；介词短语 of expression 作后置定语，修饰第二个 change。
看标点	冒号	冒号后的内容对其前面的 their first proposition 进行解释说明。

【结构分析】

一级修饰   All the same,

           ↓ 插入语

句子主干   no thinking man can refuse to accept...**proposition**:（主＋谓＋宾）

          that 引导的同位语从句，解释说明 their first proposition

一级修饰   **[that]** a great **change**...calls for **a change**

      介词短语作后置定语，修饰 change   介词短语作后置定语，修饰 a change

二级修饰   **in** our emotional life   **of** expression.

【词汇注释】

| proposition [ˌprɒpə'zɪʃn] *n.* 主张；建议；任务 |

【意群训练】

All the same, // no thinking man can refuse // to accept their first proposition: // that a great change // in our emotional life // calls for // a change of expression.

(四) 转移否定

转移否定指在主从复合句中，主句中的否定词实际上是在否定从句的内容。这一现象常见于宾语从句中，主句谓语动词（如 believe, think, suppose, expect, assume, feel, guess, imagine 等）前加 not 实际上是在否定其所引导的宾从的谓语动词。考研英语中还存在另一种否定转移的情况：not + because（of）。这种结构按照正常语序及语义理解的话，会产生歧义，因为 not 实际否定的是后面 because 引导的原因状语从句或 because of 引导的介词短语。

-------- 实例 1 --------

I don't think the findings that we have are any evidence of personal delusion. 我认为这一研究结果不能作为任何个人幻想的证据。【英语（二）2014 Text 2】

【难句类型】否定结构 + 省略 + 嵌套结构　　　　　　难度：★★★

【难句破解】

| 找主干 | 过程 | 第一步：找从句标志词，并剥离该从句。找到标志词 that：距离 that 之后最近的动词是 have，至此将该从句剥离。
第二步：识别非谓语动词，同时删除非谓语动词结构及其它修饰成分。本句无非谓语动词结构；删除修饰成分 of personal delusion。全句剩下了 I don't think the findings are any evidence。
第三步：识别并删除很像谓语动词的动词。根据辨析真假谓语动词的方法，句中剩下两个动词 don't think 和 are，且二者后分别跟有宾语和表语，故前面的 don't think 是主干谓语动词，are 则是省略 that 的宾语从句 the findings… 的系动词，any evidence 作其表语，至此将该从句剥离。全句剩下了 I don't think，这就是句子的主谓部分。 |

	结果	I don't think **(that)** the findings...are any evidence...（主＋谓＋宾从） 省略引导词 that 的宾语从句 **(that)** <u>the findings</u>...are any evidence（主＋系＋表），作 don't think 的宾语，是主干成分，故还原。 主干谓语中的 not 否定的不是 think，而是宾语从句中的 are，意为"认为……不……"，而不是"不认为……"。
理修饰	定从	that 引导的定语从句 **[that]** <u>we have</u>（宾＋主＋谓）修饰 the findings。
	定语	介词短语 of personal delusion 作后置定语，修饰 evidence。

【结构分析】

	[that] we have
一级修饰	that 引导的定语从句，修饰 the findings
	of personal delusion.
	介词短语作后置定语，修饰 evidence
句子主干	I don't think **(that) the findings**...are any **evidence**（主＋谓＋宾从）

【词汇注释】

delusion	[dɪˈluːʒn] *n.* 幻想；错觉；缪见

【意群训练】

I don't think // the findings // that we have // are any evidence // of personal delusion.

实例 2

It was argued at the end of the 19th century that humans do not cry because they are sad but that they become sad when the tears begin to flow. 19 世纪末还有人认为，人们不是因为悲伤而哭泣，而是当眼泪开始流淌时才感到悲伤。【英语（一）2011 完形】

【难句类型】否定结构＋嵌套结构＋平行结构＋非谓语动词　　难度：★★★★

【结构破解】

找主干	过程	第一步：找从句标志词，并剥离该从句。❶ 找到第一个标志词 that：距离 that 之后最近的动词是 do not cry，至此将该从句剥离；❷ 找到第二个标志词 because：距离 because 之后最近的动词是 are，sad 作其表语，至此将该从句剥离；❸ 找到第三个标志

词 that：距离 that 之后最近的动词是 become，sad 作其表语，至此将该从句剥离；❹ 找到第四个标志词 when：距离 when 之后最近的动词是 begin，至此将该从句剥离。由于 but 在这四个从句之间，起连接作用，故一并剥离。

第二步：识别非谓语动词，同时删除非谓语动词结构及其它修饰成分。删除非谓语动词 to flow；删除修饰成分 at the end of the 19th century。全句剩下了 It was argued，这就是句子的主谓部分。

第三步：识别并删除很像谓语动词的动词。（真正的谓语动词已找到，故该步骤略。）

结果	It was argued...（主 + 谓） 句中 It 为形式主语，but 连接的并列的主语从句是真正的主语。
理修饰 状语	介词短语 at the end of the 19th century 作时间状语。
理修饰 主从	but 连接两个 that 引导的主语从句 [that] humans do not cry...（主 + 谓）和 [that] they become sad...（主 + 系 + 表），第一个主语从句中的 not 虽是谓语的一部分，但这里出现了否定转移，其否定的实际上是后面 because 引导的原因状语从句。第一层：because 引导原因状语从句 [because] they are sad（主 + 系 + 表），修饰第一个主语从句，该部分是主从 + 嵌套原因状从结构；when 引导时间状语从句 [when] the tears begin to flow（主 + 谓 + 宾），修饰第二个主语从句，其中动词不定式 to flow 作宾语，该部分是主从 + 嵌套时间状从结构。

【结构分析】

句子主干

It was argued at the end of the 19th century（主 + 谓）

It 为形式主语，that 引导的主语从句作真正的主语

[that] humans do not cry

but 连接的并列主语从句

but [that] they become sad

because 引导的原因状语从句

[because] they are sad

一级修饰

when 引导的时间状语从句

[when] the tears begin to flow.

【意群训练】

It was argued // at the end of the 19th century // that humans do not cry // because they are sad // but that they become sad // when the tears //

92

begin to flow.

（五）　转换否定

转换否定即句子是肯定形式，但意义表否定；或句子是否定形式，但意义表肯定。转换否定在考研英语中较常见，在分析该类结构时，一定要明确理解句子的真正含义。

---------- 实例 1 ----------　　　　　　　　　　　　　　　　　　　　>>>>>

"Dare to be different, please don't smoke!" pleads one billboard campaign aimed at reducing smoking among teenagers—*teenagers*, who desire nothing more than fitting in. 一项旨在减少青少年吸烟的广告宣传活动请求道："敢于与众不同，请不要吸烟！"——但青少年最渴望的恰恰是融入群体中。【英语（一）2012 Text 1】

【难句类型】否定结构＋倒装＋非谓语动词＋从句　　　　难度：★★★★★
【结构破解】

找主干	过程	第一步：找从句标志词，并剥离该从句。找到标志词 who：距离 who 之后最近的动词是及物动词 desire，nothing more 作其宾语，至此将该从句剥离。 第二步：识别非谓语动词，同时删除非谓语动词结构及其它修饰成分。删除非谓语动词结构 aimed at，reducing smoking。删除修饰成分 among teenagers，*teenagers*，than fitting in。全句剩下了 "Dare to be different, please don't smoke!" pleads one billboard campaign，这就是句子的主干部分。 第三步：识别并删除很像谓语动词的动词。Dare 和 don't smoke 都是引号中祈使句的动词，因此 pleads 是主干的谓语动词。
	结果	"Dare to be different, please don't smoke!" pleads one billboard campaign...（宾＋谓＋主） 本句是主谓倒装句。引号内的祈使句作 pleads 的宾语，其中 don't 表全部否定；不定式短语 to be different 作 Dare 的宾语。
理修饰	定语	第一层：过去分词短语 aimed at reducing smoking among teenagers 作后置定语，修饰 campaign。其中动名词短语 reducing smoking 作 at 的宾语；介词短语 among teenagers 作状语，表范围。第二层：破折号之后的内容作第一个 teenagers 的同位语。第三层：who 引导非限定性定语从句 [who] desire nothing more than fitting in（主＋谓＋宾），修饰破折号后的

teenagers, 介词短语 than fitting in 作比较状语，nothing more than 是转换否定，虽然字面意义为否定，但实际表肯定，意为"最……的是……"。

看标点 破折号 破折号后面是对其前内容进行解释说明的同位语。

【结构分析】

句子主干

"Dare to be different, please don't smoke!"

↓ 直接引语作 pleads 的宾语

pleads one billboard **campaign**（倒装句：宾 + 谓 + 主）

过去分词短语作后置定语，修饰 campaign ↑

一级修饰

aimed at reducing smoking among **teenagers**

teenagers 的同位语 ↑

二级修饰

—*teenagers*,

who 引导的非限定性定语从句，修饰 *teenagers* ↑

三级修饰

[who] desire nothing more than fitting in.

【词汇注释】

| aim at | 目的在于；针对；瞄准 | fit in | 融入；适应；适合 |

【意群训练】

"Dare to be different, // please don't smoke!" // pleads one billboard campaign // aimed at // reducing smoking // among teenagers //— *teenagers*, who desire // nothing more // than fitting in.

（六） 重复否定

重复否定是指在不同时间内，对从句或主句作同一否定。与表达肯定意思的双重否定不同，重复否定的句子仍表示否定含义。

···· 实例 1 ·············

And dead markets partly reflect the paralysis of banks which will not sell assets for fear of booking losses, yet are reluctant to buy all those supposed bargains. 毫无生气的市场也在一定程度上反映出银行的瘫痪，银行担心账面损失而不愿出售资产，也不愿购买那些所谓的廉价资产。【英语（一）2010 Text 4】

【难句破解】

<table>
<tr><td rowspan="2">找主干</td><td>过程</td><td>第一步：找从句标志词，并剥离该从句。找到标志词 which：距离 which 之后最近的动词是 will not sell，assets 作其宾语，且连词 yet 连接前后两个并列谓语，故 are 也是该从句动词，reluctant 作其表语，至此将该从句剥离。
第二步：识别非谓语动词，同时删除非谓语动词结构及其它修饰成分。删除非谓语动词结构 to buy all...bargains；删除修饰成分 partly，of banks，for fear of booking losses。全句剩下了 And dead markets reflect the paralysis，这就是句子的主干部分。
第三步：识别并删除很像谓语动词的动词。（真正的谓语动词已找到，故该步骤略。）</td></tr>
<tr><td>结果</td><td>And <u>dead markets</u>...<u>reflect</u> the <u>paralysis</u>...（主 + 谓 + 宾）
句首的连词 And 表示与上文的顺接关系；副词 partly 作状语，修饰 reflect。</td></tr>
<tr><td>理修饰</td><td>定语</td><td>第一层：介词短语 of banks 作后置定语，修饰 the paralysis。第二层：which 引导定语从句 [which] will not sell assets..., yet are reluctant...（主 + 谓 + 宾 + yet + 系 + 表）修饰 banks。其中，which 代替先行词 banks 作定从的主语；not 和 yet 均表示否定，二者重复否定 banks 的动作。第三层：介词短语 for fear of booking losses 作 will not sell 的原因状语；动词不定式短语 to buy...bargains 作表语 reluctant 的补足语。</td></tr>
</table>

【结构分析】

句子主干	And <u>dead markets</u> partly <u>reflect</u> the **paralysis**（主 + 谓 + 宾）
	介词短语作后置定语，修饰 paralysis ↑
一级修饰	**of banks**
	which 引导的定语从句，修饰 banks ↑
二级修饰	**[which] will not sell** assets
	yet 连接的并列谓语
	yet are reluctant
	动词不定式短语作 reluctant 的补足语
	to buy all those supposed bargains.
三级修饰	介词短语作原因状语
	for fear of booking losses,

paralysis	[pəˈræləsɪs] *n.* 瘫痪；麻痹
reluctant	[rɪˈlʌktənt] *a.* 不情愿的；勉强的
for fear of	唯恐，以免

【意群训练】

And dead markets // partly reflect // the paralysis of banks // which will not sell assets // for fear of // booking losses, // yet are reluctant // to buy all those // supposed bargains.

实例 2

Rather, we have a certain conception of the American citizen, a character who is incomplete if he cannot competently assess how his livelihood and happiness are affected by things outside of himself. 相反，我们对美国公民有一种特定的观念：如果一个人没有能力评价外在因素如何对其生活和幸福产生影响，那么他的公民特征就是不完整的。【英语（一）1999 Passage 3】

【难句类型】 否定结构＋嵌套结构　　　　　　　难度：★★★★☆

【难句破解】

| 找主干 | 过程 | 第一步：找从句标志词，并剥离该从句。❶ 找到第一个标志词 who：距离 who 之后最近的动词是 is，incomplete 作其表语，至此将该从句剥离；❷ 找到第二个标志词 if：距离 if 之后最近的动词是 cannot assess，至此将该从句剥离；❸ 找到第三个标志词 how：距离 how 之后最近的动词是 are affected，至此将该从句剥离。
第二步：识别非谓语动词，同时删除非谓语动词结构及其它修饰成分。本句无非谓语动词结构；删除修饰成分 Rather, of the American citizen，a character，competently，by things outside of himself。全句剩下了 we have a certain conception，这就是句子的主干部分。
第三步：识别并删除很像谓语动词的动词。（真正的谓语动词已找到，故该步骤略。） |
| | 结果 | ..., we have a certain conception...（主＋谓＋宾） |

| 理修饰 | 状语 | 句首的副词 Rather 作状语，表转折。 |

理修饰　定语	第一层：介词短语 of the American citizen 作后置定语，修饰 conception。第二层：a character 作 the American citizen 的同位语。第三层：who 引导的定语从句 [who] is incomplete（主＋系＋表）修饰 a character。第四层：if 引导的条件状语从句 [if] he cannot competently assess [how]…（主＋谓＋宾从），作定从的条件状语，其中，副词 competently 作状语，修饰谓语 cannot assess。incomplete 和 cannot 重复否定，意为"如果不能……，……就不完整"；在该从句中，how 引导的嵌套宾语从句 [how] his livelihood and happiness are affected by things…（主＋谓），作 cannot assess 的宾语，该宾从的谓语使用了被动语态，by 引出动作的发出者 things。第五层：介词短语 outside of himself 作后置定语，修饰 things。

【结构分析】

句子主干　　　Rather, we have a certain **conception**（主＋谓＋宾）

介词短语作后置定语，修饰 conception

一级修饰　　　**of the American citizen**

the American citizen 的同位语

二级修饰　　　**a character**

who 引导的定语从句，修饰 a character

三级修饰　　　**[who] is incomplete**

if 引导的条件状语从句

四级修饰　　　**[if] he cannot competently assess**

how 引导的宾语从句，作 cannot assess 的宾语

[how] his livelihood and happiness are affected by things

介词短语作后置定语，修饰 things

五级修饰　　　**outside of himself.**

【词汇注释】

conception	[kən'sepʃn] *n.* 观念；概念；设想；怀孕
competently	['kɒmpɪtəntli] *ad.* 胜任地，适合地
livelihood	['laɪvlihʊd] *n.* 赚钱谋生的手段；生计

Rather, // we have a certain conception // of the American citizen, // a character // who is incomplete // if he cannot competently assess // how his livelihood and happiness // are affected // by things // outside of himself.

五 比较结构

比较结构是英语中较复杂的语法现象，用来表达人或事物的属性或特征的不同程度，常为形容词或副词的比较。考研英语中比较结构可以通过固定的句式来体现，也会以比较状语或比较状语从句的形式出现。

(一) 同级比较

同级比较中，比较的结果是二者相同。常见结构是 as + 原级 + as...，the same + 原级 + as...，so + 原级 + as...。要注意，as + 原级 + as... 的否定形式 not as + 原级 + as... 是劣等比较，而不是同级比较。

实例 1

Besides, this is unlikely to produce the needed number of every kind of professional in a country as large as ours and where the economy is spread over so many states and involves so many international corporations. 除此之外，在我们这么大的一个国家里，经济分布在这么多州，涉及到这么多的跨国公司，这样做不可能培养出所需数量的各种专业人才。
【英语（一）1999 Passage 3】

【难句类型】比较结构＋平行结构＋从句＋非谓语动词　　　　难度：★★★☆

【难句破解】

找主干	过程	第一步：找从句标志词，并剥离该从句。找到标志词 where：距离 where 最近的动词是 is spread，and 将其前后两个并列分句连接，故 and 之后的及物动词 involves 也是该从句动词，so many international corporations 作其宾语，至此将该从句剥离。 第二步：识别非谓语动词，同时删除非谓语动词结构及其它修饰成分。删除非谓语动词结构 to produce the needed number。删除修饰成分 Besides, of every kind of professional，in a country，和 as large as ours。全句剩下了 this is unlikely，这就是句子的主干部分。 第三步：识别并删除很像谓语动词的动词。（真正的谓语动词已找到，故该步骤略。）

	结果	..., this is unlikely...（主＋系＋表）
理修饰	状语	句首的副词 Besides 作状语，表示与上文的逻辑关系。
	表补	第一层：动词不定式短语 to produce the needed number 作表语补足语，对表语 unlikely 进行补充说明。第二层：介词短语 of every kind of professional 作后置定语，修饰 number；介词短语 in a country 作地点状语。第三层：as large as ours 作后置定语，修饰 a country，as large as 为同级比较结构；[where] 引导的定语从句 [where] the economy is spread...and involves so many international corporations（主＋谓 +and+ 谓＋宾），也修饰 a country，其中 and 在该定从中连接两个并列谓语。第四层：定从中，介词短语 over so many states 作 is spread 的地点状语。

【结构分析】

句子主干　　Besides, this is **unlikely**（主＋系＋表）

　　　　　　　　　　　　↑ 动词不定式短语作 unlikely 的补足语

一级修饰　　　　**to** produce the needed **number**

　　　　　介词短语作后置定语，修饰 number ↑

　　　　　　　　　　　　of every kind of professional

二级修饰　　　　　　介词短语作地点状语

　　　　　　　　　in a country

　　　　形容词短语作后置定语，修饰 a country ↑

　　　　　　　　as large as ours

　　　　　where 引导的定语从句，修饰 a country ↑

三级修饰　　　　　　and [**where**] the economy **is spread**

　　　　　　　　　　and 连接的并列谓语 ↑

and involves so many international corporations.

　　　　　介词短语作 is spread 的地点状语 ↑

四级修饰　　　　　　**over** so many states

【词汇注释】

professional	[prəˈfeʃənl] *a.* 专业的；职业的；娴熟的
corporation	[ˌkɔːpəˈreɪʃn] *n.* 大公司；法人

Besides, // this is unlikely // to produce the needed number // of every kind of professional // in a country // as large as ours // and where the economy is spread // over so many states // and involves // so many international corporations.

---- 实例 2 ----

Television is one of the means by which these feelings are created and conveyed—and perhaps never before has it served so much to connect different peoples and nations as in the recent events in Europe. 电视是引发和传递这些感受的方式之一。在欧洲近来发生的事件中，它把不同的民族和国家联系在一起，其作用之大，或许前所未有。【英语（一）2005 翻译】

【难句类型】比较结构＋倒装＋省略＋非谓语动词＋平行结构 难度：★★★☆
【难句破解】

找主干	过程	第一步：找从句标志词，并剥离该从句。找到标志词 by which：距离 by which 之后最近的动词是 are created，created 之后的 and 连接前后并列的平行结构，因此 conveyed 也是该从句的动词，至此将该从句剥离。 第二步：识别非谓语动词，同时删除非谓语动词结构及其它修饰成分。删除非谓语动词结构 to connect different peoples and nations。删除修饰成分 and perhaps...so much 和 as in the recent events in Europe。全句剩下了 Television is one of the means，这就是句子的主干部分。 第三步：识别并删除很像谓语动词的动词。（真正的谓语动词已找到，故该步骤略。）
	结果	Television is one of the means...（主＋系＋表）

理修饰	定从	by which 引导的定语从句 **[by which]** these feelings are created and conveyed（主＋谓 1＋and＋谓 2）修饰主干表语中的 the means。
	解释说明	第一层：破折号后，由于 never 提前，故使用了部分倒装 never has it served，正常语序为：and perhaps it has never served so much...（主＋谓）。第二层：副词 before 作时间状语，副词短语 so much 修饰谓语 has served，表程度；动词不定式短语 to connect...nations 作状语；as 引导比较状语从句 **[as]** (it has served) in the recent events in Europe（主＋谓），与前面的 so much 构成同级比较结构。介词短语 in the recent events in Europe 作状语，修饰比较状语从句。

看标点 破折号 破折号后面的内容是对其前内容的补充说明。

【结构分析】

句子主干　　Television is one of **the means**（主＋系＋表）

　　　　　　　　by which 引导的定语从句，修饰 the means

一级修饰　　**[by which]** these feelings are created and conveyed

　　　　　　补充说明句子主干

　　　　　　—and perhaps never before...different peoples and nations

　　　　　　　　　　　　as 引导的比较状语从句

二级修饰　　**as** in the recent events in Europe.

【词汇注释】

| means | [mi:nz] *n.* 方式；途径；财富；钱财 | convey | [kən'veɪ] *vt.* 传递，表达 |

【意群训练】

Television is one of the means // by which these feelings // are created and conveyed // —and perhaps // never before // has it served // so much // to connect different peoples and nations // as in the recent events // in Europe.

(二)　优等比较

　　两者之间的优等比较即指一方优于另一方。常见结构有：比较级＋than, better than..., more than..., superior to... 等。

　　三者及三者以上的优等比较即指一方优于其他各方。常见结构有：the most＋多音节形容词，（the）most＋多音节副词，某些特定词汇后＋est，某些词汇（如 perfect, favorite 和 super 等）的原级即体现出最高级的意义。

　　优等比较在考研英语中虽较常考，但都较简单，句意也很容易理解。

---- 实例 1 ----

But the idea that the journalist must understand the law more profoundly than an ordinary citizen rests on an understanding of the established conventions and special responsibilities of the news media.
但是"新闻记者必须比普通公民更深入地了解法律"这种观点，是建立在对新闻媒体既定规约和特殊责任的理解上的。【英语（一）2007 翻译】

【难句类型】比较结构 + 平行结构 + 从句　　　　　　　　难度：★★★★

【结构破解】

<table>
<tr><td rowspan="2">找主干</td><td>过程</td><td>第一步：找从句标志词，并剥离该从句。找到标志词 that：距离 that 之后最近的动词是 must understand，因 understand 是及物动词，故 the law 作其宾语，至此将该从句剥离。
第二步：识别非谓语动词，同时删除非谓语动词结构及其它修饰成分。本句无非谓语动词结构。删除修饰成分 more profoundly，than an ordinary citizen，of the established conventions and special responsibilities，of the news media。全句剩下了 But the idea rests on an understanding，这就是句子的主干部分。
第三步：识别并删除很像谓语动词的动词。（真正的谓语动词已找到，故该步骤略。）</td></tr>
<tr><td>结果</td><td>But the idea...rests on an understanding...（主 + 谓 + 宾）
句首的连词 But 表示与上文的逻辑关系。</td></tr>
<tr><td rowspan="2">理修饰</td><td>同位语从句</td><td>第一层：that 引导同位语从句 [that] the journalist must understand the law...（主 + 谓 + 宾），解释说明 idea。第二层：副词短语 more profoundly 修饰同位语从句的谓语 must understand，than an ordinary citizen 作比较状语，more...than 构成优等比较结构。</td></tr>
<tr><td>定语</td><td>第一层：介词短语 of the established conventions and special responsibilities 作后置定语，修饰 an understanding。第二层：介词短语 of the news media 作后置定语，修饰 the established conventions and special responsibilities。</td></tr>
</table>

【结构分析】

二级修饰	**of** the news media.
	介词短语作后置定语，修饰 the established...responsibilities
一级修饰	**of the established conventions and special responsibilities**
	介词短语作后置定语，修饰 an understanding
句子主干	But **the idea**...rests on **an understanding**（主 + 谓 + 宾）
	that 引导的同位语从句，解释说明 the idea
一级修饰	[that] the journalist must understand the law more profoundly
	than...作比较状语
二级修饰	**than** an ordinary citizen

profoundly	[prəˈfaʊndli] *ad.* 深刻地；严重地
rest on	以……为基础；基于
convention	[kənˈvenʃn] *n.* 惯例；大会；公约；传统手法

【意群训练】

But the idea // that the journalist must understand // the law // more profoundly // than an ordinary citizen // rests on an understanding // of the established conventions and special responsibilities // of the news media.

------ 实例 2

He adds humbly that perhaps he was "superior to the common run of men in noticing things which easily escape attention, and in observing them carefully." 他又谦虚地说道，或许自己"在注意容易被忽略的事物并对其加以仔细观察方面优于常人"。【英语（一）2008 翻译】

【难句类型】比较结构＋嵌套结构＋平行结构　　　　　　　难度：★★★☆

【难句破解】

| 找主干 | 过程 | 第一步：找从句标志词，并剥离该从句。❶ 找到第一个标志词 that：距离 that 之后最近的动词是 was，superior 作其表语，至此将该从句剥离；❷ 找到第二个标志词 which：距离 which 之后最近的动词是及物动词 escape，attention 作其宾语，至此将该从句剥离。
第二步：识别非谓语动词，同时删除非谓语动词结构及其它修饰成分。本句无非谓语动词结构。删除修饰成分 humbly, perhaps, to the common run of men, in noticing things esaily, in observing them carefully。句中 and 在各修饰成分之间，起连接作用，故也删除。全句剩下了 He adds，这就是句子的主谓部分。
第三步：识别并删除很像谓语动词的动词。（真正的谓语动词已找到，故该步骤略。） |
| | 结果 | He adds humbly **[that]** perhaps he was "superior to the common run of men..."（主＋谓＋宾从）
副词 humbly 作状语，修饰谓语 adds；that 引导宾语从句 **[that]** perhaps he was "superior to the common run of men..."（主＋系＋表），是主干成分，故还原。其中副词 perhaps 作状语。superior 和介词短语 to the common run of men 共同构成优等比较结构，表示"优于……"。 |

| 理修饰 | 状语 | 第一层：介词短语 to the common run of men...作状语，表对象；连词 and 连接两个并列的介词短语 in noticing things...attention 和 in observing them carefully 作状语，表方面。第二层：which 引导定语从句 [which] easily <u>escape</u> attention（主＋谓＋宾），修饰 things，其中副词 easily 作状语，修饰 escape。 |

【结构分析】

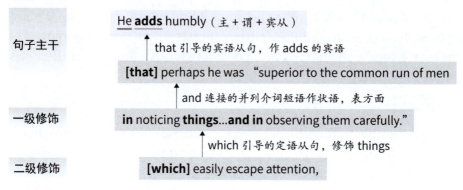

【词汇注释】

humbly	['hʌmbli] *ad.* 谦逊地；卑贱地
superior	[suː'pɪərɪə(r)] *a.* 优于……的；更高的；有优越感的 *n.* 上级；上司
run	[rʌn] *n.* 趋势，趋向；跑步

【意群训练】

He adds humbly // that perhaps he was "superior // to the common run of men // in noticing things // which easily escape attention, // and in observing them carefully".

（三） 劣等比较

两者之间的劣等比较即指一方次于另一方。常见结构有：not as (so)+原级＋as，less＋原级＋than...，worse than...，inferior to... 等。

三者及三者以上的劣等比较即一方次于其他各方。常见结构有：the most＋多音节形容词，（the）most＋多音节副词，某些特定词汇后＋est，某些词汇（如 hopeless 和 impossible）的原级即暗含着最高级的意义。

劣等比较在考研英语中也较常考，但都较简单，句意很容易理解。

Rich economies are also less dependent on oil than they were, and so less sensitive to swings in the oil price. 富裕国家对石油的依赖也比以前要小，因此，其对油价的波动也不会那么敏感。【英语（一）2002 Text 3】

【难句类型】比较结构 + 平行结构 + 从句　　　　　　难度：★ ★ ★ ☆
【难句破解】

找主干	过程	第一步：找从句标志词，并剥离该从句。找到标志词 than：距离 than 之后最近的动词是 were，至此将该从句剥离。 第二步：识别非谓语动词，同时删除非谓语动词结构及其它修饰成分。本句无非谓语动词结构。删除修饰成分 also，on oil，to swings，in the oil price。全句剩下了 Rich economies are less dependent, and so less sensitive，这就是句子的主干部分。 第三步：识别并删除很像谓语动词的动词。（真正的谓语动词已找到，故该步骤略。）
	结果	Rich economies are...less dependent..., and so less sensitive...（主 + 系 + 表 1 + and + 表 2）
理修饰	状语	第一层：副词 also 作状语。介词短语 on oil 和 to swings 均作状语，表对象。第二层：介词短语 in the oil price 作后置定语，修饰 swings。
	状从	than 引导的比较状语从句 [than] they were（主 + 系），作句子主干的比较状语，than 与第一个表语 less dependent 中的 less 构成劣等比较结构，less sensitive 也有劣等比较含义。

【结构分析】

一级修饰	[than] they were, than 引导的比较状语从句，作句子主干的比较状语
	on oil 介词短语作状语，表对象
句子主干	Rich economies are also **less dependent**（主 + 系 + 表） and 连接的并列表语 **and** so **less sensitive**
一级修饰	介词短语作状语，表对象 **to** swings in the oil price.

【词汇注释】

dependent	[dɪ'pendənt] *a.* 依赖的；依靠的
sensitive	['sensətɪv] *a.* 敏感的；体贴的；易生气的
swing	[swɪŋ] *n.* 改变；秋千 *vt.* 摆动，纵身跃向

【意群训练】

Rich economies are // also less dependent on oil // than they were, // and so less sensitive // to swings // in the oil price.

---- 实例 2 ----

In their recent work, however, some researchers have come up with the finding that influentials have far less impact on social epidemics than is generally supposed. 然而，一些研究人员在最近的研究中发现，有影响力人士对社会流行潮的影响比人们普遍认为的要小得多。【英语（一）2010 Text 3】

【难句类型】比较结构＋嵌套结构＋分隔结构＋省略　　　　难度：★★★☆

【难句破解】

找主干	过程	第一步：找从句标志词，并剥离该从句。❶找到第一个标志词 that：距离 that 之后最近的动词是及物动词 have，far less impact 作其宾语，至此将该从句剥离；❷找到第二个标志词 than：距离 than 之后最近的动词是 is supposed，至此将该从句剥离。 第二步：识别非谓语动词，同时删除非谓语动词结构及其它修饰成分。本句无非谓语动词结构。删除修饰成分 In their recent work，however，on social epidemics。全句剩下了 some researchers have come up with the finding，这就是句子的主干部分。 第三步：识别并删除很像谓语动词的动词。（真正的谓语动词已找到，故该步骤略。）
	结果	..., some researchers have come up with the finding...（主＋谓＋宾）
理修饰	状语	介词短语 In their recent work 作状语。
	插入语	however 作插入语，表转折。
	同位语从句	第一层：that 引导同位语从句 [that] influentials have far less impact（主＋谓＋宾），解释说明宾语 the finding。第二层：介词短语 on social epidemics 作后置定语，修饰 impact；than 引导的定语从句 [than] is generally supposed（主＋谓）修饰 impact，

其中谓语使用了被动语态，副词 generally 修饰谓语，本句嵌套结构为同位语从句 + 嵌套定从。far less...than... 构成了劣等比较结构。

【结构分析】

一级修饰	**In** their recent work,		however,
	介词短语作状语		插入语

句子主干　　some researchers have come up with **the finding**（主 + 谓 + 宾）

that 引导的同位语从句，解释说明 the finding

一级修饰　　[that] influentials have far less **impact** on social epidemics

than 引导的定语从句，修饰 impact

二级修饰　　　　　　　　　　　　　　　　[than] is generally supposed.

【词汇注释】

come up with	找到（答案）；想出；设法拿出
influential	[ˌɪnfluˈenʃl] n. 有影响力的人 a. 有影响的；有势力的
epidemic	[ˌepɪˈdemɪk] n. 流行；盛行；流行病

【意群训练】

In their recent work, // however, // some researchers // have come up with // the finding // that influentials // have far less impact // on social epidemics // than is generally supposed.

（四）　特殊比较结构

英语中有一些固定句式，含有比较的意义，但是和汉语的逻辑不同，甚至相反。如 no/not any...more than...; no more than...; all/only/much + the + 比较级; not so much as...; the + 比较级，the + 比较级; more and more... 等。考生需要掌握这些句式的含义，尤其是实际意义与字面意义存在差别的结构，否则会造成对原句含义的曲解。

------ 实例 **1** ------

As the Internet becomes more and more commercialized, it is in the interest of business to universalize access—after all, the more people online, the more potential customers there are. 随着互联网日趋商业化，网络普及符合商家的利益。毕竟，上网人数越多，潜在的客户就越多。【英语（一）2001 Passage 2】

【难句类型】比较结构＋从句＋非谓语动词　　　　　　　难度：★★★☆

【难句破解】

找主干	过程	第一步：找从句标志词，并剥离该从句。找到标志词 As：距离 As 之后最近的动词是系动词 becomes，more and more commercialized 作其表语，至此将该从句剥离。 第二步：识别非谓语动词，同时删除非谓语动词结构及其它修饰成分。删除非谓语动词结构 to universalize access；删除修饰成分 of business 和 after all...there are。全句剩下了 it is in the interest，这就是句子的主干部分。 第三步：识别并删除很像谓语动词的动词。（真正的谓语动词已找到，故该步骤略。）
	结果	...，it is in the interest...（主＋系＋表） it 是形式主语，真正的主语为动词不定式短语 to universalize access。
理修饰	状从	As 引导时间状语从句 [As] the Internet becomes more and more com-mercialized（主＋系＋表），more and more commercialized 是特殊比较结构。
	定语	介词短语 of business 作后置定语，修饰 the interest。
	解释说明	破折号后的内容对破折号前的主干部分进行解释说明，其中又包含了 the more..., the more... 的特殊比较结构，表示"……越多，……就越多"的含义。
看标点	破折号	破折号表示其后的句子对前面的内容进行解释说明。

【结构分析】

一级修饰　　**[As]** the Internet becomes more and more commercialized,

　　　　　　As 引导的时间状语从句，作句子主干的时间状语

句子主干　　**it** is in the interest of business（主＋系＋表）

　　　　　　it 为形式主语，动词不定式短语作真正的主语

　　　　　　to universalize access

　　　　　　解释说明句子主干

一级修饰　　—after all, the more people online, the more...there are.

【词汇注释】

commercialize	[kə'mɜːʃəlaɪz] *vt.* 商业化
in the interest of	为了……的利益

universalize	[ˌjuːnɪˈvɜːsəlaɪz] *vt.* 普及；使普遍化
potential	[pəˈtenʃl] *a.* 潜在的 *n.* 潜力；可能性

【意群训练】

As the Internet becomes // more and more commercialized, // it is // in the interest of business // to universalize access // —after all, // the more people online, // the more potential customers // there are.

<u>实例 2</u>

For the women of my generation who were urged to keep juggling through the'80s, downshifting in the mid-'90s is not so much a search for the mythical good life—growing your own organic vegetables, and risking turning into one—as a personal recognition of your limitations.

对于我们这一代在整个 80 年代曾被迫忙碌地生活的女性来说，90 年代中期的放慢生活节奏与其说是寻求神话般的美好生活——自己种植有机蔬菜并冒着使自己变成一个单调乏味的人的风险——倒不如说我们都认识到了自身的局限。【英语（一）2001 Passage 5】

【难句类型】比较结构＋从句＋非谓语动词＋平行结构　　　　难度：★★★★

【难句破解】

找主干	过程	第一步：找从句标志词，并剥离该从句。找到标志词 who：距离 who 之后最近的动词是 were urged，至此将该从句剥离。 第二步：识别非谓语动词，同时删除非谓语动词结构及其它修饰成分。删除非谓语动词结构 to keep juggling through the'80s, growing your own organic vegetables, and risking turning into one；删除修饰成分 For the women of my gene-ration, in the mid-'90s, for the mythical good life, as a personal...limitations。全句剩下了 downshifting is not so much a search，这就是句子的主干部分。 第三步：识别并删除很像谓语动词的动词。（真正的谓语动词已找到，故该步骤略。）
	结果	..., downshifting...is not so much a search...as a personal recognition...（主＋系＋表1＋as＋表2）动名词 downshifting 作主语；连词 as 连接并列的表语，not so much...as 是特殊比较结构，意为"与其……，不如……"。
理修饰	状语	第一层：介词短语 For the women of my generation...作状语，表对象。第二层：who 引导的定语从句 **[who]** were urged...（主＋谓），修饰 the women。第三层：定语从句中，动词不定式短语 to keep juggling 作 who 的补足语，介词短语 through the'80s 作时间状语。

<table>
<tr><td>定语</td><td>第一层：介词短语 in the mid-'90s 作后置定语，修饰主干主语 downshifing；介词短语 for the mythical good life 作后置定语，修饰 a search；介词短语 of your limitations 作后置定语，修饰 a personal recognition。第二层：两个破折号之间的部分是插入语，由连词 and 连接的并列动名词短语 growing your own organic vegetables 和 risking turning into one 构成，用于解释说明 the mythical good life。</td></tr>
</table>

看标点 破折号 破折号中间的内容是插入语，起解释说明的作用。

【结构分析】

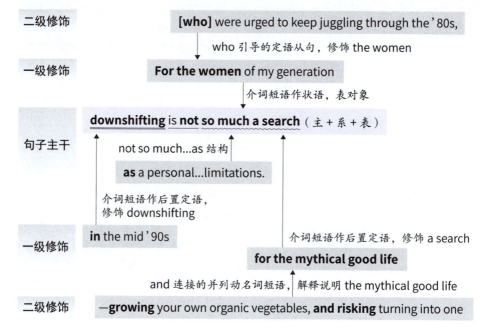

二级修饰 [who] were urged to keep juggling through the '80s,
who 引导的定语从句，修饰 the women

一级修饰 **For the women** of my generation
介词短语作状语，表对象

句子主干 **downshifting** is **not so much a search**（主 + 系 + 表）
not so much...as 结构
as a personal...limitations.

介词短语作后置定语，修饰 downshifting

一级修饰 **in** the mid '90s
介词短语作后置定语，修饰 a search
for the mythical good life

and 连接的并列动名词短语，解释说明 the mythical good life

二级修饰 **—growing** your own organic vegetables, **and risking** turning into one

【词汇注释】

recognition	[rekəg'nɪʃn] n. 认识；承认；赞誉
downshift	['daʊnʃɪft] vi. 减慢节奏；换低挡

【意群训练】

For the women // of my generation // who were urged // to keep juggling through the 80's, // downshifting in the mid-90's is not // so much a search // for the mythical good life //—growing your own organic vegetables // and risking turning into one //—as a personal recognition // of your limitations.

六　倒装

英语句子的基本语序是"主语＋谓语"，称为陈述句语序。倒装即将谓语的全部或一部分置于主语之前。英语中有两种情况需要倒装：一、由于语法结构需要倒装，此时必须使用倒装，否则会出现语法错误；二、由于修辞及语气需要倒装，这类倒装不是必须的，倒装只影响句子语气，不影响语法结构。

在倒装结构中，句子的主语不再位于谓语动词之前，在寻找谓语动词时要特别注意，如果一个句子读起来不符合日常语法习惯，或者出现了倒装结构的标志词，那么句中很有可能含有倒装结构。

（一）　全部倒装

全部倒装即谓语全部位于主语之前。常见的全部倒装句型有：

（1）There be 句型；

（2）here, there, now, then 等副词置于句首，且主语不是人称代词；

（3）作表语的形容词、分词或介词短词置于句首；

（4）表示方向、地点的状语 up, down, in, out, away, off 等置于句首；

（5）当直接引语位于句首时，后面的 sb. says 可倒装。在考研英语中全部倒装虽不常见，但广大考生一定要掌握其特点和判断方法。

> #### 实例 1
>
> Along with the many folks looking to make a permanent home in the United States came those who had no intention to stay, and who would make some money and then go home. 很多人来到美国是为了在这里安家落户，而同他们一起来的也有那些无意长久停留的暂住者，他们打算赚一些钱然后就回家。【英语（二）2013 Text 2】

【难句类型】倒装＋从句＋平行结构＋非谓语动词　　　　　　难度：★★★★

【难句破解】

找主干	过程	第一步：找从句标志词，并剥离该从句。❶找到第一个标志词 who：距离 who 之后最近的动词是 had，因 have 为及物动词，故 no intention 作其宾语，至此将该从句剥离；❷找到第二个标志词 who：距离 who 之后最近的动词是 would make，因 make 是及物动词，故 some money 作其宾语，且 and 连接的与 make 并列的动词 go，也是该从句的谓语，至此将该从句剥离。句中第一个 and 在两个从句之间，起连接作用，故也一并剥离。

	第二步：识别非谓语动词，同时删除非谓语动词结构及其它修饰成分。删除非谓语动词结构 looking to make a permanent home 和 to stay；删除修饰成分 Along with the many folks，in the United States，home。全句剩下了 came those，这就是句子的主谓部分。 第三步：识别并删除很像谓语动词的动词。（真正的谓语动词已找到，故该步骤略。）
结果	...came those...（谓＋主） 本句是倒装结构，正常语序为 those came。

理修饰	状语	第一层：介词短语 Along with the many folks...the United States 作方式状语，因其位于句首，句子主干部分全部倒装。第二层：现在分词短语 looking to make a permanent home 作后置定语，修饰 folks。第三层：介词短语 in the United States 作第二层现在分词短语的地点状语。
	定从	第一层：and 连接两个并列的定语从句 [who] had no intention to stay（主＋谓＋宾）和 [who] would make some money and then go home（主＋谓1＋宾＋and＋谓2），均修饰 those。第二层：动词不定式 to stay 在第一个定语从句中作后置定语，修饰 intention；副词 home 作状语，修饰 go。

【结构分析】

一级修饰	**and [who]** would make some money and then go home. and 连接的并列定语从句
	[who] had no intention to stay, who 引导的定语从句，修饰 those
句子主干	...came **those**（倒装句：谓＋主） 介词短语作方式状语
一级修饰	**Along** with the many **folks** 现在分词短语作后置定语，修饰 folks
二级修饰	**looking** to make a permanent home 介词短语作地点状语
三级修饰	**in** the United States

【词汇注释】

along with	与……一起，和
permanent	['pɜːmənənt] a. 永久的，永恒的

| intention | [ɪnˈtenʃn] *n.* 打算；意图；目的 |

【意群训练】

Along with the many folks // looking to make a permanent home // in the United States // came those // who had no intention to stay, // and who would make some money // and then go home.

---- 实例 2 ----

"Data is becoming an asset which needs to be guarded as much as any other asset," says Haim Mendelson of Stanford University's business school. 数据正在变成一种资产，像其他任何资产一样，它也需要受到保护，"斯坦福大学商学院的海姆·门德尔森说。【英语（一）2007 Text 4】

　　本句是一种典型的倒装结构：直接引语＋谓语＋主语。对于这类句子，我们将其中的直接引语当作宾语，按以下步骤进行处理：

　　1. 将双引号内的完整句子划成宾语；

　　2. 寻找双引号外之前或之后最近的动词，即为谓语；

　　3. 识别并删除直接引语之外的非谓语动词结构及其它修饰成分。

　　4. 最后按基础篇提到的破解长难句的三大步骤分析直接引语。

【难句类型】倒装＋从句＋非谓语动词　　　　　　　　难度：★★★☆

【难句破解】

| 找主句主干 | 过程 | 第一步：将双引号内的完整句子划成宾语："Data is becoming an asset which needs to be guarded as much as any other asset," 即为该句的宾语，暂且将其当作一个整体，不进行非谓语动词结构及其它修饰成分的删减。
第二步：寻找双引号外之前或之后最近的动词，即为谓语：双引号外之后最近的动词为 says，即为谓语。
第三步：识别并删除直接引语之外的非谓语动词结构及其它修饰成分。本句无非谓语动词结构；删除修饰成分 of Stanford University's business school。全句剩下了 "Data is...asset," says Haim Mendelson，这就是句子的主干部分。 |
| | 结果 | "Data...asset," <u>says</u> <u>Haim Mendelson</u>...（宾＋谓＋主）
由于作宾语的直接引语位于句首，主谓完全倒装。这里也可以不倒装，正常语序为 Haim Mendelson says, "Data is...asset."。 |

找直接引语主干	过程	第一步：找从句标志词，并剥离该从句。找到从句引导词 which：距离 which 之后最近的动词是 needs，至此将该从句剥离。 第二步：识别非谓语动词，同时删除非谓语动词结构及其它修饰成分。删除非谓语动词结构 to be guarded；删除修饰成分 as much as any other asset。全句剩下了 Data is becoming an asset，这就是直接引语的主干部分。 第三步：识别并删除很像谓语动词的动词。（真正的谓语动词已找到，故该步骤略。）
	结果	<u>Data</u> <u>is becoming</u> <u>an asset</u>...（主＋系＋表） is becoming 使用了现在进行时。
理修饰	定语	of Stanford University's business school 作后置定语，修饰主干主语 Haim Mendelson。
	定从	第一层：直接引语中，which 引导定语从句 **[which]** needs to be guarded as much as any other asset（主＋谓＋宾）修饰 which 前的 an asset。第二层：介词短语 as much as any other asset 作定从的比较状语。

【结构分析】

二级修饰
　　　　　　　　as much as any other asset,
　　　　　　　　　　作比较状语

一级修饰
　　　　　　　　[which] needs to be guarded
　　　　　　　　　　which 引导的定语从句，修饰 an asset

句子主干
　　　　　　"Data is...**an asset**..." says **Haim Mendelson**（倒装句：宾＋谓＋主）
　　　　　　　　介词短语作后置定语，修饰 Haim Mendelson

一级修饰
　　　　　　　　of Stanford University's business school

【词汇注释】

asset	['æset] *n.* 资产；有价值的人	guard	[gɑ:d] *vt.* 保卫；监视

【意群训练】

"Data is becoming // an asset // which needs to be guarded // as much as any other asset," // says Haim Mendelson // of Stanford University's business school.

Among the commission's 51 members are top-tier-university presidents, scholars, lawyers, judges, and business executives, as well as prominent figures from diplomacy, filmmaking, music and journalism. 该委员会的 51 名成员中，有顶尖大学的校长、学者、律师、法官和企业高管以及来自外交、电影制片、音乐和新闻界的显赫人物。【英语（一）2014 Text 4】

【难句类型】倒装 + 平行结构　　　　　　　　　　　　　难度：★★★
【难句破解】

找主干	过程	第一步：找从句标志词，并剥离该从句。（本句中无从句，故该步骤略。） 第二步：识别非谓语动词，同时删除非谓语动词结构及其它修饰成分。本句无非谓语动词结构；删除修饰成分 Among the commission's 51 members, from diplomacy, filmmaking, music and journalism。全句剩下了 are top-tier-university presidents...prominent figures，这就是句子主干的一部分。 第三步：识别并删除很像谓语动词的动词。（真正的谓语动词已找到，故该步骤略。）
	结果	Among the commission's 51 members are top-tier-university presidents...prominent figures...（表 + 系 + 主） 因介词短语 Among the commission's 51 members 作表语，是主干成分，故还原。且因其位于句首，句子完全倒装。正常语序为：Top-tier-university presidents...prominent figures are among the commission's 51 members。
理修饰	定语	介词短语 from diplomacy, filmmaking, music and journalism 作后置定语，修饰 figures。

【结构分析】

句子主干	Among...members are top-tier-university...**figures**（倒装句：表 + 系 + 主）
	介词短语作后置定语，修饰 figures
一级修饰	**from** diplomacy, filmmaking, music and journalism.

【词汇注释】

commission	[kə'mɪʃn] n. 委员会；佣金；委任 vt. 委任；委托
executive	[ɪg'zekjətɪv] n. 管理人员；行政领导；部门 a. 行政的；经营管理的
prominent	['prɒmɪnənt] a. 杰出的；显著的；卓越的

115

Among the commission's 51 members // are top-tier-university presidents, scholars, lawyers, judges, // and business executives, // as well as prominent figures // from diplomacy, filmmaking, music and journalism.

（二） 部分倒装

部分倒装即谓语的一部分（助动词或情态动词）位于主语之前。部分倒装的常见句型有：

（1）有否定或半否定意义的词或短语在句首作状语，如 never, hardly, neither, nor, no more, little, by no means, not until, hardly...when..., no sooner...than 等；

（2）虚拟语气中，若条件状语从句省略了 if，则需要部分倒装；

（3）only + 状语位于句首，即 only 修饰状语；

（4）so + *adj.* + that...和 such + *n.* + that...句型中, so + *adj.*/such + *n.* 位于句首；

（5）not until 引导状语从句, not until 位于句首时，主句需部分倒装，但从句不倒装；

（6）So + be/助动词 / 情态动词 + 主语，表示"……也……"，或 Neither/Nor/No more + be/ 助动词 / 情态动词 + 主语，表示"……也不……"；

（7）as, though 引导的让步状语从句，可倒装为名词 / 形容词 / 副词 + as/though + 主 + 谓。

考研英语复习的过程中，大家一定要掌握部分倒装的特点和判断方法。

········ 实例 1 ··▷▷▷▷

Only gradually was the by-product of the institution noted, and only more gradually still was this effect considered as a directive factor in the conduct of the institution. 人们只是渐渐地才注意到这种机构附带产生的作用，而人们把这种作用视为机构运作的指导性因素的过程则更为缓慢。
【英语（一）2009 翻译】

【难句类型】倒装 + 平行结构   难度：★★★★☆
【难句破解】

找主干	过程	第一步：找从句标志词，并剥离该从句。（本句中无从句，故该步骤略。）

		第二步：识别非谓语动词，同时删除非谓语动词结构及其它修饰成分。本句无非谓语动词结构；删除修饰成分 Only gradually, of the institution, only more gradually, still, as a directive factor, in the conduct of the institution。全句剩下了 was the by-product noted, and was this effect considered as a directive factor，这就是句子的主干部分。 第三步：识别并删除很像谓语动词的动词。（真正的谓语动词已找到，故该步骤略。）
	结果	...was the by-product...noted, and...was this effect considered...（be 动词 1 + 主 1 + 谓语动词 1 + and + be 动词 2 + 主 2 + 谓语动词 2） 连词 and 连接了两个并列的倒装句，且两个倒装句中的谓语动词均使用了被动语态。
理修饰	定语	分句一中，介词短语 of the institution 作后置定语，修饰主语 the by-product。
	主补	第一层：介词短语 as a directive factor 作主语 this effect 的补足语。 第二层：介词短语 in the conduct of the institution 作后置定语，修饰 factor。
	状语	分句一中的副词 gradually，分句二中的副词 more gradually 和 still 均作状语。由于 only 位于句首分别强调 gradually 和 more gradually，故分句一和分句二均采用了部分倒装，正常语序为：The by-product of the institution was noted only gradually, and this effect was still considered only more gradually as a directive factor in the conduct of the institution.

【结构分析】

一级修饰	**of** the institution,
	介词短语作后置定语，修饰 the by-product
句子主干	Only gradually was **the by-product**...noted,（倒装句：谓 + 主） and 连接的并列句 **and** only more gradually still was **this effect** considered（倒装句：谓 + 主）
	介词短语作 this effect 的补足语
一级修饰	**as** a directive **factor**
	介词短语作后置定语，修饰 factor
二级修饰	**in** the conduct of the institution

directive	[də'rektɪv] *a.* 指导的；指示的 *n.* 指示；命令
conduct	['kɒndʌkt] *n.* 经营方式；行为 [kən'dʌkt] *vt.* 组织；带领；举止

【意群训练】

Only gradually // was the by-product // of the institution noted, // and only more gradually // still was this effect considered // as a directive factor // in the conduct // of the institution.

实例 2

Not only did they develop such a device but by the turn of the millennium they had also managed to embed it in a worldwide system accessed by billions of people every day. 他们不仅研发出了这样的设备，而且在世纪之交，还成功地将其嵌入一个每天都有数十亿用户访问的全球系统。【英语（一）2012 新题型】

【难句类型】倒装 + 平行结构 + 非谓语动词 　　　　　　难度：★★★★☆

【难句破解】

找主干	过程	第一步：找从句标志词，并剥离该从句。（本句中无从句，故该步骤略。） 第二步：识别非谓语动词，同时删除非谓语动词结构及其它修饰成分。删除非谓语动词结构 to embed it 和 accessed by billions of people；删除修饰成分 by the turn of the millennium, also, in a worldwide system, every day。全句剩下了 Not only did they develop such a device but they had managed，这就是句子的主干部分。 第三步：识别并删除很像谓语动词的动词。（真正的谓语动词已找到，故该步骤略。）
	结果	Not only did they develop such a device but...they had...managed to embed it...（Not only + 助动词 + 主 + 谓 1 + 宾 1 + but + 主 + 谓 2 + 宾 2） Not only...but... 连接两个并列分句：分句一中，由于表否定的 Not 位于句首，句中的谓语使用了部分倒装，正常语序为 they not only developed...；分句二中，动词不定式短语 to embed it 作宾语，是主干成分，故还原。
理修饰	状语	介词短语 by the turn of the millennium 作时间状语；副词 also 作状语修饰 had managed。

状语	第一层：介词短语 in a worldwide system 作状语。第二层：过去分词短语 accessed by billions of people every day 作后置定语，修饰 system，其中 every day 作时间状语。

【结构分析】

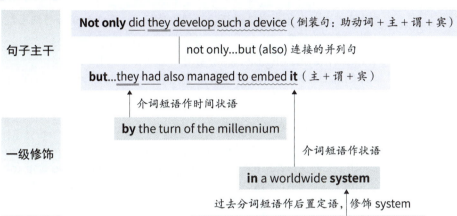

句子主干	**Not only** did they develop such a device（倒装句：助动词＋主＋谓＋宾） not only...but (also) 连接的并列句 **but**...they had also managed to embed **it**（主＋谓＋宾）
一级修饰	介词短语作时间状语 **by** the turn of the millennium 介词短语作状语 **in** a worldwide **system**
二级修饰	过去分词短语作后置定语，修饰 system **accessed** by billions of people every day.

【词汇注释】

millennium	[mɪˈleniəm] *n.* 一千年，千禧年
embed	[ɪmˈbed] *vt.* 把……牢牢地嵌入；派遣

【意群训练】

Not only did they develop // such a device // but by the turn of the millennium // they had also managed // to embed it // in a worldwide system // accessed by billions of people // every day.

──── 实例 3 ────────────────────────────────────⟩⟩⟩⟩

Only if the jobless arrive at the jobcentre with a CV, register for online job search, and start looking for work will they be eligible for benefit—and then they should report weekly rather than fortnightly. 失业者只有带上简历到就业中心，注册在线求职，并开始找工作，才有资格获得救济金。同时，他们之后应该每周而不是每两周才报到一次。【英语（一）2014 Text 1】

【难句类型】倒装＋平行结构＋从句＋非谓语动词　　　　　　难度：★★★★

【难句破解】

找主干	过程	第一步：找从句标志词，并剥离该从句。找到标志词 if：距离 if 之后最近的动词是 arrive，and 将其前后的成分并列连接，因此

119

		register for 和 start 也是该从句的动词，至此将该从句剥离。 第二步：识别非谓语动词，同时删除非谓语动词结构及其它修饰成分。删除非谓语动词结构 looking for work；删除修饰成分 Only，for benefit 和 and then...rather than fortnightly。全句剩下了 will they be eligible，这就是句子的主干部分。 第三步：识别并删除很像谓语动词的动词。（真正的谓语动词已找到，故该步骤省略。）
	结果	..., will they be eligible...（助动词＋主＋be 动词＋表） 因 Only 位于句首，故本句采用了倒装，正常语序为：they will be eligible，will 与 they 倒装。
理修饰	状语	介词短语 for benefit 作状语。
	状从	if 引导条件状语从句 Only **[if]** the jobless arrive at the jobcentre with a CV, register for online job search, and start looking for work（主＋谓1＋谓2＋宾1＋and＋谓3＋宾2）位于句首，作主句的条件状语，包含了 and 连接的三个并列的谓语，其中，介词短语 at the jobcentre 作地点状语，介词短语 with a CV 作伴随状语，副词 Only 作状语，表强调。
	补充 说明	第一层：破折号后句子结构为 and then they should report weekly rather than fortnightly（主＋谓）。第二层：then 是时间状语；rather than 连接两个并列的副词 weekly 和 fortnightly，修饰 should report，表示"是……；而不是……"。

看标点	破折号	破折号后的内容对其之前的内容进行补充说明。

【结构分析】

	Only **[if]** the jobless **arrive** at the jobcentre with a CV,
	并列谓语
一级修饰	**register for** online job search,
	and 连接的并列谓语
	and start looking for work
	if 引导的条件状语从句，作句子主干的条件状语
句子主干	will they be eligible for benefit（部分倒装：助动词＋主＋系＋表）
	补充说明
一级修饰	—and then they **should report**
	rather than 连接的并列副词作状语，修饰 should report
二级修饰	weekly **rather than** fortnightly.

【词汇注释】

| register | ['redʒɪstə(r)] *vt&vi.* 注册；登记；把……挂号邮寄 *n.* 登记表 |
| eligible | ['elɪdʒəbl] *a.* 有资格的；合格的；具备条件的 |

【意群训练】

Only if the jobless // arrive at the jobcentre // with a CV, // register for // online job search, // and start looking for work // will they be eligible // for benefit // —and then // they should report // weekly rather than fortnightly.

七 强调

　　强调就是对句中某一成分的着重说明。英语中的强调分为两种：单词强调，即通过助动词、only、so 等单词来突出某一成分；句型强调，即通过强调句型来强调某一成分。有些强调句型中还会出现倒装现象。

(一) 单词强调

　　常见的单词强调有：

　　（1）助动词强调，即助动词出现在陈述语气中，这时助动词也是谓语动词的一部分；

　　（2）only + 状语强调状语，位于句首时，要部分倒装；

　　（3）so + 主语 + 谓语 / 系动词表示同意；

　　（4）反身代词强调。需要注意，要将"so + 主 + 谓 / 系"和"so + 谓 / 系 + 主"区分开，前者表示对前文内容的同意或肯定，后者表示"……也一样……"。

实例 1

Peretti says the *Times* shouldn't waste time getting out of the print business, but only if they go about doing it the right way. 佩雷蒂表示，《纽约时报》不应在取消印刷版业务上浪费时间，除非他们采取了正确的方法。【英语（一）2016 Text 4】

【难句类型】强调 + 嵌套结构 + 省略 + 非谓语动词　　　　　难度：★★★★
【难句破解】

| 找主干 | 过程 | 第一步：找从句标志词，并剥离该从句。找到标志词 if：距离 if 之后最近的动词是 go about doing，do 是及物动词，故 it 作其宾语，至此将该从句剥离。 |

		第二步：识别非谓语动词，同时删除非谓语动词结构及其它修饰成分。删除非谓语动词结构 getting out of the print business；删除修饰成分 only 和 the right way。but 在 if 引导的从句之前，起连接作用，故一并删除。全句剩下了 Peretti says the *Times* shouldn't waste time。
		第三步：识别并删除很像谓语动词的动词。根据辨析真假谓语动词的方法，全句还剩下两个动词 says 和 shouldn't waste，二者均不缺失宾语，因此前面的 says 是主干谓语动词，shouldn't waste 是省略引导词 that 的宾语从句的谓语动词，因 waste 是及物动词，故 time 作其宾语，至此将该从句剥离。全句剩下了 Peretti says，这就是句子的主谓部分。
	结果	Peretti <u>says</u> **(that)** the *Times* shouldn't waste time...（主＋谓＋宾从） 省略引导词 that 的从句 **(that)** the *Times* shouldn't waste time...（主＋谓＋宾）作 says 的宾语，是句子的主干成分，故还原。
理修饰	状语	省略 in 的介词短语（in）getting out of the print business 作状语，表方面。
	状从	第一层：if 引导条件状语从句 only **[if]** <u>they</u> <u>go</u> about doing <u>it</u> the right way（主＋谓＋宾），作宾从的条件状语，only 在 if 从句之前表示对整个状从的强调；but 承接上文，表转折。第二层：省略 in 的介词短语（in）the right way 作方式状语。

【结构分析】

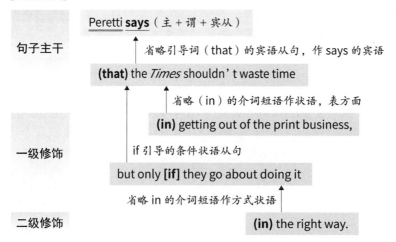

句子主干　Peretti **says**（主＋谓＋宾从）

省略引导词（that）的宾语从句，作 says 的宾语

(that) the *Times* shouldn' t waste time

省略（in）的介词短语作状语，表方面

(in) getting out of the print business,

一级修饰

if 引导的条件状语从句

but only **[if]** they go about doing it

省略 in 的介词短语作方式状语

二级修饰　　　　　　　**(in)** the right way.

【词汇注释】

get out of	放弃；逃避；摆脱	go about doing sth.	开始做某事

Peretti says // the *Times* shouldn't waste time // getting out of the print business, // but only if // they go about doing it // the right way.

-------- 实例 2 --------

But science does provide us with the best available guide to the future, and it is critical that our nation and the world base important policies on the best judgments that science can provide concerning the future consequences of present actions. 但是它确实能为我们的未来提供最好的可行性指导，而且至关重要的是我们的国家乃至整个世界在做重要决策时，都应该以科学能够提供的关于人类当前行为对未来影响最佳判断为依据。【英语（一）2005 Text 2】

【难句类型】强调＋嵌套结构＋平行结构＋非谓语动词　　　　　难度：★★★★
【难句破解】

找主干	过程	第一步：找从句标志词，并剥离该从句。❶ 找到第一个标志词 that：距离 that 之后最近的动词是及物动词 base，important policies 作其宾语，至此将该从句剥离；❷ 找到第二个标志词 that：距离 that 之后最近的动词是 can provide，至此将该从句剥离。 第二步：识别非谓语动词，同时删除非谓语动词结构及其它修饰成分。删除非谓语动词结构 concerning the future consequences。删除修饰成分 with the best available guide，to the future，on the best judgments，of present actions。全句剩下了 But science does provide us and it is critical，这就是句子的主干部分。 第三步：识别并删除很像谓语动词的动词。（真正的谓语动词已找到，故该步骤略。）
	结果	But science does provide us…，…and it is critical…（But + 主 1 + 谓 + 宾 + and + 主 2 + 系 + 表） 这是 and 连接的两个并列分句。助动词 does 强调 provide，二者一起作分句一的谓语动词。句首的连词 But 表示与上文的逻辑关系。
理修饰	状语	第一层：分句一中，介词短语 with…guide to the future 作状语，修饰 provide。第二层：介词短语 to the future 作后置定语，修饰 guide。
	主从	分句二中，it 是形式主语，真正的主语是 that 引导的主语从句 **[that]** our nation and the world base important policies…（主＋谓＋宾）。 第一层：介词短语 on the best judgments 作状语，修饰 base。第二层：that 引导定语从句 **[that]** science can provide…（宾＋主

＋谓）修饰 judgments，其中介词短语 concerning...present actions 作后置定语，亦修饰 judgments。

【结构分析】

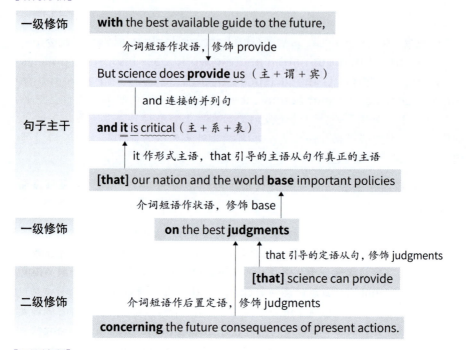

| 一级修饰 | **with** the best available guide to the future, |

介词短语作状语，修饰 provide

But science does **provide** us（主＋谓＋宾）

and 连接的并列句

| 句子主干 | **and it** is critical（主＋系＋表）|

it 作形式主语，that 引导的主语从句作真正的主语

[that] our nation and the world **base** important policies

介词短语作状语，修饰 base

| 一级修饰 | **on** the best **judgments** |

that 引导的定语从句，修饰 judgments

[that] science can provide

| 二级修饰 | 介词短语作后置定语，修饰 judgments |

concerning the future consequences of present actions.

【词汇注释】

available	[ə'veɪləbl] *a.* 可获得的；可找到的；有空的
critical	['krɪtɪkl] *a.* 关键的；批评的；挑剔的；可能有危险的

【意群训练】

But science // does provide us // with the best available guide // to the future, // and it is critical that // our nation and the world // base important policies // on the best judgments // that science can provide // concerning the future consequences // of present actions.

（二）　句型强调

　　常见的句型强调有：It is/was＋被强调成分＋that/who...，可以强调句子的各个成分；not until... 和 It was not until...that... 强调句中的时间状语，其中前者主谓必须部分倒装，后者则不需要使用倒装。要将这类句型与主语从句区分开，在主语从句中，is/was 是句子的系动词，而在强调句型中，is/was 则是强调句型中的动词，不作句子的谓语动词，考生判断强调句型的一个方法为：将强调句型整体删除后句子的语法结构完整，不缺少任何成分。

注：在句型强调结构的句子中，考生需先判断 that/who 是从句标志词还是只起强调作用，强调结构中的 that/who 在强调句中不作任何成分。

实例 1

It was within the computer age that the term "information society" began to be widely used to describe the context within which we now live. 正是在计算机时代，"信息社会"这个词开始被广泛用于描述我们现在所生活的环境。【英语（一）2002 完形】

【难句类型】强调 + 非谓语动词 + 从句　　　　　　　　难度：★★★☆

【难句破解】

找主干	过程	第一步：找从句标志词，并剥离该从句。该句中的 that 与其前的 It was 构成强调结构，并非从句引导词。找到标志词 within which：距离 within which 之后最近的动词是 live，至此将该从句剥离。 第二步：识别非谓语动词，同时删除非谓语动词结构及其它修饰成分。删除非谓语动词结构 to be widely used, to describe the context；删除修饰成分 within the computer age。 第三步：识别并删除很像谓语动词的动词。由第一步可知，该句中的 It was...that... 为强调句型，was 是该句型中的动词，故删除该句型结构。全句剩下了 the term "information society" began，这就是句子的主谓部分。
	结果	...the term "information society" began to be widely used...（主 + 谓 + 宾） 动词不定式短语 to be widely used 作宾语，是主干成分，故还原。
理修饰	状语一	句首的 It was...that... 为强调句型，强调时间状语 within the computer age。
	状语二	第一层：动词不定式短语 to describe the context...作目的状语。 第二层：介词 within+which 引导的定语从句 [within which] we now live（主 + 谓），修饰 the context，副词 now 作时间状语。

【结构分析】

一级修饰

It was...that

It was...that 为强调句型，强调时间状语 within the computer age

within the computer age

介词短语作句子主干的时间状语

句子主干 ┆ the term "information society" began to be widely used（主＋谓＋宾）

动词不定式短语作目的状语

一级修饰

to describe **the context**

介词 within+which 引导的定语从句，修饰 the context

二级修饰

[**within which**] we now live.

【意群训练】

It was within the computer age // that the term // "information society" // began to be widely used // to describe the context // within which // we now live.

┄┄┄┄ 实例 2 ┄┄┄┄┄┄┄┄┄┄┄┄┄┄┄┄┄┄┄┄┄┄┄┄┄┄ >>>>

It is only the Queen who has preserved the monarchy's reputation with her rather ordinary (if well-heeled) granny style. 只有女王以她相当平凡的（尽管相当考究的）奶奶风格保住了君主的声誉。【英语（一）2015 Text 1】

【难句类型】强调   难度：★★★

【难句破解】

找主干	过程	第一步：找从句标志词，并剥离该从句。该句中的 who 与其前的 It is 构成强调结构，并非从句引导词。本句中无从句，故该步骤略。 第二步：识别非谓语动词，同时删除非谓语动词结构及其它修饰成分。本句无非谓语动词结构；删除修饰成分 with her...granny style。 第三步：识别并删除很像谓语动词的动词。由第一步可知，该句中的 It is...who... 为强调句型，is 是该句型中的动词，故删除该句型结构。全句剩下了 the Queen has preserved the monarchy's reputation，这就是句子的主干部分。
	结果	...only the Queen...has preserved the monarchy's reputation... （主＋谓＋宾） It is...who... 是强调句型，强调状语 only 和主语 the Queen。

理修饰	状语	第一层：介词短语 with her rather ordinary...granny style 作方式状语。第二层：括号中的内容 if well-heeled 补充说明 rather ordinary。
看标点	括号	括号表示补充说明。

【结构分析】

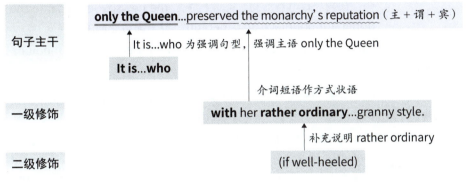

句子主干	only the Queen...preserved the monarchy's reputation（主＋谓＋宾） It is...who 为强调句型，强调主语 only the Queen **It is...who**
一级修饰	介词短语作方式状语 **with** her **rather ordinary**...granny style.
二级修饰	补充说明 rather ordinary (if well-heeled)

【词汇注释】

preserve	[prɪ'zɜːv] vt. 维护；保存；储存；保护 n. 专门领域
reputation	[ˌrepju'teɪʃn] n. 名誉；名声
well-heeled	['wel'hiːld] a. 穿着考究的；富有的

【意群训练】

It is only the Queen // who has preserved // the monarchy's reputation // with her rather ordinary // (if well-heeled) // granny style.

------ 实例 3 ------

As was discussed before, it was not until the 19th century that the newspaper became the dominant pre-electronic medium, following in the wake of the pamphlet and the book and in the company of the periodical. 正如前面所讲过的那样，直到 19 世纪，继小册子和图书之后，随着期刊的出现，报纸才成为电子时代之前的主流传播媒介。【英语（一）2002 完形】

【难句类型】强调＋非谓语动词＋从句   难度：★★★★

【难句破解】

找主干	过程	第一步：找从句标志词，并剥离该从句。该句中的 that 与其前的 it was not until 构成强调结构，并非从句引导词。找到标志词

	As：距离 As 之后最近的动词是 discussed，至此将该从句剥离。第二步：识别非谓语动词，同时删除非谓语动词结构及其它修饰成分。删除非谓语动词结构 following in the wake...periodical；删除修饰成分 before。第三步：识别并删除很像谓语动词的动词。由第一步可知，该句中的 it was not until...that 为强调句型，was 是该句型中的动词，故删除该句型结构。全句剩下了 the newspaper became the dominant pre-electronic medium，这就是句子的主干部分。
结果	...the newspaper became the dominant pre-electronic medium,... （主＋系＋表）

理修饰	定从	As 引导的非限定性定语从句 [As] was discussed before(主＋谓)，补充说明句子主干，其中 before 作时间状语。
	状语	it was not until...that... 为强调句型，强调时间状语 the 19th century；现在分词短语 following...作伴随状语，其中第二个 and 连接了两个并列的介词短语 in the wake of the pamphlet and the book 和 in the company of the periodical。

【结构分析】

一级修饰	[As] was discussed before,
	As 引导的非限定性定语从句，补充说明句子主干
	it was not until...that
	it was not until...that 为强调句型，强调时间状语 the 19th century
	the 19th century
	名词短语作句子主干的时间状语
句子主干	the newspaper became the dominant pre-electronic medium, （主＋系＋表）
	现在分词短语作伴随状语
一级修饰	**following in** the wake of the pamphlet and the book
	and 连接的并列介词短语
	and in the company of the periodical.

【词汇注释】

dominant	['dɒmɪnənt] *a.* 占优势的；显性的
in the wake of	随……之后而来；跟随在……后

pamphlet	['pæmflət] *n.* 小册子；手册
periodical	[ˌpɪəri'ɒdɪkl] *n.* 期刊

【意群训练】

As was discussed before, // it was // not until the 19th century // that the newspaper // became the dominant pre-electronic medium, // following in the wake of // the pamphlet and the book // and in the company of // the periodical.

（八）非谓语动词与独立主格

非谓语动词是英语中一个重要的语法点，也是考研英语常见的考点。它是动词的一种形式，但是不能在句中单独作谓语。非谓语动词有三种：分词、不定式、动名词，其中分词又包括现在分词和过去分词。这三种形式的非谓语动词可以在句子中充当除谓语以外的各种句子成分。在基础篇中我们已经了解了如何辨析非谓语动词和谓语动词，本节中我们将具体学习各种非谓语动词的用法和区别。

（一）非谓语动词作主语

动名词和不定式均可以在句中作主语，但二者用法不同。动名词作主语，多表示抽象的、概念性的动作，动作可能经常发生，即泛指；不定式作主语，常表示具体的动作，尤其是表示某一次的动作，即特指。疑问词＋不定式也可以在句中作主语。

非谓语动词作主语时，句中常出现形式主语it,句型为: It is/was +*adj.*/*n.* + to do/doing sth.。考研英语中对非谓语动词作主语的考查不多，不是考查重点。

·······实例 1·······

Knowing what you're good at and doing even more of it creates excellence. 只有知道自己的长处，并多去实践，才能造就卓越。【英语（一）2009 Text 1】

【难句类型】非谓语动词＋从句＋平行结构   难度：★★★☆
【难句破解】

找主干	过程	第一步：找从句标志词，并剥离该从句。找到标志词 what：距离 what 之后最近的动词是 are good at，至此将该从句剥离。

	第二步：识别非谓语动词，同时删除非谓语动词结构及其它修饰成分。删除非谓语动词结构 Knowing，doing even more of it；本句无其它修饰成分。并列连词 and 连接了两个并列的非谓语动词结构，故也删除。全句剩下了 creates excellence，这就是句子的谓宾部分。 第三步：识别并删除很像谓语动词的动词。（真正的谓语动词已找到，故该步骤略。）
结果	Knowing...and doing even more of it creates excellence.（主1 + and + 主2 + 谓 + 宾） and 连接两个并列的动名词短语 Knowing... 和 doing even more of it 作主语，是主干成分，故还原。
理修饰　宾从	what 引导的宾语从句 [what] you're good at（宾 + 主 + 谓），作 Knowing 的宾语，与 Knowing 共同构成句子主干的主语。

【结构分析】

句子主干	**Knowing**...and doing even more of it creates excellence."（主 + 谓 + 宾） ↑ what 引导的宾语从句，作 Knowing 的宾语 **[what]** you're good at

【词汇注释】

excellence	['eksələns] n. 卓越；优秀；杰出

【意群训练】

Knowing what you're good at // and doing even more of it // creates excellence.

（二）非谓语动词作宾语

　　动名词和不定式均可在句中作宾语，具体用哪种形式作宾语取决于前面的谓语动词，即我们常说的动词后面跟 to do 还是 doing。有些动词后面既可跟动名词，也可跟不定式作宾语，但意义可能不同。具体动词的用法没有明显的规律，因此在记忆单词时，要将"动词 + 非谓语动词作宾语"的用法一起记忆。常见的"动词 + 非谓语动词作宾语"的情况如下：

　　（1）只能跟动名词作宾语的动词有：consider, suggest, advise, admit, pardon, avoid, keep, finish, practice, enjoy, appreciate, forbid, allow, permit, imagine, look forward to 等；

　　（2）只能跟不定式作宾语的动词有：decide, determine, want, expect, hope, refuse, pretend, promise, choose, plan, agree, help, offer, learn 等；

（3）可以跟不定式和动名词作宾语，但意义不同的动词有：forget to do（忘记要去做），forget doing（忘记做过）；remember to do（记得要去做），remember doing（记得做过）；try to do（努力去做），try doing（试一试）等。

------ 实例 1 ------ >>>>

For these reasons, I stopped weighing myself every day and switched to a bimonthly weighing schedule instead. 基于这些原因，我不再每天称重，转而改为每月称重两次。【英语（二）2019 完形】

【难句类型】非谓语动词 + 平行结构　　　　　　　　　难度：★★★
【难句破解】

找主干	过程	第一步：找从句标志词，并剥离从句。（本句中无从句标志词，故该步骤略。） 第二步：识别非谓语动词，同时删除非谓语动词结构及其它修饰成分。删除非谓语动词结构 weighing myself；删除修饰成分 For these reasons，every day，to a bimonthly weighing schedule instead。全句剩下了 I stopped and switched，这就是句子的主谓部分。 第三步：识别并删除很像谓语动词的动词。（真正的谓语动词已找到，故该步骤略。）
	结果	I stopped weighing myself...and switched...（主 + 谓 1+ 宾 +and + 谓 2） 动名词短语 weighing myself 作谓语 1 的宾语，是主干成分，故还原。
理修饰	状语	句首的介词短语 For these reasons 作原因状语；名词短语 every day 作状语，表频次；介词短语 to a bimonthly weighing schedule 作状语，表对象，instead 作状语，两者均修饰 switched。

【结构分析】

一级修饰　　　　　　**For** these reasons,
　　　　　　　　　　│介词短语作原因状语
　　　　　　　　　　↓
I **stopped** weighing myself every day（主 + 谓 + 宾）
句子主干　　│ and 连接的并列谓语

and switched
　　　　　　│介词短语作状语，修饰 switched
　　　　　　↓
一级修饰　　**to** a bimonthly weighing schedule instead.

bimonthly	[ˌbaɪˈmʌnθli] *a./ad.* 一月两次的（地）；两月一次的（地）

【意群训练】

For these reasons, // I stopped weighing myself // every day // and switched // to a bimonthly weighing schedule instead.

---- 实例 2 ----

But don't bother trying to kill off old habits; once those ruts of procedure are worn into the brain, they're there to stay. 但不要自寻烦恼地去戒除旧习惯；一旦这些习惯的"踪迹"被印入脑海，便会根深蒂固。【英语（一）2009 Text 1】

【难句类型】非谓语动词＋从句＋平行结构　　　　　　难度：★★★☆

【难句破解】

找主干	过程	第一步：找从句标志词，并剥离该从句。找到标志词 once：距离 once 之后最近的动词是 are worn，至此将该从句剥离。 第二步：识别非谓语动词，同时删除非谓语动词结构及其它修饰成分。删除非谓语动词结构 trying to kill off old habits，to stay。删除修饰成分 into the brain，there。全句剩下了 But don't bother；they're，这就是句子主干的一部分。 第三步：识别并删除很像谓语动词的动词。（真正的谓语动词已找到，故该步骤略。）
	结果	But don't bother trying to kill off old habits; ..., they're ...there to stay...（谓＋宾＋主＋系＋表） 这是分号连接的两个并列分句，分句一是祈使句，try to do（努力去做）为固定短语，trying to kill off old habits 作宾语；分句二中的 there 作表语。均属于句子主干，故还原。句首的连词 But 表示与上文在逻辑上为转折关系。
理修饰	状从	第一层：分句二中，once 引导的条件状语从句 [once] those ruts of procedure are worn...（主＋谓），作主句的条件状语。第二层：介词短语 of procedure 作后置定语，修饰 ruts；介词短语 into the brain 作状语。
	状语	副词 there 作分句二的状语。
看标点	分号	分号表示两个句子并列，说明该句是平行结构。

132

句子主干	But don't bother trying to kill off old habits;（祈使句：谓+宾） 　　　并列句 they're there to stay.（主+系+表） 　　　↑ once 引导的条件状语从句，作句子主干的条件状语
一级修饰	[once] those ruts of procedure are worn into the brain,

【词汇注释】

kill off	除掉；大量消灭
rut	[rʌt] *n.* 惯例；车辙；刻板状态 *vt.* 使留下车辙

【意群训练】

But don't bother // trying to kill off // old habits; // once those ruts // of procedure // are worn into // the brain, // they're there // to stay.

（三）　**非谓语动词作表语**

四种非谓语动词均可在句中作表语，具体用法如下：

非谓语动词作表语	
不定式	表示具体的动作，尤其是表示某一次的动作，即特指（与作主语相同）。
动名词	表示抽象的、概念性的动作，动作可能经常发生，即泛指（与作主语相同），相当于一个名词，可以和主语互换位置。
现在分词	相当于形容词，多用于形容事物，表示事物的特征。
过去分词	相当于形容词，多用于形容人，表示人的心理感觉或状态。

注意：疑问词+不定式也可以在句中作表语

实例 **1**

Plenty of other species are able to learn, and one of the things they've apparently learned is when to stop. 许多其他的物种也有学习能力，而且很明显，它们所学到的其中一件事就是知道何时停止学习。【英语（一）2009 完形】

【难句类型】非谓语动词+省略+平行结构+从句　　　　　　　难度：★★★☆

【难句破解】

找主干	过程	第一步：找从句标志词，并剥离该从句。（本句中无从句标志词，故该步骤略。）

	第二步：识别非谓语动词，同时删除非谓语动词结构及其它修饰成分。删除非谓语动词结构 to learn, to stop。本句中无其他修饰成分。全句剩下了 Plenty of other species are able, and one of the things they've apparently learned is when。 第三步：识别并删除很像谓语动词的动词。根据辨析真假谓语动词的方法，全句剩下三个动词 are, have learned 和 is，其中 have learned 后缺失宾语，故它是省略关系词 that 的定语从句 they've apparently learned 的谓语动词，至此将该从句剥离。全句剩下了 Plenty of other species are able, and one of the things is when。这就是句子的主干成分。
结果	Plenty of other species <u>are</u> able to learn, and <u>one of the things</u> <u>is</u> when to stop. (主 1+ 系 1+ 表 1+and+ 主 2+ 系 2+ 表 2) 分句一中，不定式 to learn 作表语补足语，与表语联系紧密；分句二中，when 与动词不定式 to stop 构成表语，是主干成分，故还原。
理修饰　定从	**(that)** they've apparently <u>learned</u>（宾＋主＋谓）是省略 that 的定语从句，修饰 one of the things，其中副词 apparently 作状语，修饰谓语 have learned。

【结构分析】

句子主干	<u>Plenty of other species</u> are able to learn,（主＋系＋表） 　｜ and 连接的并列句 **and one of the things**...is when to stop.（主＋系＋表）
	↑ 省略引导词 that 的定语从句，修饰 one of the things
一级修饰	**(that)** they've apparently learned

【意群训练】

Plenty of other species // are able to learn, // and one of the things // they've apparently learned is // when to stop.

---- 实例 2 ----〉〉〉〉

Since our chief business with them is to enable them to share in a common life we cannot help considering whether or not we are forming the powers which will secure this ability. 由于我们对青年人所做的首要工作在于使他们能够融入共同生活中去，所以我们不禁要细想自己是否正在形成让他们获得这种本领的能力。【英语（一）2009 翻译】

【难句类型】非谓语动词＋嵌套结构＋从句　　　　　　　难度：★★★★☆

【难句破解】

找主干	过程	第一步：找从句标志词，并剥离该从句。❶ 找到第一个标志词 Since：距离 Since 之后最近的动词是 is，至此将该从句剥离；❷ 找到第二个标志词 whether：距离 whether 之后最近的动词是 are forming，因 form 是及物动词，故 the powers 作其宾语，至此将该从句剥离；❸ 找到第三个标志词 which：距离 which 之后最近的动词是 will secure，因 secure 是及物动词，故 this ability 作其宾语，至此将该从句剥离。 第二步：识别非谓语动词，同时删除非谓语动词结构及其它修饰成分。删除非谓语动词结构 to enable them，to share。删除修饰成分 in a common life。全句剩下了 we cannot help considering，这就是句子主干的一部分。 第三步：识别并删除很像谓语动词的动词。（真正的谓语动词已找到，故该步骤略。）
	结果	...we cannot help considering **[whether]** or not we are forming the powers（主＋谓＋宾） 在固定搭配 can't help doing sth. 这一结构中，can't help 作谓语，doing sth. 作宾语。whether 引导的宾语从句 **[whether]** or not we are forming the powers（主＋谓＋宾），作 considering 的宾语，应还原。
理修饰	状从	第一层：Since 引导的原因状语从句 **[Since]** our chief business with them is to enable...life（主＋系＋表），作主句的原因状语，其中动词不定式短语 to enable them...life 作表语。第二层：第二个 them 作 to enable 的宾语，动词不定式短语 to share in a common life 作 them 的补足语。
	定从	which 引导的定语从句 **[which]** will secure this ability（主＋谓＋宾）修饰宾从中的 the powers。

【结构分析】

二级修饰	**to** share in a common life
	动词不定式短语作 them 的补足语 ↓
一级修饰	**[Since]** our chief business with them is to enable **them**
	↓ Since 引导的原因状语从句，作句子主干的原因状语
句子主干	we cannot help **considering**（主＋谓＋宾）
	↑ whether 引导的宾语从句，作 considering 的宾语
	[whether] or not we are forming **the powers**
	which 引导的定语从句，修饰 the powers ↑
一级修饰	**[which]** will secure this ability.

> secure [sɪˈkjʊə(r)] *vt.* 获得；扣紧；使安全 *a.* 牢固的；有把握的

【意群训练】

Since our chief business with them // is to enable them // to share in a common life // we cannot help considering // whether or not // we are forming the powers // which will secure // this ability.

（四）非谓语动词作补语

现在分词、过去分词和不定式均可在句中作补语，即我们常说的 *v.*+sb./ sth.+ to do/doing/done。常见的情况有两种：

（1）感官动词 see, watch, observe, look at, notice, hear, listen to, feel + 非谓语动词作补语；

（2）使役动词 make, get, have + 非谓语动词作补语。考研英语中对非谓语动词作补语的用法考查较少，但在记忆单词时最好能将相关用法一起记忆。

实例 1

Fruit flies who were taught to be smarter than the average fruit fly tended to live shorter lives. 训练得比普通果蝇聪明的那些果蝇，寿命往往比较短。【英语（一）2009 完形】

【难句类型】非谓语动词 + 从句 + 比较结构　　　　　　　难度：★★★★
【难句破解】

找主干	过程	第一步：找从句标志词，并剥离该从句。找到标志词 who：距离 who 之后最近的动词是 were taught，至此将该从句剥离。 第二步：识别非谓语动词，同时删除非谓语动词结构及其它修饰成分。删除非谓语动词结构 to be smarter, to live shorter lives。删除修饰成分 than the average fruit fly。全句剩下了 Fruit flies tended，这就是句子的主谓部分。 第三步：识别并删除很像谓语动词的动词。（真正的谓语动词已找到，故该步骤略。）
	结果	<u>Fruit flies...tended to live shorter lives.</u>（主＋谓＋宾） tended to live 整体作谓语，shorter lives 作宾语，都是句子的主干成分，故均还原。

理修饰	定从	第一层：定语从句 [who] were taught to be smarter（主＋谓）修饰 fruit flies。第二层：动词不定式短语 to be smarter 是定从主语 who 的补足语；than the average fruit fly 作定从的比较状语。

【结构分析】

句子主干	**Fruit flies**...tended to live shorter lives.（主＋谓＋宾）

↑ who 引导的定语从句，修饰 Fruit flies

一级修饰	**[who]** were taught to be smarter

↑ 介词短语作比较状语

二级修饰	**than** the average fruit fly

【意群训练】

Fruit flies // who were taught // to be smarter // than the average fruit fly // tended to // live shorter lives.

----- 实例 2 ---»»»»

It is financially terrifying, psychologically embarrassing and you know that support is minimal and extraordinarily hard to get. 失业在经济上令人害怕、在心理上让人尴尬，并且你知道，失业救济是微乎其微的，也很难得到。【英语（一）2014 Text 1】

【难句类型】非谓语动词＋从句＋平行结构　　　　　　难度：★★★⭐︎☆

【难句破解】

找主干	过程	第一步：找从句标志词，并剥离该从句。找到标志词 that：距离 that 之后最近的动词是 is，minimal and extraordinarily hard 作其表语，至此将该从句剥离。 第二步：识别非谓语动词，同时删除非谓语动词结构及其它修饰成分。删除非谓语动词结构 terrifying，embarrassing，to get。删除修饰成分 financially，psychologically。全句剩下了 It is and you know，这就是句子的主谓部分。 第三步：识别并删除很像谓语动词的动词。（真正的谓语动词已找到，故该步骤略。）
	结果	It is...terrifying, ...embarrassing and you know [that] support is minimal and extraordinarily hard to get.（主 1 ＋系＋表＋and ＋主 2 ＋谓＋宾从） 逗号连接的两个并列的现在分词作表语，that 引导的宾语从句 [that] support is minimal and extraordinarily hard（主＋系＋表1＋

137

	and +表2）作 know 的宾语，二者都是句子的主干成分，故均还原。副词 financially、psychologically 和 extraordinarily 均作状语，分别修饰 terrifying、embarrassing 和 hard。
理修饰　表补	动词不定式 to get 作表语 hard 的补足语。

【结构分析】

句子主干

It is financially terrifying, psychologically embarrassing（主＋系＋表）

　　　and 连接的并列句

and you **know**（主＋谓＋宾从）

　　　that 引导的宾语从句，作 know 的宾语

[**that**] support is minimal and extraordinarily **hard**

　　　动词不定式短语作 hard 的补足语

一级修饰　　　　　　　　　　　　　　　　**to** get.

【词汇注释】

embarrassing	[ɪm'bærəsɪŋ] *a.* 使人难堪的
extraordinarily	[ɪk'strɔːdənərɪli] *ad.* 很，十分，特别

【意群训练】

It is financially terrifying, // psychologically embarrassing // and you know // that support is minimal // and extraordinarily hard // to get.

（五）　非谓语动词作定语

　　四种非谓语动词均可在句中作定语，具体用法如下：

非谓语动词作定语	
不定式	与被修饰词之间常为动宾关系，或修饰序数词、最高级、no、all、any 等限定的词。
动名词	用于说明事物的用途，与被修饰词没有主谓关系，不能改为定语从句。
现在分词	与被修饰词有主谓关系，或者分词动作与谓语动词所表示的动作同时发生，可以改为定语从句。
过去分词	与被修饰词有主谓关系，或者表示分词动作已经完成，可以改为定语从句。

　　考研英语中，对分词和动名词作定语的考查都较简单，重点考查不定式作定语的用法。

138

When our ancestors were hunters and gatherers 10,000 years ago, they didn't have time to wonder much about anything besides finding food.

1 万年以前，当我们的祖先还在围猎和采集野果时，他们除了寻找食物以外，没有时间思考别的事情。【英语（一）2009 Text 3】

【难句类型】非谓语动词 + 从句 + 否定结构　　　　　　难度：★ ★ ★ ☆

【难句破解】

找主干	过程	第一步：找从句标志词，并剥离该从句。找到标志词 When：距离 When 之后最近的动词是 were，hunters and gatherers 作其表语，至此将该从句剥离。第二步：识别非谓语动词，同时删除非谓语动词结构及其它修饰成分。删除非谓语动词结构 to wonder much about anything。删除修饰成分 10,000 years ago，besides finding food。全句剩下了 they didn't have time，这就是句子的主干部分。第三步：识别并删除很像谓语动词的动词。（真正的谓语动词已找到，故该步骤略。）
	结果	..., they didn't have time...（主 + 谓 + 宾）
理修饰	状从	第一层：When 引导的时间状语从句 [When] our ancestors were hunters and gatherers 10,000 years ago（主 + 系 + 表），作句子主干的时间状语。第二层：10,000 years ago 作该从句的时间状语。
	定语	第一层：动词不定式短语 to wonder much about anything 作后置定语，修饰 time。第二层：介词短语 besides finding food 作定语，修饰 anything。

【结构分析】

二级修饰	10,000 years ago,
	时间状语
一级修饰	**[When]** our ancestors were hunters and gatherers
	When 引导的时间状语从句，作句子主干的时间状语
句子主干	they didn't have **time**（主 + 谓 + 宾）
	动词不定式短语作后置定语，修饰 time
一级修饰	**to** wonder much about **anything**
	介词短语作定语，修饰 anything
二级修饰	**besides** finding food.

【词汇注释】

gatherer	['gæðərə(r)] *n.* 收集者；采集者

【意群训练】

When our ancestors were // hunters and gatherers // 10,000 years ago, // they didn't have time // to wonder much about anything // besides finding food.

-------- 实例 2 --------

Mr. Nye, a former dean of the Kennedy School of Government at Harvard and one-time chairman of America's National Intelligence Council, is best known for promoting the idea of "soft power", based on persuasion and influence, as a counterpoint to "hard power", based on coercion and force. 作为哈佛大学肯尼迪政府学院的前任院长以及曾经的美国国家情报委员会主席, 奈先生因为提倡推广"软实力"而被人们所熟知。"软实力"是相对于"硬实力"的一个概念, "硬实力"的基础是强制力和军事武力, 而"软实力"的基础则是说服力和影响力。【英语（二）2009 Text 3】

【难句类型】非谓语动词 + 平行结构　　　　　　难度：★★★★★

【难句破解】

<table>
<tr>
<td rowspan="2">找主干</td>
<td>过程</td>
<td>第一步：找从句标志词, 并剥离从句。（本句中无从句标志词, 故该步骤略。）。
第二步：识别非谓语动词, 同时删除非谓语动词结构及其它修饰成分。删除非谓语动词结构 promoting the idea of "soft power", based on persuasion and influence, based on coercion and force; 删除修饰成分 a former dean, of the Kennedy School of Government, at Harvard, and one-time chairman, of America's National Intelligence Council, for, as a counterpoint to "hard power"。全句剩下了 Mr. Nye is best known, 这就是句子的主干部分。
第三步：识别并删除很像谓语动词的动词。（真正的谓语动词已找到, 故该步骤略。）</td>
</tr>
<tr>
<td>结果</td>
<td>Mr. Nye is best known...（主 + 谓）
副词 best 作状语, 修饰谓语。</td>
</tr>
<tr>
<td rowspan="2">理修饰</td>
<td>同位语</td>
<td>第一层：and 连接并列的名词短语 a former dean 和 one-time chairman, 作主语 Mr. Nye 的同位语, 对主语进行解释说明。</td>
</tr>
<tr>
<td></td>
<td>第二层：介词短语 of the Kennedy...at Harvard 作后置定语, 修饰</td>
</tr>
</table>

	dean；介词短语 of America's National Intelligence Council 作后置定语，修饰 chairman。
状语	第一层：介词短语 for promoting the idea of "soft power" 作原因状语，其中动名词短语 promoting... 作介词 for 的宾语。第二层：过去分词短语 based on persuasion and influence 作后置定语，修饰 "soft power"；介词短语 as a counterpoint to "hard power" 作 "soft power" 的补足语。第三层：过去分词短语 based on coercion and force 作后置定语，修饰 "hard power"。

【结构分析】

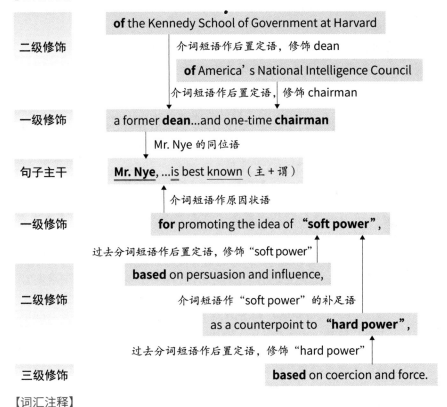

【词汇注释】

coercion	[kəʊ'ɜːʃn] *n.* 强制；强迫

【意群训练】

Mr. Nye, // a former dean of the Kennedy School of Government // at Harvard and one-time chairman // of America's National Intelligence Council, // is best known // for promoting the idea of "soft power",

// based on persuasion and influence, // as a counterpoint to "hard power", // based on coercion and force.

(六) 非谓语动词作状语

不定式、现在分词和过去分词均可在句中作状语，这是考研英语中对非谓语动词用法重点考查的内容，其具体用法如下：

非谓语动词作状语	
不定式	作目的、结果、原因状语。
现在分词	与句子主语有主谓关系，作各种状语，动作与谓语动词动作同时发生。
过去分词	与句子主语有主谓关系，作各种状语，动作已经完成，或表示句子主语的状态。

非谓语动词作状语时，有一个基本原则：非谓语动词的逻辑主语和句子的主语一致，非谓语动词的时态、语态与句子主语搭配。

---- 实例 1 >>>>

We believe that if animals ran the labs, they would test us to determine the limits of our patience, our faithfulness, our memory for locations.
我们认为如果动物掌管实验室的话，它们会对我们进行测试，以确定我们的忍耐度、忠诚度以及方位记忆力。【英语（一）2009 完形】

【难句类型】非谓语动词 + 嵌套结构 + 虚拟 + 平行结构　　　　难度：★★★★

【难句破解】

找主干	过程	第一步：找从句标志词，并剥离该从句。找到第一个标志词 that 和第二个标志词 if（因二者同时出现，故一起分析）：距离 if 之后最近的动词是 ran，因 run 是及物动词，故 the labs 作其宾语，至此将该从句剥离；剥离后距离 that 之后最近的动词是 would test，因 test 是及物动词，故 us 作其宾语，至此将该从句剥离。 第二步：识别非谓语动词，同时删除非谓语动词结构及其它修饰成分。删除非谓语动词结构 to determine...memory for locations，因 determine 为及物动词，故其宾语 the limits of...for locations 也一起删除；本句无修饰成分。全句剩下了 We believe，这就是句子的主谓部分。 第三步：识别并删除很像谓语动词的动词。（真正的谓语动词已找到，故该步骤略。）
	结果	We believe [that]...they would test us...（主 + 谓 + 宾从） that 引导的宾语从句 [that]... they would test us...（主 + 谓 + 宾）作 believe 的宾语，是句子主干成分，故还原。

142

理修饰	状从	if 引导的条件状语从句 **[if]** <u>animals</u> <u>ran</u> <u>the labs</u>（主 + 谓 + 宾），作宾语从句的条件状语，该从句使用了虚拟语气，表示与现在事实相反。
	状语	第一层：宾语从句中，动词不定式短语 to determine the limits..., our faithfulness, our memory... 作目的状语，其中，三个并列的名词（短语）作 determine 的宾语。第二层：在该动词不定式短语中，介词短语 of our patience 作后置定语，修饰 the limits；介词短语 for locations 作后置定语，修饰 our memory。

【结构分析】

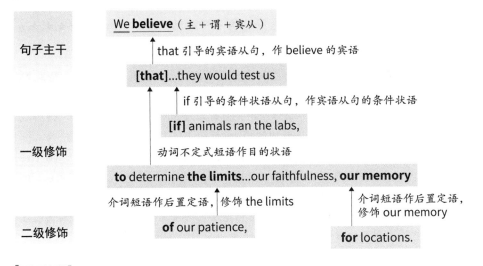

句子主干
一级修饰
二级修饰

【词汇注释】

faithfulness	['feɪθflnəs] *n.* 忠诚；诚实；正确
location	[ləʊ'keɪʃn] *n.* 位置；地点；定位

【意群训练】

We believe that // if animals ran the labs, // they would test us // to determine the limits // of our patience, // our faithfulness, // our memory // for locations.

This group generally do well in IQ test, scoring 12−15 points above the mean value of 100, and have contributed disproportionately to the intellectual and cultural life of the West, as the careers of their elites, including several world-renowned scientists, affirm. 这一族群在智商测试中普遍表现优秀，得分比 100 分这一平均值高出 12−15 分。他们对西方知识和文化生活的发展做出了与其人口数量不成比例的贡献。他们之中的杰出人士（包括好几位世界著名的科学家）的职业证实了这一点。【英语（一）2008 完形】

【难句类型】非谓语动词 + 从句 + 分隔结构 + 平行结构　　　难度：★★★★★
【难句破解】

找主干	过程	第一步：找从句标志词，并剥离该从句。找到标志词 as：距离 as 之后最近的动词是 affirm，至此将该从句剥离。 第二步：识别非谓语动词，同时删除非谓语动词结构及其它修饰成分。删除非谓语动词结构 scoring 12−15...of 100。删除修饰成分 generally，well，in IQ test，disproportionately，to the intellectual and cultural life，of the West。全句剩下了 This group do，and have contributed，这就是句子的主干部分。 第三步：识别并删除很像谓语动词的动词。（真正的谓语动词已找到，故该步骤略。）
	结果	This group...do..., and have contributed...（主 + 谓 1 + and + 谓 2）连词 and 连接了并列的谓语 do 和 have contributed。
理修饰	状语	副词 generally 和 well 均作状语，修饰 do；介词短语 in IQ test 作状语；现在分词短语 scoring 12−15...of 100 作伴随状语；副词 disproportionately 作状语，修饰 have contributed；介词短语 to the intellectual and cultural life of the West 作状语，表对象，其中介词短语 of the West 作后置定语，修饰 the...life。
	定从	第一层：as 引导的非限定性定语从句 **[as]** the careers of their elites...affirm（宾 + 主 + 谓），补充说明其前的句子。第二层：介词短语 of their elites 作后置定语，修饰 the careers。第三层：介词短语 including several world-renowned scientists 作插入语，补充说明 their elites，该插入语造成了从句的主谓分隔。
看标点	逗号	including...scientists 前后的逗号将该插入语分隔出来。

【结构分析】

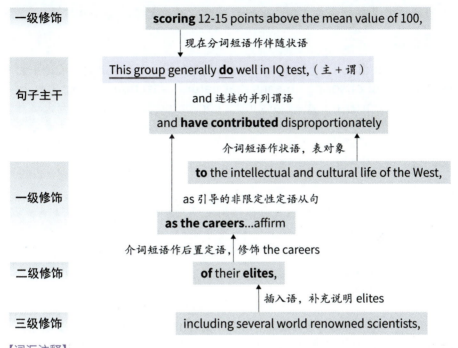

一级修饰　**scoring** 12-15 points above the mean value of 100,
现在分词短语作伴随状语

句子主干　This group generally **do** well in IQ test,（主＋谓）
and 连接的并列谓语

and **have contributed** disproportionately
介词短语作状语，表对象

一级修饰　**to** the intellectual and cultural life of the West,
as 引导的非限定性定语从句

as the careers...affirm
介词短语作后置定语，修饰 the careers

二级修饰　**of** their **elites**,
插入语，补充说明 elites

三级修饰　including several world renowned scientists,

【词汇注释】

contribute	[kən'trɪbjuːt] *vi.* (为……) 做贡献
disproportionately	[ˌdɪsprə'pɔːʃənɪtli] *ad.* 不成比例地；不相称地
elite	[eɪ'liːt] *n.* 社会精英；上层集团
renowned	[rɪ'naʊnd] *a.* 有名的；闻名的；受尊敬的
affirm	[ə'fɜːm] *vt.* 肯定属实；申明；断言

【意群训练】

This group generally do well // in IQ test, // scoring 12−15 points // above the mean value of 100, // and have contributed disproportionately to // the intellectual and cultural life // of the West, // as the careers of their elites, // including several world-renowned scientists, // affirm.

（七）　**独立主格结构**

　　非谓语动词或 with/without + 非谓语动词作状语时，其逻辑主语与主句的主语应保持一致。但有一种特殊情况：如果出现了非谓语动词的主语，且该主语与主句的主语不一致，则非谓语动词的时态和语态应与其自身的主语搭配，而无需考虑主句的主语。这就是独立主格结构。独立主格结构在考研英语中考查的频率不高，但形式特殊，因此大家也要了解其用法。

实例 1

The grand mediocrity of today—everyone being the same in survival and number of offspring—means that natural selection has lost 80% of its power in upper-middle-class India compared to the tribes. 今天这种极其显著的平均化——每个人的生存机会和子女数量都相同——意味着与部落相比较，自然选择在印度中上层家庭已经失去了 80% 的效力。【英语（一）2000 Passage 2】

【难句类型】

独立主格 + 从句 + 非谓语动词 + 分隔结构 + 平行结构　　难度：★★★★☆

【难句破解】

找主干	过程	第一步：找从句标志词，并剥离该从句。找到标志词 that：距离 that 之后最近的动词是 has lost，因 lose 是及物动词，故 80% 作其宾语，至此将该从句剥离。 第二步：识别非谓语动词，同时删除非谓语动词结构及其它修饰成分。删除非谓语动词结构 compared to the tribes。删除修饰成分 of today，everyone…offspring，of its power，in upper-middle-class India。全句剩下了 The grand mediocrity means，这就是句子的主谓部分。 第三步：识别并删除很像谓语动词的动词。（真正的谓语动词已找到，故该步骤略。）
	结果	The grand mediocrity…means **[that]** natural selection has lost 80%…（主 + 谓 + 宾从） that 引导的宾语从句 **[that]** natural selection has lost 80%（主 + 谓 + 宾）作 means 的宾语，也是主干成分，故还原。
理修饰	定语	介词短语 of today 作后置定语，修饰 mediocrity；介词短语 of its power 作后置定语，修饰 80%。
	独立主格	第一层：破折号中，现在分词 being 前出现了 everyone，二者逻辑上为主谓关系，说明这是独立主格结构，being 与其逻辑主语 everyone 搭配，而不与句子主语 The grand mediocrity 搭配，the same 作 being 的表语。第二层：破折号中，介词短语 in survival and number of offspring 作状语。
	状语	介词短语 in upper-middle-class India 作宾从的状语，表范围；过去分词短语 compared to the tribes 作宾从的比较状语。
看标点	破折号	破折号之间的内容是对 grand mediocrity 的解释说明，且破折号将主语和谓语分隔开。

146

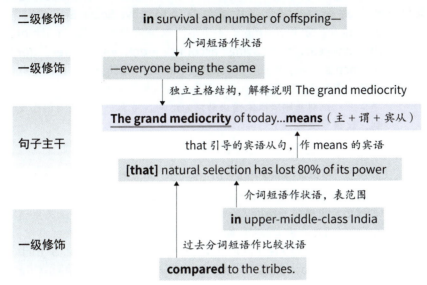

二级修饰　　**in** survival and number of offspring—
　　　　　　　↓ 介词短语作状语
一级修饰　　—everyone being the same
　　　　　　　↓ 独立主格结构，解释说明 The grand mediocrity
句子主干　　**The grand mediocrity** of today...**means**（主＋谓＋宾从）
　　　　　　　　that 引导的宾语从句，作 means 的宾语
　　　　　　[that] natural selection has lost 80% of its power
　　　　　　　　　　介词短语作状语，表范围
　　　　　　　　　　in upper-middle-class India
一级修饰　　　　过去分词短语作比较状语
　　　　　　compared to the tribes.

【词汇注释】

mediocrity	[ˌmiːdiˈɒkrəti] *n.* 平庸；原文引申为"平均化"

【意群训练】

The grand mediocrity // of today //—everyone being the same // in survival and number // of offspring— // means that // natural selection has lost // 80% of its power // in upper-middle-class India // compared to the tribes.

---- 实例 2 ----

For much of the past year, President Bush campaigned to move Social Security to a savings-account model, with retirees trading much or all of their guaranteed payments for payments depending on investment returns. 去年的大部分时间里，布什总统发起了将社会保障体系转化成储蓄账户模式的运动，让退休人员把大部分或者全部有保障的退休金换成依赖于投资收益的报酬。【英语（一）2007 Text 3】

【难句类型】独立主格＋非谓语动词　　　　　　　难度：★★★★★
【难句破解】

找主干	过程	第一步：找从句标志词，并剥离该从句。（本句中无从句，故该步骤略。）

	第二步：识别非谓语动词，同时删除非谓语动词结构及其它修饰成分。删除非谓语动词结构 to move Social Security，depending on investment returns。删除修饰成分 For much of the past year，to a savings-account model，with retirees...for payments。全句剩下了 President Bush campaigned，这就是句子的主谓部分。 第三步：识别并删除很像谓语动词的动词。（真正的谓语动词已找到，故该步骤略。）
结果	..., President Bush campaigned...（主＋谓）
理修饰　状语	第一层：介词短语 For much of the past year 作时间状语；动词不定式短语 to move Social Security...model 作目的状语。第二层：with 之后出现了 retirees 和现在分词 trading，二者逻辑上为主谓关系，说明这是独立主格结构，trading 与其逻辑主语 retirees 搭配，而不与句子主语 President Bush 搭配，其中 much or all of their guaranteed payments 作 trading 的宾语。第三层：介词短语 for payments...returns 作 with 独立主格结构的目的状语。第四层：现在分词短语 depending on investment returns 作后置定语，修饰第二个 payments。

【结构分析】

一级修饰　　**For** much of the past year,

　　　　　　　　↓ 介词短语作时间状语

句子主干　　President Bush campaigned（主＋谓）

　　　　　　　　　↓ 动词不定式短语作目的状语

一级修饰　　**to** move Social Security to a savings-account model,

　　　　　　　↑ with 独立主格结构作伴随状语

二级修饰　　**with** retirees trading much or all of their guaranteed payments

　　　　　　　　　　↑ 介词短语作目的状语

三级修饰　　　　　　**for payments**

　　　　　　　现在分词短语作后置定语，修饰 payments

四级修饰　　　　　　　**depending** on investment returns.

campaign	[kæm'peɪn] *vi.* 参加运动；领导运动 *n.* 运动；战役
retiree	[rɪˌtaɪə'ri:] *n.* 退休人员；退休者

148

For much of the past year, // President Bush campaigned // to move Social Security // to a savings-account model, // with retirees trading // much or all of their guaranteed payments // for payments // depending on investment returns.

九　虚拟

　　虚拟语气通过谓语动词的特殊形式来体现，表示假设、愿望、怀疑或推测，与真实情况相反。虚拟语气是英语中一个重要的语法点，虽然考研英语不常考查，但是大家仍需要掌握其结构和用法。

（一）　if 虚拟语气

　　if 引导条件状语从句，若从句内容为假设情况，与事实相反，则要用虚拟语气。if 虚拟语气中，主句与从句的谓语动词常有固定的时态形式，原则如下表：

	虚拟条件句	主句
与过去事实相反	if + 主语 + had done	主语 + should/would/might/could + have done
与现在事实相反	if + 主语 + 动词的过去式（be 动词用 were）	主 语 + should/would/might/could + 动词原形
与将来事实相反	if + 主语 + 动词的过去式（be 动词用 were） if + 主语 + were to + 动词原形 if + 主语 + should + 动词原形	主语 + should/would/might/could + 动词原形

　　此外，需注意：在使用虚拟语气的 if 条件句中，当从句的谓语动词含有 were，should，had 时，if 可以省略，这时从句需要使用部分倒装，即把 were，should，had 等词置于句首。

---- 实例 1 ----

First, most researchers would accept such a prize if they were offered one. 首先，如果被授予这样一个奖项，大多数研究人员都会接受。【英语（一）2014 Text 3】

【难句类型】虚拟　　　　　　　　　　　　　　　　　　难度：★★★

找主干	过程	第一步：找从句标志词，并剥离该从句。找到标志词 if：距离 if 之后最近的动词是 were offered，因 offer 是及物动词，故 one 作其宾语，至此将该从句剥离。 第二步：识别非谓语动词，同时删除非谓语动词结构及其它修饰成分。本句无非谓语动词结构；删除修饰成分 First。全句剩下了 most researchers would accept such a prize，这就是句子的主干部分。 第三步：识别并删除很像谓语动词的动词。（真正的谓语动词已找到，故该步骤略。）
	结果	..., most researchers would accept such a prize...（主＋谓＋宾）
理修饰	状语	句首的副词 First 作状语。
	状从	if 引导的条件状语从句 **[If]** they were offered one（主＋谓＋宾）使用了虚拟语气，从句谓语动词采用了一般过去式的被动语态 were offered，表示与现在事实相反，主句为与之相对应的 would ＋ 动词原形（accept）形式。

【结构分析】

句子主干　　　First, most researchers would accept such a prize（主＋谓＋宾）

↑ if 引导的条件状语从句，作句子主干的条件状语

一级修饰　　　**[if]** they were offered one.

【意群训练】

First, // most researchers // would accept // such a prize // if they were offered one.

─── 实例 2 ───────────────────────────────────>>>>

If it did, it would open up its diversity program, now focused narrowly on race and gender, and look for reporters who differ broadly by outlook, values, education, and class. 如果它注意到了这个问题，就会开设多样化项目，使其不像目前这样只单纯地考虑招收不同种族和性别的员工，而是进一步寻找那些世界观、价值观、教育水平和社会阶层各不相同的记者。

【英语（一）2001 Passage 3】

【难句类型】虚拟＋省略＋平行结构＋非谓语动词　　　　　难度：★★★☆

【难句破解】

| 找主干 | 过程 | 第一步：找从句标志词，并剥离该从句。❶找到第一个标志词 If： |

距离 If 之后最近的动词是 did，至此将该从句剥离；❷ 找到第二个标志词 who：距离 who 之后最近的动词是 differ，至此将该从句剥离。

第二步：识别非谓语动词，同时删除非谓语动词结构及其它修饰成分。删除非谓语动词结构 focused narrowly on...gender。删除修饰成分 now，broadly，by outlook...class。全句剩下了 it would open up its diversity program, and look for reporters，这就是句子的主干部分。

第三步：识别并删除很像谓语动词的动词。（真正的谓语动词已找到，故该步骤略。）

	结果	...it would open up its diversity program, ...and (would) look for reporters...（主＋谓 1＋宾 1＋and＋谓 2＋宾 2） 连词 and 连接了两个并列的谓宾结构，第二个谓语省略了 would。
理修饰	状从	If 引导的条件状语从句 **[If]** it did（主＋谓）使用了虚拟语气，表示与现在事实相反，从句谓语动词为一般过去式 did，主句则相应地采用了 would＋动词原形（open up 和 look for）的形式。
	状语	now 作时间状语。
	定语	过去分词短语 focused narrowly on race and gender 作后置定语，修饰 program。
	定从	第一层：who 引导的定语从句 **[who]** differ broadly by outlook, values, education, and class（主＋谓），修饰 reporters。第二层：副词 broadly 作状语，修饰定从的谓语 differ；介词短语 by outlook, values, education, and class 作状语，表方面。

【结构分析】

一级修饰	**[If]** it did, If 引导的条件状语从句，作句子主干的条件状语
	now **focused** narrowly on race and gender, 过去分词短语作后置定语，修饰 program
句子主干	it **would open up** its diversity **program**,（主＋谓＋宾） and 连接的并列谓宾 **and (would) look for reporters**
一级修饰	who 引导的定语从句，修饰 reporters **[who]** differ broadly
二级修饰	介词短语作状语，表方面 **by** outlook, values, education, and class.

diversity	[daɪ'vɜːsəti] *n.* 多样性；差异

【意群训练】

If it did, // it would open up // its diversity program, // now focused narrowly on // race and gender, // and look for reporters // who differ broadly // by outlook, values, education, // and class.

（二） 混合式虚拟语气

　　在虚拟条件句中，当句中出现时间状语，表明条件状语从句动作和主句动作时间不一致时，或者句意表明主从句动作时间不一致时，主从句动词的时态可根据时间状语而变化，不遵循常规的时态搭配原则。此外，在 if 引导的混合式虚拟条件句中，当从句的谓语动词含有 were、should、had 时，if 亦可以省略，这时从句需要使用部分倒装，即把 were、should、had 等词置于句首。混合式虚拟语气有时比较难判断，常常需要通过对句意的理解来辨别。

实例 1

This might sound small, but to undo the effects of such a decrease a candidate would need 30 more GMAT points than would otherwise have been necessary. 这也许听起来微乎其微，但是要消除这一下降所带来的影响，申请者的 GMAT 分数则要比原本所需的多出 30 分。【英语（一）2013 完形】

【难句类型】虚拟＋非谓语动词＋平行结构　　　　　　难度：★★★★

【难句破解】

找主干	过程	第一步：找从句标志词，并剥离该从句。找到标志词 than：距离 than 之后最近的动词是 would have been，因 be 是系动词，故 necessary 作其表语，至此将该从句剥离。 第二步：识别非谓语动词，同时删除非谓语动词结构及其它修饰成分。删除非谓语动词结构 to undo...decrease；本句无其它修饰成分。全句剩下了 This might sound small, but a candidate would need 30 more GMAT points，这就是句子的主干部分。 第三步：识别并删除很像谓语动词的动词。（真正的谓语动词已找到，故该步骤略。）
	结果	This might sound small, but...a candidate would need 30 more GMAT points...（主 1 ＋系＋表＋but＋主 2 ＋谓＋宾） 连词 but 连接了两个并列分句，表转折。其中分句一为主系表结构，分句二为主谓宾结构。

理修饰	状语	分句二中，动词不定式短语 to undo the effects of such a decrease 作目的状语。
	定从	than 引导的定语从句 [than] would otherwise have been necessary（主＋系＋表）修饰 30 more GMAT points，该从句使用了虚拟语气，从句谓语动词采用现在完成式 would have been，表示实际情况与过去事实相反。而主干陈述的是将来的事实，因此没有与该定从动词的时态搭配。副词 otherwise 作状语。

【结构分析】

句子主干

This might sound small,（主＋系＋表）

　　　but 连接的并列句，表转折

but...a candidate would need **30 more GMAT points**（主＋谓＋宾）

　　动词不定式短语作目的状语

to undo the effects of such a decrease

　　　　　　than 引导的定语从句，修饰 30 more GMAT points

一级修饰

[than] would otherwise have been necessary.

【词汇注释】

undo	[ʌn'duː] *vt.* 消除；松开；打败
candidate	['kændɪdət] *n.* 应试者；候选人，申请人

【意群训练】

This might sound small, // but to undo the effects // of such a decrease // a candidate would need // 30 more GMAT points // than would otherwise // have been necessary.

───实例 2─────────────────────────────────────>>>>

But had Entergy kept its word, that debate would be beside the point.
但是如果安特吉公司能遵守诺言，这样的争议就无关紧要了。【英语（一）2012 Text 2】

【难句类型】虚拟＋省略＋倒装　　　　　　　　　　　　难度：★★★★
【难句破解】

找主干	过程	第一步：找从句标志词，并剥离该从句。（本句中无从句标志词，故该步骤略。）第二步：识别非谓语动词，同时删除非谓语动词结构及其它修饰成

		分。本句无非谓语动词结构，也没有其它修饰成分。
		第三步：识别并删除很像谓语动词的动词。全句出现了两个动词 had kept 和 would be，而逗号前后都是完整的句子，且逗号前的句子的主语 Entergy 位于 had 和 kept 之间，这说明前一句是省略引导词 if 的条件状语从句，因此采用了倒装结构，故 had kept 是该从句的谓语动词，因 keep 是及物动词，故 its word 作其宾语，至此将该从句剥离。全句剩下了 But, that debate would be beside the point，这就是句子的主干部分。
	结果	But..., that debate <u>would be</u> beside the point.（主 + 系 + 表） 句首的连词 But 承接上句，表转折。
理修饰	状从	had Entergy kept its word（助动词 + 主 + 谓语动词 + 宾）是省略了 if 的条件状语从句，由于省略 if，故使用了倒装，将 had 置于主语之前。若还原 if，正常语序为：**[if]** Entergy had kept its word；本句使用了虚拟语气，从句谓语动词使用了过去完成式 had done，表示实际情况与过去事实相反，主句则描述与现在相反的情况，因此谓语动词没有遵循时态搭配原则，而是使用了 would + 动词原形 be 的形式。

【结构分析】

一级修饰　　　　　But had Entergy kept its word,

↓省略 if 的条件状语从句，作句子主干的条件状语

句子主干　　　　　that debate <u>would be</u> beside the point.（主 + 系 + 表）

【意群训练】

But had Entergy kept // its word, that debate would be // beside the point.

----- 实例 3 -----　　　　　　　　　　　　　　　　　　　　　　　　　　　　　　>>>>

They should be quick to respond to letters to the editor, lest animal rights misinformation go unchallenged and acquire a deceptive appearance of truth. 他们应该及时回复编辑的来信，以免动物权利的误导言论畅行无阻，披上真理的外衣行骗。【英语（一）2003 Text 2】

【难句类型】虚拟 + 省略 + 非谓语动词　　　　　　　　　难度：★ ★ ★ ★
【难句破解】

		第一步：找从句标志词，并剥离该从句。找到标志词 lest：距离 lest 之后最近的动词是 go，且并列连词 and 连接 go 与其后的动词 acquire。因 go 为系动词，故其与 unchallenged 构成复合谓语；因 acquire 为及物动词，故 a deceptive appearance of truth 作
找主干	过程	

acquire 的宾语，至此将该从句剥离。

第二步：识别非谓语动词，同时删除非谓语动词结构及其它修饰成分。删除非谓语动词结构 to respond to letters；删除修饰成分 to the editor。全句剩下了 They should be quick，这就是句子的主干部分。

第三步：识别并删除很像谓语动词的动词。（真正的谓语动词已找到，故该步骤略。）

结果	They should be quick...（主＋系＋表）

理修饰	状语	第一层：动词不定式短语 to respond to letters 作状语。第二层：介词短语 to the editor 作后置定语，修饰 letters。
	状从	lest 引导的目的状语从句 [lest] animal rights misinformation (should) go unchallenged and (should) acquire a deceptive appearance of truth（主＋系＋表＋and＋谓＋宾）使用了虚拟语气，从句谓语动词 go 和 acquire 前均省略了 should。lest 在引导状语从句时，常使用虚拟语气，从句谓语为 should ＋ 动词原形的形式，且 should 可省略。

【结构分析】

句子主干　　They should be **quick**（主＋系＋表）

　　　　　　　　　　　　动词不定式短语作状语

一级修饰　　　　　　　**to** respond to **letters**

　　　　　　　　　介词短语作后置定语，修饰 letters

二级修饰　　　　　　　　　　　　**to** the editor,

　　　　　lest 引导的目的状语从句，作句子主干的目的状语

一级修饰　　**[lest]** animal rights misinformation **(should) go unchallenged**

　　　　　　　　　　　　　　and 连接的并列谓语

　　　　　　　　　and (should) acquire a deceptive appearance of truth.

【词汇注释】

deceptive	[dɪˈseptɪv] a. 欺骗性的；误导的；骗人的

【意群训练】

They should be quick // to respond to letters // to the editor, // lest animal rights misinformation // go unchallenged // and acquire a deceptive appearance of truth.

在名词性从句，即主语从句、表语从句、宾语从句和同位语从句中，当主句中出现意为"建议、要求、命令"的动词或名词时（如 demand, require, propose, suggestion 等），也会出现虚拟语气，即名词性从句中的谓语为 should＋动词原形，其中 should 常可以省略。

实例 1

European ministers instantly demanded that the International Accounting Standards Board (IASB) do likewise. 欧洲各国的部长随即要求国际会计准则理事会（IASB）也这样做。【英语（一）2010 Text 4】

【难句类型】虚拟＋省略　　　　　　　　　　　　　　难度：★★★☆

【难句破解】

找主干	过程	第一步：找从句标志词，并剥离该从句。找到标志词 that：距离 that 之后最近的动词是 do，至此将该从句剥离。 第二步：识别非谓语动词，同时删除非谓语动词结构及其它修饰成分。本句无非谓语动词结构；删除修饰成分 instantly, likewise。全句剩下了 European ministers demanded，这就是句子的主谓部分。 第三步：识别并删除很像谓语动词的动词。（真正的谓语动词已找到，故该步骤略。）
	结果	European ministers...demanded **[that]** the International Accounting Standards Board (IASB) (should) do...（主＋谓＋宾从） that 引导的宾语从句 **[that]** the International Accounting Standards Board (IASB) (should) do（主＋谓）作 demanded 的宾语，是主干成分，故还原。由于主句谓语为 demanded，故该宾从使用了虚拟语气，且省略了 should。
理修饰	状语	副词 instantly 作状语，修饰主干的谓语 demanded；副词 likewise 作状语，修饰宾从的谓语 do。

【结构分析】

句子主干	European ministers instantly **demanded**（主＋谓＋宾从） that 引导的宾语从句，作 demanded 的宾语 **[that]** the International Accounting Board (IASB)（should）do likewise.

【词汇注释】

instantly	['ɪnstəntli] *ad.* 立即；马上

【意群训练】

European ministers // instantly demanded // that the International Accounting Standards Board (IASB) // do likewise.

------ 实例 2 ------ »»»

This year, it was proposed that the system be changed: Horizon 2020, a new program to be enacted in 2014, would not have such a category. 今年，有人提议改变这一体制："地平线 2020"这项将在 2014 年实施的新计划不会再设置这一类别。【英语（一）2013 新题型】

【难句类型】虚拟＋省略＋分隔结构　　　　　　　　难度：★★★☆

【难句破解】

<table>
<tr><td rowspan="2">找主干</td><td>过程</td><td>第一步：找从句标志词，并剥离该从句。找到标志词 that：距离 that 之后最近的动词是 be changed，至此将该从句剥离。
第二步：识别非谓语动词，同时删除非谓语动词结构及其它修饰成分。浏览该句子可发现，句中出现了表解释说明的冒号，其后内容整体上对其前内容进行解释说明，故可将冒号后内容作为对其前内容的修饰部分而整体剥离掉；删除修饰成分 This year。全句剩下了 it was proposed，这就是句子的主谓部分。
第三步：识别并删除很像谓语动词的动词。（真正的谓语动词已找到，故该步骤略。）</td></tr>
<tr><td>结果</td><td>..., it was proposed...（主＋谓）
本句中 it 作形式主语，真正的主语是 that 引导的主语从句 [that] the system (should) be changed（主＋谓），由于主干的谓语是 proposed，故该从句使用了虚拟语气，且省略了 should。</td></tr>
<tr><td rowspan="2">理修饰</td><td>状语</td><td>句首的 This year 作时间状语。</td></tr>
<tr><td>解释说明</td><td>第一层：冒号后的句子 Horizon 2020, a new program to be enacted in 2014, would not have such a category（主＋谓＋宾）解释说明其前内容。第二层：名词短语 a new program to be enacted in 2014 作 Horizon 2020 的同位语，对其进行补充说明，其中动词不定式短语 to be enacted 作后置定语，修饰 program；介词短语 in 2014 作时间状语。</td></tr>
<tr><td>看标点</td><td>冒号</td><td>冒号表示其后的内容对其前的内容进行解释说明。</td></tr>
</table>

句子主干	This year, **it** was proposed（主 + 谓）
	↳ it 作形式主语，that 引导的主语从句作真正的主语
	[that] the system be changed:
	↳ 解释说明冒号前面的内容
一级修饰	**Horizon 2020**, ...would not have such a category.
	↳ Horizon 2020 的同位语
二级修饰	a new program to be enacted in 2014,

【词汇注释】

enact	[ɪ'nækt] *vt.* 颁布；制定法律；扮演

【意群训练】

This year, // it was proposed // that the system be changed: // Horizon 2020, // a new program // to be enacted in 2014, // would not have // such a category.

十 省略

省略是为了避免重复、突出新信息并使上下文紧密连接的一种语法修辞手段，省略在英语中是一种十分普遍的现象。英语中的省略常见于平行结构、虚拟语气及各类从句中。而考研英语中对于省略现象的考查多出现在从句中，常见于定语从句、宾语从句和状语从句中。

（一）平行结构中的省略

英语平行结构中常出现省略的情况，这在考研英语中也有所体现。若各平行结构中有相同的部分，为避免重复，后面的部分可以承前省略。

在长难句中，由于某些成分被省略，考生可能会错误地判断句子成分，从而妨碍其对句意的理解。要避免此类问题的产生，考生必须炼就一双"火眼金睛"，识别出这一类省略情况。

实例 1

The teachers' unions keep an eye on schools, the CCPOA on prisons and a variety of labor groups on health care. 教师工会监察学校的预算，加州监狱和平促进委员会监察监狱的预算，而很多劳工组织则紧盯着医疗保健部门的预算。【英语（一）2012 Text 4】

【难句类型】平行结构 + 省略 　　　　　　　　　　　难度：★★★☆

找主干	过程	第一步：找从句标志词，并剥离该从句。（本句中无从句，故该步骤略。） 第二步：识别非谓语动词，同时删除非谓语动词结构及其它修饰成分。本句无非谓语动词结构，也无修饰成分。全句剩下了 The teachers' unions keep an eye on schools, the CCPOA (keeps an eye) on prisons and a variety of labor groups (keep an eye) on health care，这就是句子的主干部分。 第三步：识别并删除很像谓语动词的动词。（真正的谓语动词已找到，故该步骤略。）
	结果	The teachers' unions keep an eye on schools , the CCPOA (keeps an eye) on prisons and a variety of labor groups (keep an eye) on health care. （主 1 + 谓 1 + 宾 1 + 主 2 + 谓 2 + 宾 2 + and + 主 3 + 谓 3 + 宾 3） 连词 and 连接三个并列分句，三个分句的谓语动词均为 keep(s) an eye on，为避免重复，分句二和分句三的 keep(s) an eye 均被省略。
理修饰	状语	本句中无修饰成分，故该步骤省略。

【结构分析】

句子主干

The teachers' unions keep an eye on schools, （主 + 谓 + 宾）
　　　　　┃并列句
the CCPOA (keeps an eye) on prisons （主 + 谓 + 宾）
　　　　　┃and 连接的并列句
and a variety...groups (keep an eye) on health care. （主 + 谓 + 宾）

【意群训练】

The teachers' unions // keep an eye on schools, // the CCPOA // （keeps an eye） on prisons // and a variety of labor groups // （keep an eye） on health care.

---- 实例 2 ----

Mental health allows us to view others with sympathy if they are having troubles, with kindness if they are in pain, and with unconditional love no matter who they are. 心理健康让我们在他人遇到困难时心怀同情，在他人遭受痛苦时心怀善念，并且无论对待任何人，都心怀无条件的关爱。【英语（一）2016 翻译】

【难句类型】平行结构 + 从句 + 省略　　　　　　　　难度：★★★★

【难句破解】

找主干	过程	第一步：找从句标志词，并剥离该从句。❶ 找到第一个标志词 if：距离 if 之后最近的动词是 are having，因 have 是及物动词，故 troubles 作其宾语，至此将该从句剥离；❷ 找到第二个标志词 if：距离 if 之后最近的动词是 are，in pain 作其表语，至此将该从句剥离；❸ 找到第三个标志词 no matter who：距离 no matter who 之后最近的动词是 are，至此将该从句剥离。 第二步：识别非谓语动词，同时删除非谓语动词结构及其它修饰成分。删除非谓语动词结构 to view others；删除修饰成分 with sympathy, with kindness, with unconditional love。因 and 在几个修饰成分之间，起连接作用，故也删除。全句剩下了 Mental health allows us，这就是句子的主干部分。 第三步：识别并删除很像谓语动词的动词。（真正的谓语动词已找到，故该步骤略。）
	结果	Mental health allows us to view others... (to view others)..., and (to view others)... （主＋谓＋宾＋宾补） and 连接的三个并列动词不定式短语 to view others 作宾语 us 的补足语，与宾语联系紧密，故还原。其中后两个 to view others 均被省略。
理修饰	状语	介词短语 with sympathy, with kindness 和 with unconditional love 作状语，分别修饰 and 连接的三个并列的动词不定式短语 to view others。if 引导的条件状从 [if] they are having troubles（主＋谓＋宾）修饰第一个 to view others；if 引导的条件状从 [if] they are in pain（主＋系＋表）修饰第二个 to view others；no matter who 引导的让步状从 [no matter who] they are（表＋主＋系）修饰第三个 to view others。

【结构分析】

句子主干	Mental health allows **us** （主＋谓＋宾＋宾补）
	↑动词不定式短语作宾语 us 的补足语
	to view others with sympathy
	↑if 引导的条件状语从句
一级修饰	**[if]** they are having troubles,
	并列的动词不定式短语
句子主干	(**to** view others) with kindness
	↑if 引导的条件状语从句
一级修饰	**[if]** they are in pain,
	and 连接并列的动词不定式短语
句子主干	**and** (**to** view others) with unconditional love
	↑no matter who 引导的让步状语从句
一级修饰	**[no matter who]** they are

【意群训练】

Mental health allows us // to view others // with sympathy // if they are having troubles, // (to view others) with kindness // if they are in pain, // and (to view others) with unconditional love // no matter who they are.

（二） 虚拟语气中的省略

在虚拟语气中，有时 should 可以省略。该部分内容在虚拟一章中已经进行了详细的讲解，故这里不再赘述。

（三） 从句中的省略

1. 宾语 / 表语从句省略

宾语 / 表语从句中，引导词 that 在从句中不作任何成分，也没有实际意义，只起到引导从句的作用，因此 that 可以省略。宾语 / 表语从句省略的判断方法：如果句中出现连续的两个主谓结构或系表结构，且没有任何连词连接，即出现了谓语动词或动词短语后无宾语，系动词后无表语的情况，则第二个主谓或系表结构是省略了 that 的宾语 / 表语从句。考研英语中常考查宾语从句引导词 that 的省略，但表语从句引导词 that 的省略较少考查，故本节将重点讲解宾语从句引导词的省略。

当然，在一些特殊情况下，宾语从句的引导词 that 不能省略：（1）当多个 that 引导的宾从并列时，只有第一个宾从的引导词 that 可以省略，其它均不能省略；（2）当主句谓语动词和 that 引导的宾语从句之间有插入语时；（3）当 that 引导的宾语从句是双宾语中的直接宾语时；（4）当 it 作形式宾语时。

-------- 实例 1 --------------------------------------≫≫≫

Though several fast-fashion companies have made efforts to curb their impact on labor and the environment—including H&M, with its green Conscious Collection line—Cline believes lasting change can only be effected by the customer. 尽管多家快时尚公司已经努力地去控制他们对劳工和环境的影响——包括 H&M 公司，它推出了"绿色环保"系列产品——克莱恩认为只有消费者才能带来持久性的改变。【英语（一）2013 Text 1】

【难句类型】 省略＋分隔结构＋从句＋非谓语动词　　　　　难度：★★★★

【难句破解】

| 找主干 | 过程 | 第一步：找从句标志词，并剥离该从句。找到标志词 Though：距离 Though 之后最近的动词是 have made，因 make 是及物动词，故 efforts 作其宾语，至此将该从句剥离。 |
| | | 第二步：识别非谓语动词，同时删除非谓语动词结构及其它修饰成分。删除非谓语动词结构 to curb their impact。删除修饰成分 on labor and the environment，including H&M，with its green |

		Conscious Collection line，by the customer。全句剩下了 Cline believes lasting change can only be effected。
		第三步：识别并删除很像谓语动词的动词。根据辨析真假谓语动词的方法，句中剩下两个动词 believes 和 can only be effected，其中 can only be effected 与 lasting change 构成主谓结构，则二者中前面的动词 believes 是主干谓语动词，其后的 lasting change can only be effected... 作它的宾语，是省略 that 的宾语从句，故将该从句剥离。全句剩下了 Cline believes，这就是句子的主谓部分。
	结果	...Cline <u>believes</u> **(that)** <u>lasting change</u> can only be effected by the customer（主＋谓＋宾从） 省略 that 的宾语从句 **(that)** <u>lasting change</u> can only be effected...（主＋谓）作 believes 的宾语，是主干成分，故还原。其中介词短语 by the customer 作状语，表示动作的执行者。
理修饰	状从	第一层：Though 引导的让步状语从句 **[Though]** several fast-fashion <u>companies</u> <u>have made</u> <u>efforts</u> to curb their impact on labor and the environment（主＋谓＋宾）作主句的让步状语。 第二层：该从句中，动词不定式短语 to curb...environment 作目的的状语，其中介词短语 on...environment 作后置定语，修饰 impact。破折号中的内容作插入语，对破折号前面的内容进行举例说明，其中介词短语 with its...line 作状语。
看标点 破折号		破折号分隔插入语。

【结构分析】

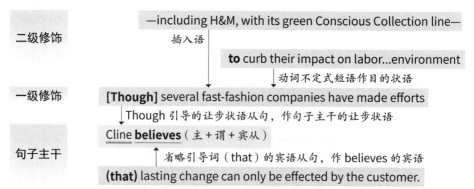

【意群训练】

Though several fast-fashion companies // have made efforts // to curb their impact // on labor and the environment // —including H&M, // with its green Conscious Collection line— // Cline believes （that） // lasting change can only be effected // by the customer.

Shippers who feel they are being overcharged have the right to appeal to the federal government's Surface Transportation Board for rate relief, but the process is expensive, time-consuming, and will work only in truly extreme cases. 如果运货商认为收费过高，他们有权向联邦政府的"地面运输委员会"上诉以争取降低费用，但是这个过程既耗财又耗时，并且只有在真正极端的情况下才有作用。【英语（一）2003 Text 3】

【难句类型】省略＋嵌套结构＋平行结构＋非谓语动词　　　　难度：★★★★★
【难句破解】

找主干	过程	第一步：找从句标志词，并剥离该从句。找到标志词 who：距离 who 之后最近的动词是 feel，至此将该从句剥离。 第二步：识别非谓语动词，同时删除非谓语动词结构及其它修饰成分。删除非谓语动词结构 to appeal to...Board。删除修饰成分 for rate relief，only in truly extreme cases。全句剩下了 Shippers they are being overcharged have the right, but the process is expensive, time-consuming, and will work。 第三步：识别并删除很像谓语动词的动词。根据辨析真假谓语动词的方法，句中还剩下四个动词 are being overcharged，have，is 和 will work，其中 are being overcharged 与其逻辑主语 they 构成完整的主谓结构，且位于 feel 之后，作 feel 的宾语，故 they are being overcharged 是省略引导词 that 的宾语从句，故将该从句剥离。而其它三个动词分别是由 but 和 and 连接的并列成分，均是主干谓语动词。至此，全句剩下了 Shippers have the right, but the process is expensive, time-consuming, and will work，这就是句子的主干部分。
	结果	Shippers... have the right..., but the process is expensive, time-consuming, and will work... 连词 but 连接两个并列句，分句一为"主＋谓＋宾"结构，分句二为"主＋系＋表＋and＋谓"结构。
理修饰	定从	第一层：who 引导的定语从句 [who] feel (that) they are being over-charged（主＋谓＋宾），修饰 Shippers。定从中的宾语是省略了 that 的嵌套宾从 (that) they are being overcharged（主＋谓），宾从的谓语使用了被动语态。
	定语	动词不定式短语 to appeal to the federal government's Surface Transportation Board for rate relief 作后置定语，修饰分句一的宾语 the right。

| 状语 | 介词短语 only in truly extreme cases 作条件状语，修饰 will work。 |

【结构分析】

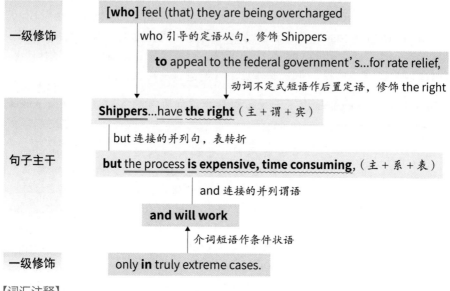

一级修饰

[who] feel (that) they are being overcharged

who 引导的定语从句，修饰 Shippers

to appeal to the federal government's...for rate relief,

动词不定式短语作后置定语，修饰 the right

句子主干

Shippers...have **the right**（主 + 谓 + 宾）

but 连接的并列句，表转折

but the process **is expensive, time consuming**,（主 + 系 + 表）

and 连接的并列谓语

and will work

介词短语作条件状语

一级修饰

only **in** truly extreme cases.

【词汇注释】

| appeal to | 上诉；要求；对……有吸引力 |

【意群训练】

Shippers who feel // (that) they are being overcharged // have the right // to appeal to // the federal government's Surface Transportation Board // for rate relief, // but the process is // expensive, time-consuming, // and will work // only in truly extreme cases.

2. 定语从句省略

　　由于非限定性定语从句的引导词不能省略，因而如果名词或代词后紧接着出现了一个句子，那么它很有可能是省略了关系词的限定性定语从句。在下列情况下，限定性定语从句的关系词可以省略：

　　（1）关系代词 who, whom, which, that 在定语从句中作及物动词或介词的宾语；（2）关系代词 that 在定语从句中作表语或宾语补足语；（3）关系副词 when 的先行词是 day, year, time 等表示时间概念的词；（4）关系副词 where 的先行词是 place, somewhere, anywhere, everywhere 等表地点概念的词；（5）关系副词 why 的先行词是 the reason。

　　考研英语中经常会考查 that/which 在从句中作宾语被省略的情况，其它情况则很少涉及。

Every month on pay day, she banks hundreds of dollars into a savings account she keeps from her husband. 每个月发工资的那一天，她都瞒着丈夫将几百美元存入一个储蓄账户。【英语（二）2008 Text 3】

【难句类型】省略＋从句   难度：★★★✫

【难句破解】

找主干	过程	第一步：找从句标志词，并剥离该从句。（本句中无从句标志词，故该步骤略。） 第二步：识别非谓语动词，同时删除非谓语动词结构及其它修饰成分。本句无非谓语动词结构；删除修饰成分 Every month on pay day，into a savings account。全句还剩下 she banks hundreds of dollars she keeps from her husband。 第三步：识别并删除很像谓语动词的动词。根据辨析真假谓语动词的方法，句中还剩下两个动词 banks 和 keeps，其中及物动词 keeps 缺失宾语，则它是假的谓语动词，而 banks 才是主干谓语动词。实际上，keeps 是省略关系词 that/which 的定语从句（that/which）she keeps from her husband 的谓语动词，故将该从句剥离。全句剩下了 she banks hundreds of dollars，这就是句子的主干部分。
	结果	..., she banks hundreds of dollars...（主＋谓＋宾）
理修饰	状语	第一层：Every month on pay day 作时间状语；介词短语 into a savings account 作地点状语。第二层：省略关系词 that/which 的定语从句 **(that/which)** she keeps from her husband（宾＋主＋谓），修饰 a savings account；其中介词短语 from her husband 作状语。

【结构分析】

一级修饰	Every month on pay day,
	↓ 时间状语
句子主干	she banks hundreds of dollars（主＋谓＋宾）
	↑ 介词短语作地点状语
一级修饰	**into a savings account**
	↑ 省略关系词（that/which）的定语从句，修饰 a savings account
二级修饰	**(that/which)** she keeps from her husband.

165

【词汇注释】

saving	['seɪvɪŋ] *n.* 储蓄；存款

【意群训练】

Every month on pay day, // she banks hundreds of dollars // into a savings account // （that/which）she keeps // from her husband.

---- 实例 2

These rules say they must value some assets at the price a third party would pay, not the price managers and regulators would like them to fetch. 这些准则要求他们必须以第三方愿意支付的价格，而不是管理者和监管机构期望它们售得的价格来评估某些资产。【英语（一）2010 Text 4】

【难句类型】 省略＋平行结构＋嵌套结构＋非谓语动词　　　　难度：★★★★
【难句破解】

找主干	过程	第一步：找从句标志词，并剥离该从句。（本句中无从句标志词，故该步骤略。） 第二步：识别非谓语动词，同时删除非谓语动词结构及其它修饰成分。删除非谓语动词结构 to fetch。删除修饰成分 at the price, not the price。全句剩下了 These rules say they must value some assets a third party would pay, managers and regulators would like them。 第三步：识别并删除很像谓语动词的动词。根据辨析真假谓语动词的方法，句中剩下四个动词 say, must value, would pay 和 would like。其中 would pay 后缺失宾语，说明 a third party would pay 是省略 that/which 的定语从句，故将该从句剥离；would like 虽不缺宾语，但其后的 to fetch 缺失宾语，故 managers and regulators would like them to fetch 是省略 that/which 的定语从句，故将该从句剥离；剩下的两个动词均不缺失宾语，故前面的 say 是主干谓语动词，后面的 must value 是省略 that 的宾语从句 they must value some assets 的谓语动词，故将该宾语从句剥离。全句剩下了 These rules say，这就是句子的主谓部分。
	结果	These rules <u>say</u> **(that)** they must value some assets...（主＋谓＋宾从） 省略 that 的宾语从句 **(that)** <u>they</u> must value some assets（主＋谓＋宾）也是主干成分，故还原。
理修饰	状语一	第一层：介词短语 at the price 作宾从的方式状语。第二层：**(that/which)** <u>a third party</u> would pay（宾＋主＋谓）是省略了 that/which 的定语从句，修饰 the price。

	第一层：省略 at 的介词短语 not (at) the price 是与 at the price 并列的方式状语。第二层：**(that/which)** <u>managers and regulators</u> <u>would like</u> <u>them</u> to fetch（主＋谓＋宾＋宾补）也是省略了 that/which 的定语从句，关系词 that/which 与 to fetch 一起作从句的宾补，且关系词 that/which 代替先行词 the price 作 fetch 的宾语。
状语二	

【结构分析】

句子主干	These rules **say**（主＋谓＋宾从）
	省略引导词（that）的宾语从句，作 say 的宾语
	(that) they must value some assets
	介词短语作方式状语
	at the price
一级修饰	并列的介词短语
	not (at) the price
	省略关系词（that/which）的定语从句，修饰 the price
	(that/which) a third party would pay,
二级修饰	省略关系词（that/which）的定语从句，修饰 the price
	(that/which) managers and regulators would like them to fetch.

【词汇注释】

value sth. at sth.	给……估价；给……定价
fetch	[fetʃ] *v.* 售得；拿；取来；请来

【意群训练】

These rules say //（that）they must value // some assets // at the price //（that/which）a third party // would pay, // not the price //（that/which）managers and regulators // would like them // to fetch.

3. 状语从句省略

在有些情况下，状语从句也会出现省略：

（1）在时间、地点、让步、条件、方式、比较状语从句中，如果状语从句的主语和主句的主语一致，或者从句的主语是 it，且从句的谓语动词是系动词 be 的某种形式，从句中的主语 /it 和 be 动词可以一起省略。因此，如果状从引导词后面是不完整的系表或谓宾结构，很有可能是出现了主谓省略。

（2）在使用虚拟语气的 if 条件状语从句中，当从句的谓语动词含有 were，should，had 时，if 可以省略，这时从句要使用部分倒装，谓语动词的一部分在主语之前（详见混合式虚拟语气实例 2）。

---- 实例 1 ----

The bans, if fully enforced, would suggest to women (and many men) that they should not let others be arbiters of their beauty. 这些禁令如果得以全面执行，将提醒女性（以及许多男性）不应让他人决定自己的美丑。
【英语（一）2016 Text 1】

【难句类型】省略＋从句　　　　　　　　　　　　　　　难度：★★★
【难句破解】

找主干	过程	第一步：找从句标志词，并剥离该从句。❶找到第一个标志词 if：距离 if 之后最近的动词是 enforced，至此将该从句剥离；❷找到第二个标志词 that：距离 that 之后最近的动词是 should not let，因 let 是及物动词，根据其固定搭配 let sb. do sth.，故 others 作其宾语，be arbiters 为宾语补足语，至此将该从句剥离。 第二步：识别非谓语动词，同时删除非谓语动词结构及其它修饰成分。本句无非谓语动词结构；删除修饰成分 fully，to women (and many men)，of their beauty。全句剩下了 The bans，would suggest，这就是句子的主谓部分。 第三步：识别并删除很像谓语动词的动词。（真正的谓语动词已找到，故该步骤略。）
	结果	The bans, ..., would suggest...[that] they should not let others be arbiters...（主＋谓＋宾从） that 引导的宾语从句 [that] they should not let others be arbiters...（主＋谓＋宾＋宾补）作 suggest 的宾语，是句子的主干成分，故还原。
理修饰	状从	[if] (they are)...enforced（主＋谓）是省略了主语 they 和 be 动词 are 的条件状语从句，从句谓语使用了被动语态，其中副词 fully 修饰谓语。
	状语	介词短语 to women (and many men) 作状语，表对象。
	定语	of their beauty 作后置定语，修饰宾从中的 arbiters。
看标点	括号	括号中的内容起补充说明的作用。

句子主干

The bans, ...**would suggest** to women (and many men)（主＋谓＋宾从）

that 引导的宾语从句，作 would suggest 的宾语

[that] they should not let others be **arbiters**

if 引导的条件状语从句，作句子主干的条件状语

一级修饰

[if] (they are) fully enforced,

介词短语作后置定语，修饰 arbiters

of their beauty.

【意群训练】

The bans, // if (they are) fully enforced, // would suggest // to women (and many men) // that they should not let others // be arbiters // of their beauty.

------ 实例 2 ------------------------------------ >>>>

Some use them to keep a close watch on the demand for their line of work or gather information on compensation to arm themselves when negotiating for a raise. 有些人借助这一代理密切关注本行业的需求情况，或者收集有关薪酬待遇的信息，以备加薪谈判时使用。【英语（一）2004 Text 1】

【难句类型】省略＋平行结构＋从句　　　　　　　　难度：★★★★

【难句破解】

找主干	过程	第一步：找从句标志词，并剥离该从句。找到标志词 when：距离 when 之后最近的动词是 negotiating，至此将该从句剥离。第二步：识别非谓语动词，同时删除非谓语动词结构及其它修饰成分。删除 or 连接的两个非谓语动词结构 to keep...work 和 (to) gather information on compensation 以及 to arm themselves；删除修饰成分 for a raise。全句剩下了 Some use them，这就是句子的主干部分。第三步：识别并删除很像谓语动词的动词。（真正的谓语动词已找到，故该步骤略。）
	结果	Some use them...（主＋谓＋宾）

理修饰	状语	第一层：or 连接的两个动词不定式短语 to keep a close watch on the demand... 和 (to) gather information... 作目的状语。第二层：介词短语 for their line of work 作后置定语，修饰 the demand；介词短语 on compensation 作后置定语，修饰 information；动词不定式短语 to arm themselves 作第二个不定式短语 (to) gather...compensation 的目的状语。
	状从	第一层：when 引导的时间状语从句，省略了主语 they 和 be 动词 are，作句子主干的时间状语，补充完整为 [when] (they are) negotiating for a raise（主＋谓）。第二层：介词短语 for a raise 作 are negotiating 的目的状语。

【结构分析】

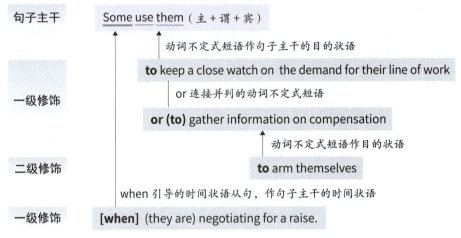

句子主干　Some use them（主＋谓＋宾）

动词不定式短语作句子主干的目的状语

一级修饰　to keep a close watch on the demand for their line of work

or 连接并列的动词不定式短语

or (to) gather information on compensation

动词不定式短语作目的状语

二级修饰　to arm themselves

when 引导的时间状语从句，作句子主干的时间状语

一级修饰　[when] (they are) negotiating for a raise.

【词汇注释】

compensation	[ˌkɒmpenˈseɪʃn] *n.* 补偿；赔偿金

【意群训练】

Some use them // to keep a close watch // on the demand // for their line of work // or gather information // on compensation // to arm themselves // when (they are) negotiating // for a raise.

第三章 提高篇

多种结构的复杂糅合

在英语中，一个句子里经常会出现多种结构，这种情况我们称为结构糅杂。考研英语长难句中，最常见的是两种、三种或四种结构的糅杂，有时也会出现四种以上结构的糅杂。对于这类句子，能明确划分句内各个成分结构是理解句意的关键。

一 两种结构的杂糅

两种结构的杂糅在考研英语试题中很常见，且大多比较简单。但也有仅包含两种结构，却比较难理解的长难句，这类句子常包含从句和平行结构、虚拟和分隔结构、从句和省略、从句和倒装、省略和嵌套结构、倒装和嵌套结构等。

实例 1

If he had played last season, however, he would have been one of 42. 然而，假如他参加了上个赛季的比赛，那他就是 42 名这样的球员中的一员了。
【英语（一）2008 Text 3】

【难句类型】分隔结构 + 虚拟 　　　　　　　　　　　　　　难度：★★★
【难句破解】

找主干	过程	第一步：找从句标志词，并剥离该从句。找到标志词 If：距离 If 之后最近的动词是 had played，至此将该从句剥离。 第二步：识别非谓语动词，同时删除非谓语动词结构及其它修饰成分。本句无非谓语动词结构。删除修饰成分 last season，however。全句剩下了 he would have been one of 42，这就是句子的主干部分。 第三步：识别并删除很像谓语动词的动词。（真正的谓语动词已找到，故该步骤略。）
	结果	..., he would have been one of 42.（主 + 系 + 表）
理修饰	状从	第一层：If 引导的条件状语从句 [If] he had played last season（主 + 谓）使用了虚拟语气，谓语动词采用过去完成式 had played，表示与过去事实相反，因此主句也相应地采用了 would + 现在完成式（have been）形式。第二层：last season 作时间状语。

171

插入语	however 是插入语，表示转折，将从句与主句分隔。
看标点　逗号	however 前后的两个逗号将其与前后内容分隔开。

【结构分析】

二级修饰	last season,
	↓ 作时间状语
一级修饰	**[If]** he had played
	↓ If 引导的条件状语从句，作句子主干的条件状语
句子主干	however, <u>he</u> would have been one of 42.（主＋系＋表）

【意群训练】

If he had played // last season, // however, // he would have been // one of 42.

--- 实例 2 ---

"Hugging protects people who are under stress from the increased risk for colds that's usually associated with stress," notes Sheldon Cohen, a professor of psychology at Carnegie. 拥抱保护那些处于压力之下的人免受感冒增加的风险，而这一风险往往和压力有关"，卡耐基大学的心理学教授谢尔顿·科恩提到。【英语（一）2017 完形】

【难句类型】倒装＋从句　　　　　　　　　　　　难度：★★★☆

【难句破解】

找主句主干	过程	第一步：将双引号内的完整句子划成宾语："Hugging protects people who are under stress from the increased risk for colds that's usually associated with stress," 即为该句的宾语，暂且将其当作一个整体，不进行非谓语动词结构及其它修饰成分的删减。
		第二步：寻找双引号外之前或之后最近的动词，即为谓语：双引号外之后最近的动词为 notes，即为谓语。
		第三步：识别并删除直接引语之外的非谓语动词结构及其它修饰成分。直接引语外无非谓语动词结构；删除修饰成分 a professor of psychology at Carnegie。全句剩下了 "Hugging protects...stress," notes Sheldon Cohen，这就是句子的主干部分。
	结果	"Hugging protects...stress," <u>notes</u> <u>Sheldon Cohen</u>,...（宾＋谓＋主）主干是倒装结构，将作宾语的直接引语提前，构成主谓倒装。
	过程	第一步：找从句标志词，并剥离该从句。❶找到第一个标志词 who：距离 who 之后最近的动词是 are，under stress 作其表语，

找直接引语主干	过程	至此将该从句剥离；❷找到第二个标志词 that：距离 that 之后最近的动词是 is associated，至此将该从句剥离。 第二步：识别非谓语动词，同时删除非谓语动词结构及其它修饰成分。直接引语中无非谓语动词结构；删除修饰成分 from the increased risk for colds, usually, with stress。全句剩下了 Hugging protects people，这就是直接引语的主干部分。 第三步：识别并删除很像谓语动词的动词。（真正的谓语动词已找到，故该步骤略。）
	结果	<u>Hugging</u> <u>protects</u> <u>people</u>（主＋谓＋宾）
理修饰	同位语	a professor of psychology at Carnegie 作同位语，补充说明主句主语 Sheldon Cohen。
	定从	在直接引语中，who 引导定语从句 **[who]** <u>are</u> <u>under</u> <u>stress</u>（主＋系＋表），修饰 people。
	状语	第一层：介词短语 from the increased risk 作状语。第二层：介词短语 for colds 作后置定语，修饰 risk。第三层：that 引导的定语从句 **[that]**'<u>s</u> <u>usually associated</u> with stress（主＋系＋表），修饰 colds，其中副词 usually 和介词短语 with stress 均作状语。

【结构分析】

三级修饰　　　　　　　　　　[that]'s usually associated with stress,"

　　　　　　　　　　　　　that 引导的定语从句，修饰 colds

一级修饰　　　　　　[who] are under stress

　　　　　　who 引导的定语从句，修饰 people

"Hugging protects **people**...from the increased risk for **colds**

句子主干　　　　直接引语作 notes 的宾语

　　　　　　notes **Sheldon Cohen**,（倒装句：宾＋谓＋主）

　　　　　　　　　Sheldon Cohen 的同位语

一级修饰　　a professor of psychology at Carnegie.

【意群训练】

"Hugging protects people // who are under stress // from the increased risk for colds // that's usually associated with stress," // notes Sheldon Cohen, // a professor of psychology // at Carnegie.

（二）三种结构的杂糅

　　三种结构的杂糅在考研英语长难句中出现的频率很高，其中多有从句的出现。如在一个长句中出现分隔结构、平行结构和从句的杂糅，省略、平行结构和嵌套结构的杂糅，倒装、省略和从句的杂糅等。

实例 1

But we're going to have questions like that where we have things we're doing that don't make sense when the market changes and the world changes. 但是，当市场和世界形势发生变化，我们所作之事又不明智时，我们也会遇到类似的问题。【英语（一）2016 Text 4】

【难句类型】省略＋嵌套结构＋平行结构　　　　　　　　　难度：★★★★
【难句破解】

找主干	过程	第一步：找从句标志词，并剥离该从句。❶找到第一个标志词 where：距离 where 之后最近的动词是及物动词 have，things 作其宾语，至此将该从句剥离；❷找到第二个标志词 that：距离 that 之后最近的动词是 don't make，因 make 是及物动词，故 sense 作其宾语，至此将该从句剥离；❸找到第三个标志词 when：距离 when 之后最近的动词是 and 连接的两个 changes，至此将该从句剥离。
		第二步：识别非谓语动词，同时删除非谓语动词结构及其它修饰成分。本句无非谓语动词结构；删除修饰成分 like that。全句剩下 But we're going to have questions we're doing。
		第三步：识别并删除很像谓语动词的动词。根据辨析真假谓语动词的方法，句中剩下两个动词 are going to have 和 are doing，其中 are doing 后缺失宾语，说明 we're doing 是省略关系词 that/which 的定语从句，故将该从句剥离。全句剩下了 But we're going to have questions，这就是句子的主干部分。
	结果	But we're going to have questions...（主＋谓＋宾） 句首的连词 But 表示与上文的逻辑关系，表转折。
理修饰	定语	介词短语 like that 作后置定语，修饰宾语 questions。
	地点状从	第一层：where 引导的地点状语从句 [where] we have things（主＋谓＋宾），作主句的地点状语。第二层：定语从句 (that/which) we're doing（宾＋主＋谓）和 [that] don't make sense（主＋谓＋宾）修饰 things，其中 we're doing 省略了作宾语的关系词 that/which。本句为状从＋嵌套定从结构。
	时间状从	when 引导的时间状语从句 [when] the market changes and the world changes（主1＋谓1＋and＋主2＋谓2），作主句的时间状语，其中连词 and 连接了两个并列分句。

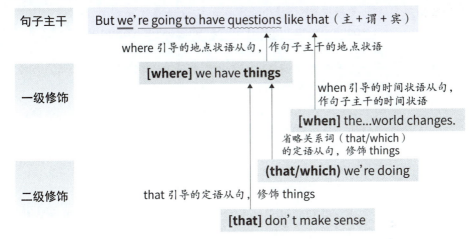

句子主干　But <u>we're going</u> to have <u>questions</u> like that（主＋谓＋宾）

where 引导的地点状语从句，作句子主干的地点状语

[where] we have **things**

when 引导的时间状语从句，
作句子主干的时间状语

一级修饰

[when] the...world changes.

省略关系词（that/which）
的定语从句，修饰 things

(that/which) we're doing

二级修饰　　　　that 引导的定语从句，修饰 things

[that] don't make sense

【意群训练】

But we're going to have questions // like that // where we have things //
we're doing // that don't make sense // when the market changes // and
the world changes.

---- 实例2 ----

In an experiment published in 1988, social psychologist Fritz Strack of
the University of Würzburg in Germany asked volunteers to hold a pen
either with their teeth—thereby creating an artificial smile—or with their
lips, which would produce a disappointed expression. 在 1988 年公布的
一项实验中，德国维尔茨堡大学的社会心理学家弗里茨·斯特拉克要求志愿
者用牙齿咬住钢笔——从而做出假笑的表情——或者用嘴唇衔住钢笔，从而
做出失望的表情。【英语（一）2011 完形】

【难句类型】分隔结构＋从句＋平行结构　　　　　　　难度：★★★★
【难句破解】

找主干	过程	第一步：找从句标志词，并剥离该从句。找到标志词 which：距离 which 之后最近的动词是 would produce，因 produce 是及物动词，故 a disappointed expression 作其宾语，至此将该从句剥离。第二步：识别非谓语动词，同时删除非谓语动词结构及其它修饰成分。删除非谓语动词结构 to hold a pen。删除修饰成分 In an experiment published in 1988，of the University of Würzburg in Germany，either with...with their lips。全句剩下了 social psychologist Fritz Strack asked volunteers，这就是句子的主干部分。

		第三步：识别并删除很像谓语动词的动词。（真正的谓语动词已找到，故该步骤略。）
	结果	..., social psychologist Fritz Strack...asked volunteers to hold a pen...（主＋谓＋宾＋宾补） 动词不定式短语 to hold a pen 作宾语 volunteers 的补足语，与宾语联系紧密，故还原。
理修饰	状语一	第一层：介词短语 In an experiment published in 1988 作状语。 第二层：过去分词短语 published in 1988 作后置定语，修饰 an experiment。
	定语	介词短语 of the University of Würzburg in Germany 作后置定语，修饰主语 social psychologist Fritz Strack。
	状语二	第一层：either...or... 连接并列的介词短语 with their teeth 和 with their lips 作方式状语，补充说明宾补 to hold a pen。第二层：破折号后引出的插入语用于说明 to hold a pen with their teeth 这一行为可能导致的结果；which 引导非限定性定语从句 [which] would produce a disappointed expression（主＋谓＋宾），则用于说明 to hold a pen with their lips 这一行为可能导致的结果。
看标点	破折号	破折号之间的内容是插入语，将 either...or... 连接的两个并列的介词短语分隔开。

【结构分析】

二级修饰　　　　　　　　**published** in 1988,

　　　　　　过去分词短语作后置定语，修饰 an experiment

一级修饰　　　　　　　　**In an experiment**

　　　　　　　　　　　　介词短语作状语

句子主干　　social psychologist **Fritz Strack**...asked volunteers **to hold a pen**

　　　　介词短语作后置定语，修饰 Fritz Strack

of the University of Würzburg in Germany

一级修饰　　　　either...or 连接的并列介词短语作方式状语，修饰 to hold a pen

either with their teeth...**or with** their lips,

　　　　　　　　　　　插入语

—thereby creating an artificial smile—

二级修饰　　　　which 引导的非限定性定语从句

[which] would produce a disappointed expression.

【词汇注释】

| artificial | [ɑːtɪˈfɪʃl] *a.* 虚假的；人造的，假的；人为的 |

【意群训练】

In an experiment published in 1988, // social psychologist // Fritz Strack // of the University of Würzburg in Germany // asked volunteers // to hold a pen // either with their teeth //—thereby creating an artificial smile—// or with their lips, // which would produce // a disappointed expression.

---- 实例 3 ----

The most loyal customers would still get the product they favor, the idea goes, and they'd feel like they were helping sustain the quality of something they believe in. 他的理念是：最忠实的顾客仍然会购买他们喜欢的产品，他们会觉得像是在帮助维护自己所信赖的某个产品的质量。【英语（一）2016 Text 4】

【难句类型】平行结构＋省略＋嵌套结构　　　　难度：★★★★☆

【难句破解】

<table>
<tr>
<td rowspan="2">找主干</td>
<td>过程</td>
<td>第一步：找从句标志词，并剥离该从句。（本句无从句标志词，故该步骤略。）

第二步：识别非谓语动词，同时删除非谓语动词结构及其它修饰成分。本句无非谓语动词结构。删除修饰成分 still, the idea goes 和 of something。

第三步：识别并删除很像谓语动词的动词。根据辨析真假谓语动词的方法，句中剩下五个动词 would get，favor，would feel like，were helping, sustain 和 believe in。句中 and 表并列，从此处将全句分为两部分。在前半部分中，及物动词 favor 后缺失宾语，说明 they favor 是省略关系词 that/which 的定语从句，至此将该从句剥离。在后半部分中，❶ believe 后的介词 in 缺失宾语，说明 they believe in 是省略关系词 that/which 的定语从句，至此将该从句剥离；❷ sustain 位于 were helping 之后，说明 sustain the quality 是省略 to 的动词不定式短语，作 were helping 的宾语。而 they were helping 位于 would feel like 之后，说明 they were helping sustain the quality 是省略引导词 that 的宾语从句，作 would feel like 的宾语，至此将该从句剥离。全句剩下了 The most loyal customers would get the product, and they'd feel like，这就是句子的主干部分。</td>
</tr>
<tr>
<td>结果</td>
<td>The most loyal customers would…get the product…and they'd feel like **(that)** they were helping sustain the quality…</td>
</tr>
</table>

		（主1＋谓1＋宾＋and＋主2＋谓2＋宾从） and 连接了两个并列分句，在分句一中，副词 still 作状语，修饰谓语 would get；在分句二中，省略引导词 that 的宾语从句作谓语 would feel like 的宾语，是主干成分，故还原。
理修饰	定从	分句一中，省略关系词 that/which 的定语从句 **(that/which)** they favor（宾＋主＋谓）修饰 the product。
	插入语	the idea goes 作插入语。
	宾从	分句二中，省略引导词 that 的宾语从句 **(that)** they were helping sustain the quality...（主＋谓＋宾）作 would feel like 的宾语；其中，介词短语 of something 作后置定语，修饰 the quality。第一层：省略关系词 that/which 的定语从句 **(that)** they believe in（宾＋主＋谓）修饰 something。本句为宾从＋嵌套定从结构。
看标点	逗号	成对出现的逗号表明 the idea goes 是插入语。

【结构分析】

【词汇注释】

sustain	[səˈsteɪn] *vt.* 维持；支撑；证明；经受

【意群训练】

The most loyal customers // would still get // the product // they favor, // the idea goes, // and they'd feel like // they were helping // sustain the quality // of something // they believe in.

178

在考研英语中,四种结构的杂糅也很常见,且往往伴随着从句的出现。虽然出现了四种结构,但只要先抓住句子主干,再层层分析,整个句意便不难理解。

实例 1

Says Korn/Ferry senior partner Dennis Carey: "I can't think of a single search I've done where a board has not instructed me to look at sitting CEOs first." 光辉国际有限公司的资深合伙人丹尼斯·凯里说:"我所做的每一次招聘,董事会都会让我首先从在任的 CEO 中寻找人选。"【英语(一)2011 Text 2】

【难句类型】倒装 + 省略 + 否定结构 + 从句   难度:★★★☆

【难句破解】

找主句主干	过程	第一步:将双引号内的完整句子划成宾语:"I can't think of a single search I've done where a board has not instructed me to look at sitting CEOs first." 即为该句的宾语,暂且将其当作一个整体,不进行非谓语动词结构及其它修饰成分的删减。第二步:寻找双引号外之前或之后最近的动词,即为谓语:双引号外之前最近的动词为 Says,即为谓语。第三步:识别并删除直接引语之外的非谓语动词结构及其它修饰成分。直接引语外无非谓语动词结构及其它修饰成分。全句剩下了 Says Korn/Ferry senior partner Dennis Carey: "I can't think of a single search...",这就是句子的主干部分。
	结果	Says Korn/Ferry senior partner Dennis Carey: "I can't think of a single search..."(谓 + 主 + 宾) 该句使用了主谓倒装结构。
找直接引语主干	过程	第一步:找从句标志词,并剥离该从句。找到标志词 where:距离 where 之后最近的动词是 has not instructed,因 instruct 是及物动词,故 me 作其宾语,至此将该从句剥离。 第二步:识别非谓语动词,同时删除非谓语动词结构及其它修饰成分。删除非谓语动词结构 to look at sitting CEOs。删除修饰成分 first。全句剩下 I can't think of a single search I've done。 第三步:识别并删除很像谓语动词的动词。根据辨析真假谓语动词的方法,句中剩下两个动词 can't think of 和 have done,其中 have done 后缺失宾语,说明 I've done 是省略关系词 that/which 的定语从句,故将该从句剥离。全句剩下了 I can't think of a

	single search，这就是直接引语的主干部分。
结果	I can't think of a single search（主＋谓＋宾）

		在直接引语中，省略了关系词 that/which 的定语从句 **(that/ which)** I've done（宾＋主＋谓）修饰 search；where 引导的定语从句 **[where]** a board has not instructed me to look at sitting CEOs first（主＋谓＋宾＋宾补）也修饰 search，其中动词不定式短语 to look at sitting CEOs first 作该定从的宾语 me 的补足语；sitting 为形容词，修饰 CEOs；副词 first 作状语，修饰 look at。
理修饰	定从	

【结构分析】

	Says Korn/Ferry senior partner Dennis Carey:（倒装句：谓＋主＋宾）
句子主干	↑ 直接引语作 Says 的宾语
	"I can't think of a single **search**
	省略关系词（that/which）的定语从句，修饰 search
	(that/which) I've done
一级修饰	where 引导的定语从句，修饰 search
	[where] a board has...me to look at sitting CEOs first."

【词汇注释】

instruct	[ɪn'strʌkt] *vt.* 指示，吩咐，命令

【意群训练】

Says Korn/Ferry senior partner // Dennis Carey: // "I can't think of // a single search // I've done // where a board has not instructed me // to look at sitting CEOs first."

---- 实例 2 ----

Michael Lynn, an associate professor of consumer behavior and marketing at Cornell's School of Hotel Administration, has conducted dozens of studies of tipping and has concluded that consumers' assessments of the quality of service correlate weakly to the amount they tip. 康奈尔大学酒店管理学院的消费者行为和市场营销学副教授迈克尔·林恩通过开展多项

有关小费行为的研究得出结论：消费者对于服务质量的评价与他们支付小费的数额联系不大。【英语（二）2007 Text 3】

【难句类型】平行结构 + 嵌套结构 + 省略 + 分隔结构　　　　　难度：★★★★

【难句破解】

<table>
<tr>
<td rowspan="2">找主干</td>
<td>过程</td>
<td>第一步：找从句标志词，并剥离该从句。找到标志词 that：距离 that 之后最近的动词是 correlate，至此将该从句剥离。
第二步：识别非谓语动词，同时删除非谓语动词结构及其它修饰成分。本句无非谓语动词；删除修饰成分 an associate...Administration, of tipping, weakly 和 to the amount。全句还剩下 Michael Lynn has conducted dozens of studies and has concluded they tip。
第三步：识别并删除很像谓语动词的动词。根据辨析真假谓语动词的方法：句中剩下三个动词 has conducted, has concluded 和 tip，其中及物动词 tip 后缺失宾语，说明 they tip 是省略关系词 that/which 的定语从句，至此将该从句剥离。剩下的两个动词由连词 and 连接，故均是主干谓语动词。全句剩下了 Michael Lynn has conducted dozens of studies and has concluded，这就是句子的主干部分。</td>
</tr>
<tr>
<td>结果</td>
<td>Michael Lynn...has conducted dozens of studies and has concluded [that]...（主 + 谓1 + 宾 + and + 谓2 + 宾从）
that 引导的宾语从句 [that] consumers' assessments of the quality of service correlate（主 + 谓），作 has concluded 的宾语，也是主干成分，故还原。and 连接了两个并列的谓宾结构。</td>
</tr>
<tr>
<td rowspan="3">理修饰</td>
<td>同位语</td>
<td>第一层：an associate professor...Administration 作主语 Michael Lynn 的同位语。第二层：介词短语 of consumer behavior and marketing 和 at Cornell's School of Hotel Administration 均作后置定语，修饰 professor。</td>
</tr>
<tr>
<td>定语</td>
<td>介词短语 of tipping 作后置定语，修饰 studies；介词短语 of the quality of service 作后置定语，修饰 assessments。</td>
</tr>
<tr>
<td>状语</td>
<td>第一层：副词 weakly 作状语，修饰宾语从句的谓语 correlate；介词短语 to the amount 在宾语从句中作状语。第二层：省略关系词 that/which 的嵌套定语从句 (that/which) they tip（宾 + 主 + 谓）修饰 the amount。</td>
</tr>
</table>

【结构分析】

at Cornell's School of Hotel Administration,

二级修饰   介词短语作后置定语，修饰 professor

of consumer behavior and marketing

介词短语作后置定语，修饰 professor

一级修饰   an associate **professor**   **of** tipping

Michael Lynn 的同位语   介词短语作后置定语，修饰 studies

句子主干   <u>**Michael Lynn**</u>,...**has conducted** dozens of **studies**（主＋谓＋宾）

and 连接的并列谓宾

and has concluded [that] consumers' **assessments**...weakly

介词短语作后置定语，修饰 assessments   介词短语作状语

一级修饰   **of** the quality of service   **to the amount**

省略关系词（that/which）的定语从句，修饰 the amount

二级修饰   **(that/which)** they tip.

【意群训练】

Michael Lynn, // an associate professor // of consumer behavior and marketing // at Cornell's School of Hotel Administration, // has conducted dozens of studies // of tipping // and has concluded // that consumers' assessments // of the quality of service // correlate weakly // to the amount // they tip.

─── 实例 3 ───────────────────────────────>>>>

"The traditional rule was it's safer to stay where you are, but that's been fundamentally inverted," says one headhunter. 一位猎头说道："按照传统规则，待在原来的职位会更保险，但是这一规则已经被彻底颠覆了。"
【英语（一）2011 Text 2】

【难句类型】平行结构＋省略＋嵌套结构＋倒装   难度：★★★★★
【难句破解】

找主语主干	过程	第一步：将双引号内的完整句子划成宾语："The traditional rule was it's safer to stay where you are, but that's been fundamentally inverted,"即为该句的宾语，暂且将其当作一个整体，不进行非谓语动词结构及其它修饰成分的删减。 第二步：寻找双引号外之前或之后最近的动词，即为谓语：双引号外之后最近的动词为 says，即为谓语。

		第三步：识别并删除直接引语之外的非谓语动词结构及其它修饰成分。直接引语之外无非谓语动词结构及其它修饰成分，全句剩下了"The traditional rule...inverted," says one headhunter，这就是句子的主干部分。
	结果	"The traditional rule...inverted", <u>says</u> <u>one headhunter</u>.（宾＋谓＋主）主干是倒装结构，将作宾语的直接引语提前，构成主谓倒装。
找直接引语主干	过程	第一步：找从句标志词，并剥离该从句。找到标志词 where：距离 where 之后最近的动词是 are，至此将该从句剥离。 第二步：识别非谓语动词，同时删除非谓语动词结构及其它修饰成分。删除非谓语动词结构 to stay；删除修饰成分 fundamentally。全句剩下了 The traditional rule was it's safer, but that's been inverted。 第三步：识别并删除很像谓语动词的动词。全句剩下三个动词 was, is 和 has been inverted，前两者均是不缺失表语的系动词，故位于前面的 was 是主干系动词，is 是省略引导词 that 的表语从句 it's safer 的系动词，至此将该从句剥离；而 has been inverted 使用了被动语态，but 将其与 was 并列，故其亦为直接引语主干的谓语动词。全句剩下了 The traditional rule was, but that's been inverted，这就是直接引语的主干部分。
	结果	The traditional rule <u>was</u> **(that)** it's safer..., but <u>that</u>'s <u>been</u> <u>inverted</u>（主1＋系＋表从＋but＋主2＋谓） 省略引导词 that 的表语从句 **(that)** <u>it</u>'s safer...（主＋系＋表）作直接引语中分句一的表语，也是主干部分，故还原。其中 it 为形式主语，动词不定式短语 to stay where you are 作真正的主语。该直接引语为 but 连接的并列句。
理修饰	状从	where 引导的地点状语从句 **[where]** <u>you</u> <u>are</u>（表＋主＋系）作表语从句中 to stay 的地点状语，即分句一的表语是表从＋嵌套状从结构。

【结构分析】

一级修饰　　　　　　　　　　　　　　　**[where]** you are,
　　　　　　　where 引导的地点状语从句，作 stay 的地点状语

　　　　　　　　　　　　　　(that) it's safer to **stay**
　　　　　　　　　　　　省略引导词 (that) 的表语从句

　　　　　　　　　"The traditional rule was
句子主干　　　　　　　　　　but 连接的并列句

　　　　　　　　　but that's been fundamentally inverted,"
　　　　　　　直接引语作 says 的宾语

　　　　　says one headhunter.（倒装句：宾＋谓＋主）

fundamentally	[ˌfʌndə'mentəli] *ad.* 根本上；基本上
invert	[ɪn'vɜːt] *vt.* 使倒转，颠倒，倒置

【意群训练】

"The traditional rule was // it's safer // to stay // where you are, // but that's been fundamentally inverted," // says one headhunter.

----- 实例 4 -----

Their analysis ruled out the possibility that it was firms' political influence, rather than their CSR stand, that accounted for the leniency: Companies that contributed more to political campaigns did not receive lower fines. 他们的分析排除了如下可能性：公司受到宽大处理是因为其政治影响力，而非 CSR 立场。为政治运动做出了更多贡献的公司并没有得到较低的处罚。【英语（一）2016 Text 3】

【难句类型】从句＋强调＋平行结构＋否定结构　　　　　难度：★★★★★

【难句破解】

找主干	过程	第一步：找从句标志词，并剥离该从句。❶找到第一个标志词 that：距离 that 之后最近的动词是 was，但因该句中存在 it was...that... 强调结构，故该强调结构中 that 之后最近的动词 accounted for 才是该从句的谓语动词，介词 for 后需跟宾语，故 the leniency 作其宾语，至此将该从句剥离；❷找到第二个标志词 that：距离 that 之后最近的动词是 contributed，因 contribute 为及物动词，故 more 作其宾语，至此将该从句剥离。 第二步：识别非谓语动词，同时删除非谓语动词结构及其它修饰成分。本句无非谓语动词结构。删除修饰成分 Companies...did not receive lower fines。全句剩下了 Their analysis ruled out the possibility，这就是句子的主干部分。 第三步：识别并删除很像谓语动词的动词。（真正的谓语动词已找到，故该步骤略。）
	结果	<u>Their analysis</u> <u>ruled out</u> <u>the possibility</u>...（主＋谓＋宾）
理修饰	同位语从句	that 引导的同位语从句 **[that]** it was firms' political influence... that <u>accounted for</u> <u>the leniency</u>（主＋谓＋宾），解释说明宾语 the possibility，其中 it was...that... 是强调结构，强调主语 firms' political influence；rather than 连接并列主语 firms' political influence 和 their CSR stand，肯定前者，否定后者。

| 解释说明 | 第一层：冒号后的内容 Companies...did not receive lower fines（主＋谓＋宾）对前文进行补充说明，did not 表否定。第二层：that 引导的定语从句 [that] contributed more to political campaigns（主＋谓＋宾）修饰 Companies，其中介词短语 to political campaigns 作状语，表对象。 |

| 看标点 | 冒号 | 冒号表示对前文内容进行补充说明。 |

【结构分析】

| 句子主干 | Their analysis ruled out **the possibility**（主＋谓＋宾） |

that 引导的同位语从句，解释说明 the possibility

[that] it was **firms' political influence**...the leniency:

rather than 连接并列主语，肯定前者，否定后者

rather than their CSR stand,

补充说明

Companies...did not receive lower fines.

一级修饰

that 引导的定语从句，修饰 companies

二级修饰 | **[that]** contributed more to political campaigns

【词汇注释】

| rule out | 排除；不予考虑；阻止 |
| account for | 导致；说明；对……负有责任 |

【意群训练】

Their analysis // ruled out // the possibility // that it was // firms' political influence, // rather than their CSR stand, // that accounted for the leniency: // Companies that contributed more // to political campaigns // did not receive // lower fines.

实例 5

In a society that so persistently celebrates procreation, is it any wonder that admitting you regret having children is equivalent to admitting you support kitten-killing? 在这个如此执着于颂扬生育的社会，承认后悔生孩子就等于赞同虐杀小猫，这又有什么奇怪的呢？【英语（一）2011 Text 4】

【难句破解】

找主干	过程	第一步：找从句标志词，并剥离该从句。❶找到第一个标志词 that：距离 that 之后最近的动词是及物动词 celebrates，procreation 作其宾语，至此将该从句剥离；❷找到第二个标志词 that，因其后有完整的主谓宾结构 you regret having children，暂时无法确定谓语动词，故在第三步分析。 第二步：识别非谓语动词，同时删除非谓语动词结构及其它修饰成分。删除非谓语动词结构两个 admitting 和 having children；删除修饰成分 In a society 和 to。全句剩下 is it any wonder that you regret is equivalent you support kitten-killing？ 第三步：识别并删除很像谓语动词的动词。根据辨析真假谓语动词的方法，句中剩下四个动词 is，regret，is equivalent to（由于 be equivalent to 为固定搭配，在辨别真假谓语动词时需看作一个整体的谓语动词）和 support。其中后三者都在第二个 that 之后，由于三者均不缺失宾语，is equivalent to 表明其前后内容语义上存在并列关系，且前后两个 admitting 后分别跟有完整的主谓宾结构，故 regret 和 support 分别是两个 admitting 后省略引导词 that 的宾语从句中的谓语动词，其宾语分别为 having children 和 kitten-killing，至此将这两个从句剥离。全句剩下了 is it any wonder that is equivalent to，而 is equivalent to 是 that 引导的从句的谓语动词，至此将该从句剥离。全句剩下了 is it any wonder，这就是句子的主干部分。
	结果	..., is it any wonder...?（系 + 主 + 表）
理修饰	状语	第一层：介词短语 In a society 作地点状语。第二层：that 引导的定语从句 [that] so persistently celebrates procreation（主 + 谓 + 宾）修饰 a society，so persistently 修饰谓语 celebrates。
	主从	主句中 it 是形式主语，真正的主语是 that 引导的主语从句 [that] admitting... is equivalent to admitting...（主 + 系 + 表）。省略引导词 that 的嵌套宾从 (that) you regret having children（主 + 谓 + 宾），作第一个 admitting 的宾语，该从句的宾语是动名词短语 having children；省略引导词 that 的嵌套宾从 (that) you support kitten-killing（主 + 谓 + 宾）作第二个 admitting 的宾语。

二级修饰 　[that] so persistently celebrates procreation,

　　　　　that 引导的定语从句，修饰 a society

一级修饰 　**In a society**

　　　　　介词短语作地点状语

句子主干 　is **it** any wonder（一般疑问句：系＋主＋表）

　　　　　it 作形式主语，that 引导的主语从句为真正的主语

　　　　　[that] admitting...is equivalent to **admitting**

　　　　　省略引导词 that 的宾语从句，作 admitting 的宾语

　　　　　(that) you regret having children

　　　　　　省略引导词 that 的宾语从句，作 admitting 的宾语

　　　　　　　(that) you support kitten-killing?

【词汇注释】

procreation	[ˌprəʊkriˈeɪʃn] *n.* 生殖；生育；繁殖
equivalent	[ɪˈkwɪvələnt] *a.* 相等的，相同的

【意群训练】

In a society // that so persistently celebrates procreation, // is it any wonder // that admitting you regret having children // is equivalent to // admitting you support kitten-killing?

四　四种以上结构的杂糅

在考研英语中，偶尔可见四种以上更为复杂结构的杂糅，这种句式复杂多变，层层嵌套，乍一看，很容易让人眼花缭乱，搞不清所云，但只要先抓住句子主干，再层层分析，突破句意并不难。

实例 1

Those forced to exercise their smiling muscles reacted more enthusiastically to funny cartoons than did those whose mouths were contracted in a frown, suggesting that expressions may influence emotions rather than just the other way around. 那些被迫锻炼笑肌的人

对滑稽漫画的反应比那些皱眉噘嘴的人更为强烈，这表明表情也可以影响情绪，而不仅仅是情绪影响表情。【英语（一）2011 完形】

【难句类型】

嵌套结构 + 倒装 + 非谓语动词 + 比较结构 + 平行结构 + 从句　难度：★★★★★

【难句破解】

找主干	过程	第一步：找从句标志词，并剥离该从句。❶找到第一个标志词 than：距离 than 之后最近的动词是 did，those 作其宾语，至此将该从句剥离；❷找到第二个标志词 whose：距离 whose 之后最近的动词是 were contracted，至此将该从句剥离；❸找到第三个标志词 that：距离 that 之后最近的动词是 may influence，因 influence 是及物动词，emotions 作其宾语，并列连词 rather than 前后内容存在并列关系，故 rather than just the other way around 也为该从句的一部分，至此将该从句剥离。 第二步：识别非谓语动词，同时删除非谓语动词结构及其它修饰成分。删除非谓语动词结构 forced...muscles 和非谓语动词 suggesting；删除修饰成分 more enthusiastically, to funny cartoons 和 in a frown。全句剩下了 Those reacted，这就是句子的主干部分。 第三步：识别并删除很像谓语动词的动词。（真正的谓语动词已找到，故该步骤略。）
	结果	<u>Those</u>...<u>reacted</u>...（主 + 谓） 副词比较级 more enthusiastically 作状语，修饰谓语 reacted。
理修饰	定语	过去分词短语 forced to exercise their smiling muscles 作后置定语，修饰主语 Those。
	状从	第一层：than 引导的比较状语从句 **[than]** <u>did</u> <u>those</u>（谓 + 主）使用了倒装语序，正常语序为：than those did，虽然在找主干过程中我们将 did 之后的 those 视为其宾语，但将该处倒装语序还原为正常语序后可知，those 其实作 did 的主语。第二层：whose 引导的定语从句 **[whose]** <u>mouths</u> <u>were contracted</u> in a frown（主 + 谓）修饰 those，介词短语 in a frown 作方式状语。本句为状从 + 嵌套定从结构。
	状语	介词短语 to funny cartoons 作状语，表对象；现在分词短语 suggesting... 作伴随状语，其中 that 引导的宾语从句 **[that]** <u>expressions</u> <u>may influence</u> <u>emotions</u> rather than just the other way around（主 + 谓 + 宾）作 suggesting 的宾语。其中连词 rather than 表示"而不是……"，肯定前者，否定后者。从整个句意角度来讲，其后的 just the other way around 等同于"emotions may influence expressions"。

【结构分析】

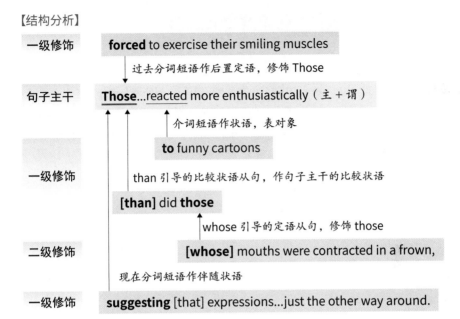

一级修饰   **forced** to exercise their smiling muscles

　　　　　过去分词短语作后置定语，修饰 Those

句子主干   **Those**...**reacted** more enthusiastically（主＋谓）

　　　　　介词短语作状语，表对象

　　　　　to funny cartoons

一级修饰   than 引导的比较状语从句，作句子主干的比较状语

　　　　　[than] did **those**

　　　　　whose 引导的定语从句，修饰 those

二级修饰   **[whose]** mouths were contracted in a frown,

　　　　　现在分词短语作伴随状语

一级修饰   **suggesting** [that] expressions...just the other way around.

【词汇注释】

enthusiastically	[ɪnˌθjuːzɪˈæstɪkli] *ad.* 热心地；满腔热情地
contract	[kənˈtrækt] *v.* 收缩；感染 [ˈkɒntrækt] *n.* 合同；协议
frown	[fraʊn] *n./v.* 皱眉
the other way around	相反地；从相反方向

【意群训练】

Those // forced to exercise their smiling muscles // reacted more enthusiastically //to funny cartoons // than did those // whose mouths were contracted // in a frown, // suggesting that expressions may influence emotions // rather than // just the other way around.

"叮!"课间休息时间到喽!☺

学习累了吧,和"闪过"一起来做个小游戏吧~最近,天南海北考研的小伙伴们给"闪过"发来了很多有意思的短诗,"闪过"特别挑选了几则,制成了"短诗福袋",并在里面放进了小惊喜~你喜欢哪一首呢?选出来你的"最爱",去本书P198领取研友们为你准备的惊喜吧!

英雄,王者,部落,传说
放下了;
英语,政治,数学,专业
拿起了。
　　　　——武当扫地僧

有多少人告诉我考研无望
有多少时刻我也曾这样想
还好,心有不甘
我没有被这些浅见削弱我
的锋芒
　　　　——两勺豆豆

春朝背书时落下的木棉
夏日思考时轻摇的蒲扇
秋夜做题时浮动的婵娟
最后拼成了这个冬天的考研
　　　　——城北徐公

图书馆老排队
自习室占座位
数学,英语轮番上
考研的心儿不疲惫~
　　　　——还能再学100天

考研难,考研难
考研到底难不难?
书本,真题,视频课
一刷二刷不再难
　　　　——输出刷题机器

第四章 挑战篇

"变态"难句的巅峰训练

在上一章，我们讲解了考研英语中常见的结构杂糅。但在英语中，尤其是学术类的期刊论文中，可能会出现包含多个结构的更为复杂的长句。遇到这类句子，我们同样首先要找出句子的谓语动词，通过谓语动词锁定主干成分，并剥离出从句，再对其它成分进行分析，一步一步将长难句破解。

本章根据考研英语真题改编了两个"超级长难句"，分别是包含了所有结构和包含了五大标点的"变态"长难句。当然，考研英语中不会出现结构如此复杂的超级长难句，本章的目的就是希望大家通过对这两个长难句的逐层分析，能达到"一览众山小"的效果。想想如此"超级长难句"都能攻克，破解考研英语长难句岂不是易如反掌？

（一）十一种结构的"变态"杂糅

实例

Nor, if regularity and conformity to a standard pattern were as desirable to the scientist as the writing of his papers would appear to reflect—which means he has already made conclusions that he expects to draw before the results are presented—would management be, undoubtedly, to be blamed for discriminating against the "odd balls" that carry innovative ideas among researchers in favor of more conventional thinkers who consider it is working well with the team that is more important. 如果当科学家像他的论文所反映的那样，期待规律性与某种标准模式的一致性，也就是说，在得到研究成果前，他已经设定了所期待的结果，那么毫无疑问，管理层歧视研究人员中有创新理念的"标新立异者"，而赞赏认为善于合作更重要的、思想较为循规蹈矩的人，也是无可指责的。【根据英语（一）1999 Passage 5 中原句改编】

1.剥离枝蔓法

【难句类型】

倒装＋否定结构＋从句＋非谓语动词＋嵌套结构＋分隔结构＋比较结构＋省略＋虚拟＋强调＋平行结构

难度：变态难

【难句破解】

找主干	过程	第一步：找从句标志词，并剥离该从句。❶找到第一个标志词 if：距离 if 之后最近的动词是 were，as desirable 作其表语，至此将该从句剥离；❷找到第二个标志词 as：距离 as 之后最近的动词是 would appear，至此将该从句剥离；❸找到第三个标志词 which：距离 which 之后最近的动词是 means，至此将该从句剥离；❹找到第四个标志词 that：距离 that 之后最近的动词是 expects，至此将该从句剥离；❺找到第五个标志词 before：距离 before 之后最近的动词是 are presented，至此将该从句剥离；❻找到第六个标志词 that：距离 that 之后最近的动词是及物动词 carry，innovative ideas 作其宾语，至此将该从句剥离；❼找到第七个标志词 who：距离 who 之后最近的动词是 consider，至此将该从句剥离。 第二步：识别非谓语动词，同时删除非谓语动词结构及其它修饰成分。删除非谓语动词结构 to reflect, to draw, to be blamed。删除修饰成分 to the scientist，already，undoubtedly，for discriminating against the "odd balls"，among researchers，in favor of more conventional thinkers，with the team。全句剩下了 Nor, he has made conclusions would management be, it is working well that is more important。 第三步：识别并删除很像谓语动词的动词。根据辨析真假谓语动词的方法，句中剩下四个动词 has made，would be，is working 和 is：❶第一个动词 has made 不缺失宾语，且位于动词 means 之后，说明 he has already made conclusions 是省略引导词 that 的宾语从句，作 means 的宾语，故将该从句剥离；❷ is working 位于 it is...that... 的强调结构中，必然不可能是主干谓语动词；❸剩下两个动词 would be 和第二个 is，其中 is 不缺失表语，故前面的 would be 是主干谓语动词，is 之前是及物动词 consider，故 consider 之后是省略引导词that 的宾语从句,is 为该从句的系动词,more important 作其表语，至此将该从句剥离。全句剩下了 Nor, would management be，这就是句子的主系部分。

结果	Nor, ...would <u>management be</u>, ...<u>to be blamed</u>...（Nor ＋ 情态动词 ＋ 主 ＋ 系动词 ＋ 表） 动词不定式短语 to be blamed 作表语，是主干成分，故还原。表否定的 Nor 位于句首，因此使用了部分倒装结构，将 would 提前。正常语序为：management would not be to be blamed...。

状从	第一层：if 引导条件状语从句 **[if]** <u>regularity and conformity</u> to a standard pattern <u>were</u> as desirable...（主 ＋ 系 ＋ 表），该从句使用了虚拟语气，从句谓语动词为 be 动词的一般过去式 were，表示与现在事实相反，主句则相应地采用了 would be。第二层：该条件状从中，介词短语 to a standard pattern 作后置定语，修饰 conformity，介词短语 to the scientist 作状语，表对象；as 引导的比较状语从句 **[as]** <u>the writing of his papers</u> <u>would appear</u> to reflect（主 ＋ 系 ＋ 表），作条件状语从句的比较状语；which 引导非限定性定语从句 **[which]** <u>means</u> <u>he has...made conclusions</u>（主 ＋ 谓 ＋ 宾），补充说明条件状从，其中 already 作状语，该定语从句的宾语是省略引导词 that 的宾语从句 **(that)** <u>he</u> <u>has...made</u> conclusions（主 ＋ 谓 ＋ 宾）。第三层：that 引导的定语从句 **[that]** <u>he</u> <u>expects</u> to draw（主 ＋ 谓 ＋ 宾），修饰第二层中的 conclusions；before 引导的时间状语从句 **[before]** <u>the results</u> <u>are presented</u>（主 ＋ 谓），作第二层中宾从的时间状语。

理修饰	
插入语	副词 undoubtedly 作插入语。
状语	第一层：介词短语 for discriminating against the "odd balls" ... 作原因状语。第二层：that 引导的定语从句 **[that]** <u>carry</u> innovative ideas（主 ＋ 谓 ＋ 宾），修饰 "odd balls"；介词短语 among researchers 作后置定语，修饰 "odd balls"；介词短语 in favor of more conventional thinkers 作伴随状语，修饰原因状语。第三层：who 引导的定语从句 **[who]** <u>consider</u>...（主 ＋ 谓），修饰 thinkers，其中省略引导词 that 的宾语从句 **(that)** <u>it</u> <u>is</u> <u>working well with the team</u> that <u>is</u> <u>more important</u>（主 ＋ 系 ＋ 表），作定语从句中 consider 的宾语，其中，it is...that... 为强调结构，强调作主语的动名词短语 working well with the team，形容词比较级构成的优等比较结构 more important 作表语。

看标点	破折号	破折号将非限定性定语从句分隔开。

2. 丰富主干法

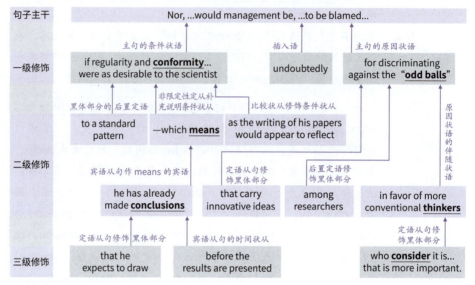

【词汇注释】

regularity	[ˌrɡjuˈlærəti] *n.* 规律性；匀称；有规律的事物
conformity	[kənˈfɔːməti] *n.* 遵从，遵守
discriminate	[dɪˈskrɪmɪneɪt] *vi.* 歧视 *v.* 辨别；区分
be blamed for	因……被责备
conventional	[kənˈvenʃənl] *a.* 传统的；依照惯例的；常规的

【意群训练】

Nor, // if regularity and conformity // to a standard pattern // were as desirable // to the scientist // as the writing of his papers // would appear to reflect //—which means // he has already made conclusions // that he expects to draw // before the results are presented //—would management be, // undoubtedly, // to be blamed // for discriminating against the "odd balls" // that carry innovative ideas // among researchers // in favor of // more conventional thinkers // who consider // it is working well with the team // that is more important.

实例

When asked about his opinion, Orin Kerr, a law professor, compares the explosion and accessibility of digital information in the 21st century with the establishment of automobile use as a virtual necessity of life in the 20th, which was caused by the popularity of vehicles: The justices had to specify novel rules for the new personal domain of the passenger car (private car and taxi) then; they must sort out how the Fourth Amendment applies to digital information now—meaning that they may need to amend this amendment. 当被问及他的看法时，法学教授奥林·科尔把 21 世纪的数字信息大爆炸及其易获取性与由机动车的普及引起的 20 世纪汽车使用成为生活实际需要的确立进行了比较：当时法官不得不为私人用车（私家车和出租车）中的个人空间明确新的规则；而当下他们必须解决第四条修正案如何应用于数据信息的问题——意味着他们可能需要修改该修正案。【根据英语（一）2015 Text 2 中原句改编】

1. 剥离枝蔓法

【难句类型】

五大标点＋从句＋非谓语动词＋省略＋平行结构＋分隔结构　难度：变态难

【难句破解】

找主干	过程	**第一步**：找从句标志词，并剥离该从句。❶找到第一个标志词 When：距离 When 之后最近的动词是 asked ，至此将该从句剥离；❷找到第二个标志词 which：距离 which 之后最近的动词是 was caused，至此将该从句剥离；❸找到第三个标志词 how：距离 how 之后最近的动词是 applies，至此将该从句剥离；❹找到第四个标志词 that：距离 that 之后最近的动词是 may need，至此将该从句剥离。 **第二步**：识别非谓语动词，同时删除非谓语动词结构及其它修饰成分。删除非谓语动词结构 meaning 和 to amend this amendment。删饰成分 about his opinion，a law professor，of digital information，in the 21st century，with the establishment...in the 20th，by the popularity of vehicles，for the new personal domain，of the passenger car，(private car and taxi)，then，to digital information 和 now。全句剩下了 Orin Kerr, compares the explosion and accessibility: The justices had to specify novel rules; they must sort out.

		第三步：识别并删除很像谓语动词的动词。冒号后的句子表示解释说明，其中的动词 had to specify 和 must sort out 分别是由分号连接的两个分句的谓语动词，所以不是主干谓语动词，故将这两句删除。全句剩下了 Orin Kerr, compares the explosion and accessibility，这就是句子的主干部分。
	结果	..., <u>Orin Kerr</u>, ...<u>compares</u> <u>the explosion and accessibility</u>...（主＋谓＋宾）
理修饰	状从	第一层：When 引导时间状语从句 **[When]** (he was) <u>asked</u>（主＋谓），该从句的主语和主句主语相同，故省略了主语＋be 动词。第二层：介词短语 about his opinion 作状语，表方面。
	同位语	名词短语 a law professor 作主语 Orin Kerr 的同位语。
	定语	介词短语 of digital information 和 in the 21st century 均作后置定语，修饰 the explosion and accessibility。
	状语	第一层：介词短语 with the establishment 作主句的方式状语，与谓语构成 compare...with... 结构。第二层：介词短语 of automobile use...in the 20th 作后置定语，修饰 the establishment；which 引导的非限定性定从 **[which]** <u>was caused</u> by the popularity of vehicles（主＋谓），补充说明 the establishment，该定从的谓语是被动语态，介词 by 引出动作的发出者 the popularity of vehicles。第三层：介词短语 as a virtual necessity of life in the 20th 作后置定语，修饰 use，其中介词短语 of life in the 20th 又是修饰 necessity 的后置定语。
	解释说明	第一层：冒号后的内容解释说明主干，分号分隔两个并列分句，分句一是 <u>The justices</u> <u>had to specify</u> <u>novel rules</u>（主＋谓＋宾）；分句二是 <u>they</u> <u>must sort out</u> <u>how</u>...（主＋谓＋宾从）；how 引导的宾语从句 **[how]** <u>the Fourth Amendment</u> <u>applies</u>（主＋谓）作分句二的宾语，其中 now 作时间状语。第二层：介词短语 for the new personal domain of the passenger car 作状语，表对象，副词 then 作时间状语；介词短语 to digital information 是修饰 applies 的状语，表对象；破折号后的现在分词短语 meaning...表补充说明；其中，that 引导的宾语从句 **[that]** <u>they</u> <u>may need</u> <u>to amend this amendment</u>（主＋谓＋宾）作现在分词 meaning 的宾语。第三层：分句一中的介词短语 of the passenger car 作后置定语，修饰 domain。
看标点	逗号	a law professor 前后的逗号将主语和谓语隔开。
	冒号	冒号后的内容表示对主句的解释说明。
	分号	分号表示其前后两个句子是平行关系。

196

| 看标点 | 括 号 | 括号中的 private car and taxi 是对 passenger car 的解释说明。 |
| | 破折号 | 破折号后的现在分词短语对破折号前的内容进行补充说明。 |

2. 丰富主干法

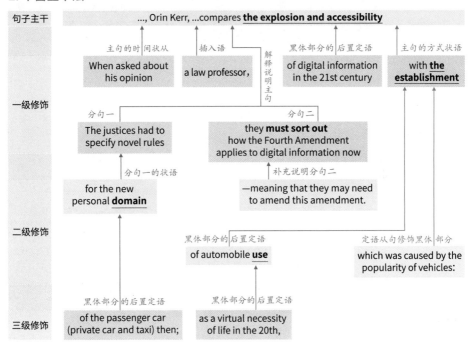

【词汇注释】

accessibility	[əkˌsesəˈbɪləti] *n.* 易接近；可到达
domain	[dəˈmeɪn] *n.* 领域；领土；域；区域
amend	[əˈmend] *vt.* 修正，修订

【意群训练】

When asked about // his opinion, // Orin Kerr, // a law professor, // compares the explosion and accessibility // of digital information // in the 21st century // with the establishment // of automobile use // as a virtual necessity // of life in the 20th, // which was caused // by the popularity of vehicles: // The justices had to specify novel rules // for the new personal domain // of the passenger car // (private car and taxi) then; // they must sort out // how the Fourth Amendment // applies to // digital information now //—meaning that // they may need // to amend this amendment.

"叮!"课间休息时间到喽!😊

　　你还记得之前选的"短诗福袋"吗(不记得的小伙伴,去本书P190再去回顾下吧)?接下来快对号入座,找出自己喜欢的福袋,看看那些研友们给你准备了什么惊喜吧~

放下,说得轻而易举
拿起,说得云淡风轻
做,却要拼尽全力
愿你克制自律,言行如一!
——武当扫地僧

这一路上
累过,哭过,崩溃过
但仍然相信,考研值得
愿你不忘初心,坚定前行!
——两勺豆豆

一路相伴,你的累我看在眼里
你的努力记在心里
愿你逐梦成功
成为更好的自己!
——城北徐公

考研就像一条摸黑行走的路
身处其中,只能不断前进
愿你无所畏惧,终迎曙光!
——还能再学100天

你熬过了酷暑寒冬
抗下了晨霜雨露
考研让你成长了太多
愿你不惧挫折,勇往直前!
——输出刷题机器

　　没错,小小的惊喜,就是研友们的祝福和问候,只想告诉你,考研路上,你不是一个人在奋斗,我们都是并肩的战友,快带着研友们的祝福,继续上路吧!相信你一定会摘得硕果,收获满满!

◆ 真题例句的实战演练 ◆

在前四章，我们用"找主干、理修饰、看标点"的解析方法分析了各种结构的考研英语长难句，大家到底掌握得如何呢？在这一章，我们将利用考研英语真题让大家进行实战演练。例句解析只给出【难句类型】和【结构分析】，具体的三步骤和意群划分则需由大家自己完成。本章的例句难度虽是逐渐增加的，但大家只要利用我们的长难句三步破解法，并结合第一章的基础语法，就一定能将这 30 个实例逐个击破。

（一） 基础演练

—— 实例 1 ——

An emerging body of research shows that positive health habits—as well as negative ones—spread through networks of friends via social communication. 不断涌现的大量研究表明，积极健康的生活习惯和不良的生活习惯一样，都可通过社交在朋友圈中传播。【英语（一）2012 Text 1】

【难句类型】分隔结构 + 从句 + 平行结构　　　　　　　　　难度：★★★
【结构分析】

句子主干

An emerging body of research **shows**（主 + 谓 + 宾从）

that 引导的宾语从句，作 shows 的宾语

[that] positive health habits...spread

插入语

—as well as negative ones—

介词短语作状语

一级修饰

through networks of friends

介词短语作状语

via social communication.

—— 实例 2 ——

Its scientists were the world's best, its workers the most skilled. 它拥有世界上最优秀的科学家和技术最娴熟的工人。【英语（一）2000 Passage 1】

【难句类型】比较结构 + 独立主格　　　　　　　　　难度：★★★

【结构分析】

句子主干　　Its scientists were the world's best,（主 + 系 + 表）

　　　　　　　　　　　　　↑ 独立主格结构作伴随状语
一级修饰　　its workers the most skilled.

---- 实例 3 ----

The court would be recklessly modest if it followed California's advice.
如果法院听取了加州政府的建议，那它就太过于谦虚了。【英语（一）2015 Text 2】

【难句类型】虚拟 + 从句　　　　　　　　　　　　难度：★★★

【结构分析】

句子主干　　The court would be recklessly modest（主 + 系 + 表）

　　　　　if 引导的条件状语从句，作句子主干的条件状语　↑
一级修饰　　[if] it followed California's advice.

---- 实例 4 ----

The company seems to have concluded that its reputation in Vermont is already so damaged that it has nothing left to lose by going to war with the state. 安特吉公司似乎已经断定，它在佛蒙特州已经名誉扫地，和州政府开战也不会再损失什么。【英语（一）2012 Text 2】

【难句类型】嵌套结构 + 否定结构 + 非谓语动词　　　难度：★★★

【结构分析】

句子主干　　The company seems to **have concluded**（主 + 系 + 表）

　　　　　　that 引导的宾语从句，作 have concluded 的宾语　↑
　　　　　　[that] its reputation in Vermont is already **so** damaged

　　　　　　　　　　so...that 引导的结果状语从句　↑
一级修饰　　[that] it has nothing left to lose

　　　　　　　　　　介词短语作方式状语　↑
二级修饰　　**by** going to war with the state.

Adding to a woman's increased dose of stress chemicals, are her increased "opportunities" for stress. 加重女性体内更多压力化学物质剂量的，是她们增多的压力"机会"。【英语（一）2008 Text 1】

【难句类型】倒装　　　　　　　　　　　　　　　　难度：★★★☆

【结构分析】

句子主干　　Adding to a...increased **dose**...are her increased **"opportunities"**

　　　　　　　　　　　　　　　　介词短语作后置定语，修饰 "opportunities"

　　　　　　　　　　　　　　　　　　　　　　for stress.

一级修饰　　介词短语作后置定语，修饰 dose

　　　　　　　　　　　　　of stress chemicals,

At the end of adolescence, however, the brain shuts down half of that capacity, preserving only those modes of thought that have seemed most valuable during the first decade or so of life. 然而，在青春期结束时，大脑关闭了其中一半的能力，只留下在生命最初大约十年中看起来最有价值的思维方式。【英语（一）2009 Text 1】

【难句类型】非谓语动词＋从句＋分隔结构　　　　　难度：★★★☆

【结构分析】

一级修饰　　**At** the end of adolescence,

　　　　　　　　　　　介词短语作时间状语

句子主干　　however, the brain shuts down half of that capacity,（主＋谓＋宾）

　　　　　　　　　　　　　　　　现在分词短语作伴随状语

一级修饰　　　　**preserving** only those **modes of thought**

　　　　　　　　　that 引导的定语从句，修饰 modes of thought

二级修饰　　　　　**[that]** have seemed most valuable

　　　　　　　　　　　　介词短语作时间状语

三级修饰　　　　　**during** the first decade or so of life.

The sensible place to build new houses, factories and offices is where people are, in cities and towns where infrastructure is in place. 人群集中的地方，也就是基础设施完备的城市和乡村，通常适合建造新的房屋、工厂和办公室。【英语（一）2016 Text 2】

【难句类型】嵌套结构 + 平行结构 + 非谓语动词　　　　　难度：★★★☆

【结构分析】

一级修饰	**to** build new houses, factories and offices

动词不定式短语作后置定语，修饰 place

句子主干	The sensible **place**...is [where] people are, （主 + 系 + 表从）

解释说明

一级修饰	in **cities and towns**

where 引导的定语从句，修饰 cities and towns

二级修饰	[where] infrastructure is in place.

Mr. McWhorter's academic speciality is language history and change, and he sees the gradual disappearance of "whom", for example, to be natural and no more regrettable than the loss of the case-endings of Old English. 麦克沃特先生的学术专长是语言史和语言演变。举例来说，他认为"whom"一词的逐渐消失是很自然的，和古英语中词格尾缀的消失一样没有什么可惋惜的。【英语（一）2005 Text 4】

【难句类型】比较结构 + 平行结构 + 非谓语动词 + 分隔结构　　难度：★★★☆

【结构分析】

句子主干	Mr. McWhorter's...speciality is language...change, （主 + 系 + 表）

and 连接的并列分句

and he sees the... "whom" to be...regrettable （主 + 谓 + 宾 + 宾补）

插入语

for example,

一级修饰	介词短语作比较状语

than the loss of the case-ending of Old English.

Only when humanity began to get its food in a more productive way was there time for other things. 只有当人类开始用更有效的方法获取食物时，他们才有时间考虑其他事情。【英语（一）2009 Text 3】

【难句类型】倒装＋从句＋非谓语动词　　　　　　　　　难度：★★★☆

【结构分析】

二级修饰	**in** a more productive way
	↓ 介词短语作方式状语
一级修饰	Only [**when**] humanity began to get its food
	↓ when 引导的时间状语从句，作句子主干的时间状语
句子主干	was there **time**（there be 句型的倒装：was + there + 主）
	↑ 介词短语作后置定语，修饰 time
一级修饰	**for** other things.

But that does not mean coercion should now take a back seat to persuasion, Mr. Nye argues. 但奈先生认为，这并不意味着强制力现在应次于说服力，位居第二。【英语（二）2009 Text 3】

【难句类型】省略＋从句＋否定结构　　　　　　　　　难度：★★★☆

【结构分析】

句子主干	But that **does not mean**（主＋谓＋宾从）
	↓ 省略引导词（that）的宾语从句，作 does not mean 的宾语
	(that) coercion should now take a back seat to persuasion,
	↑ 插入语
一级修饰	Mr. Nye argues.

（二）提升演练

Open-source spying does have its risks, of course, since it can be difficult to tell good information from bad. 当然，公源谍报活动的确有风险，因为

很难区分情报的真伪。【英语（一）2003 Text 1】

【难句类型】强调 + 非谓语动词 + 从句 + 分隔结构　　　　　　难度：★★★★

【结构分析】

句子主干　Open-source spying does have its risks,（主 + 谓 + 宾）

插入语
of course,

一级修饰　since 引导的原因状语从句，作句子主干的原因状语

[since] it can be difficult to tell good information from bad.

---------- 实例12 ----------

They are motivated by the desire for a better job or the need to hang on to the one they've got. 他们的动机在于寻求一份更好的职业或保持现有的职位。【英语（二）2006 Text 2】

【难句类型】省略 + 平行结构 + 非谓语动词　　　　　　难度：★★★★

【结构分析】

句子主干　They are motivated by the desire（主 + 谓）

介词短语作后置定语，修饰 desire

一级修饰　for a better job or the need

动词不定式短语作后置定语，修饰 the need

二级修饰　to hang on to the one

省略关系词（that）的定语从句，修饰 the one

三级修饰　(that) they've got.

---------- 实例13 ----------

Though not biologically related, friends are as "related" as fourth cousins, sharing about 1% of genes. 朋友之间虽然没有血缘关系，但却"亲"如第四代表亲，约有 1% 的基因相同。【英语（一）2015 完形】

【难句类型】省略 + 非谓语动词 + 从句 + 比较结构　　　　　　难度：★★★★

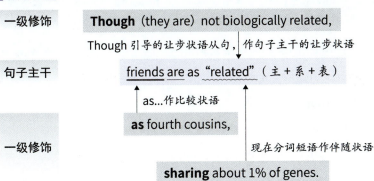

一级修饰　　**Though** (they are) not biologically related,

　　　　　　Though 引导的让步状语从句，作句子主干的让步状语

句子主干　　friends are as "related" （主＋系＋表）

　　　　　　as...作比较状语

　　　　　　as fourth cousins,

　　　　　　　　　　　　　　　　现在分词短语作伴随状语

一级修饰

　　　　　　sharing about 1% of genes.

-------- 实例14 --------

When CareerSite's agent sends out messages to those who have signed up for its service, for example, it includes only three potential jobs—those it considers the best matches. 比如，"职业网站"的代理向注册服务的用户发送信息时，它只提供三个它认为最可能匹配的职位。【英语（一）2004 Text 1】

【难句类型】嵌套结构＋省略＋分隔结构　　　　　　　　难度：★★★★
【结构分析】

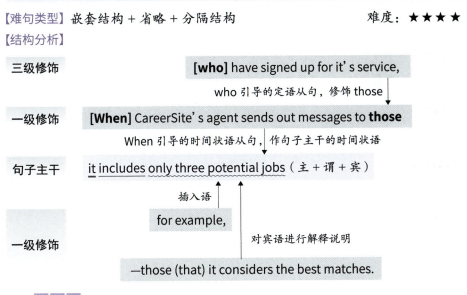

三级修饰　　　　　　　　　　[who] have signed up for it's service,

　　　　　　　　　　who 引导的定语从句，修饰 those

一级修饰　　[When] CareerSite's agent sends out messages to **those**

　　　　　When 引导的时间状语从句，作句子主干的时间状语

句子主干　　it includes only three potential jobs （主＋谓＋宾）

　　　　　　　　　　插入语

　　　　　　　　　　for example,

　　　　　　　　　　　　　　对宾语进行解释说明

一级修饰

　　　　　　　　　　—those (that) it considers the best matches.

-------- 实例15 --------

It is this implicit or explicit reference to nature that fully justifies the use of the word *garden*, though in a "liberated" sense, to describe these synthetic constructions. 虽然有"扩大词义外延"的意味，但正是这种对

大自然或含蓄或明显的参照，充分证明了使用"花园"一词来描述这些人造建筑的合理性。【英语（一）2013 翻译】

【难句类型】从句 + 强调 + 省略 + 非谓语动词　　　　　　难度：★★★★
【结构分析】

句子主干	**It is...that**　↓　It is...that...强调句型，强调主语 this implicit...nature **this implicit...nature** fully justifies **the use**（主 + 谓 + 宾）
一级修饰	though 引导的让步状语从句　　　　　　　介词短语作 the use 的后置定语 **though** (it is) in a "liberated" sense,　**of the word _garden_**,
二级修饰	动词不定式短语作后置定语，修饰 the word _garden_ **to** describe these synthetic constructions.

─── 实例16 ──

It is also the reason why when we try to describe music with words, all we can do is articulate our reactions to it, and not grasp music itself.
这也解释了为什么当我们试图用语言来描述音乐时，只能清楚地表达自己的感受，却无法领会音乐本身。【英语（一）2014 翻译】

【难句类型】嵌套结构 + 非谓语动词 + 否定结构 + 平行结构 + 省略　难度：★★★★
【结构分析】

句子主干	It is also **the reason**（主 + 系 + 表）
一级修饰	why 引导的定语从句，修饰 the reason **[why]**...all we can do is (to) articulate our reactions to it, and 连接的并列表语 **and** not (to) grasp music itself.
二级修饰	when 引导的时间状语从句 **[when]** we try to describe music with words,

─── 实例17 ──

Even today, in our industrial life, apart from certain values of industriousness and thrift, the intellectual and emotional reaction of the

206

forms of human association under which the world's work is carried on receives little attention as compared with physical output. 即使在我们工业化生活的今天，除了勤劳和节俭等某些价值观以外，与物质的产出相比，我们很少关注人类各种形式的交往所产生的智力和情感上的反应。而这个世界就是依靠这些反应来运作的。【英语（一）2009 翻译】

【难句类型】比较结构＋平行结构＋从句＋分隔结构＋省略　　难度：★★★★
【结构分析】

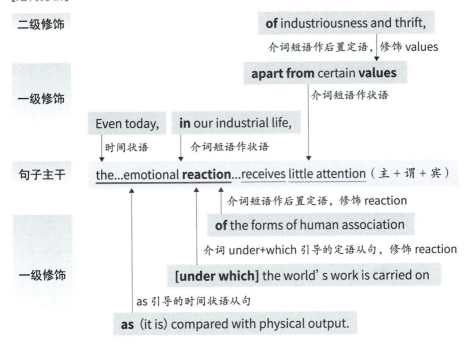

---------- 实例18 ----------

The potential evolution of today's technology, and its social consequences, is dazzlingly complicated, and it's perhaps best left to science fiction writers and futurologists to explore the many possibilities we can envisage. 现今技术的潜在发展及其社会影响复杂得令人眩晕，或许最好的办法是把我们所能想象到的诸多可能性留给科幻小说家和未来学家去探索。【英语（一）2013 Text 3】

【难句类型】省略＋平行结构＋非谓语动词＋分隔结构　　　　难度：★★★★

一级修饰

of today's technology,   and its social consequences,

介词短语作后置定语，修饰 potential evolution   插入语

The **potential evolution**...is dazzlingly complicated,（主＋系＋表）

and 连接的并列句

句子主干

and it's perhaps best left to science...and futurologists（主＋谓）

it 作形式主语，动词不定式短语为真正的主语

to explore the many **possibilities**

省略关系词（that/which）的定语从句，修饰 possibilities

一级修饰

(that/which) we can envisage.

实例19 >>>>>

The Greeks assumed that the structure of language had some connection with the process of thought, which took root in Europe long before people realized how diverse languages could be. 希腊人认为，语言结构与思维过程之间存在着某种联系。这种观点早在人们认识到语言的千差万别之前就在欧洲根深蒂固了。【英语（一）2004新题型】

【难句类型】嵌套结构   难度：★★★★☆

【结构分析】

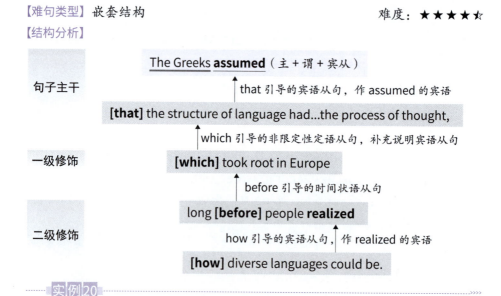

句子主干

The Greeks **assumed**（主＋谓＋宾从）

that 引导的宾语从句，作 assumed 的宾语

[that] the structure of language had...the process of thought,

which 引导的非限定性定语从句，补充说明宾语从句

一级修饰

[which] took root in Europe

before 引导的时间状语从句

long [before] people **realized**

二级修饰

how 引导的宾语从句，作 realized 的宾语

[how] diverse languages could be.

实例20 >>>>>

Symbolic of national unity as they claim to be, their very history—and sometimes the way they behave today—embodies outdated and indefensible privileges and inequalities. 虽然他们声称自己是民族团结的象征,但他们的历史本身——有时还包括其当下的行为方式——体现着过时、不合理的特权和不平等。【英语（一）2015 Text 1】

【难句类型】省略＋倒装＋平行结构＋分隔结构＋从句　　　难度：★★★★☆
【结构分析】

一级修饰	Symbolic of national unity [as] they claim to be,

as 引导的让步状语从句，作句子主干的让步状语

句子主干	their...history...embodies...privileges and inequalities.（主＋谓＋宾）

插入语

一级修饰	—and sometimes **the way**

省略关系词（that/in which）的定语从句，修饰 the way

二级修饰	**(that/in which)** they behave today—

------- 实例21 ------->>>>>

I have excluded him because, while his accomplishments may contribute to the solution of moral problems, he has not been charged with the task of approaching any but the factual aspects of those problems. 我之所以将普通科学家排除在外，是因为尽管他的成果可能有助于解决道德问题，但他承担的任务只不过是研究这些问题的事实层面。【英语（一）2006 翻译】

【难句类型】嵌套结构＋分隔结构＋否定结构　　　难度：★★★★☆
【结构分析】

句子主干	I have excluded him（主＋谓＋宾）

because 引导的原因状语从句，作句子主干的原因状语

一级修饰	[because],...he has not been charged with **the task**

介词短语作后置定语，修饰 the task

二级修饰	**of** approaching any but...aspects of those problems.

while 引导的让步状语从句

	[while] his accomplishments may contribute to **the solution**

介词短语作后置定语，修饰 the solution

三级修饰	**of** moral problems,

Often it's the delivery which causes the audience to smile, so speak slowly and remember that a raised eyebrow or an unbelieving look may help to show that you are making a light-hearted remark. 通常引人发笑的是你的说话方式，所以语速要放慢一些，并且要记住，扬扬眉毛或摆出难以置信的神情可能会有助于让人知道你在开玩笑。【英语（一）2002 Text 1】

【难句类型】嵌套结构 + 平行结构 + 强调 + 非谓语动词　　　　难度：★★★★☆

【结构分析】

句子主干

it's...which

↓ it's...which 为强调句型，强调主语 the delivery

Often...**the delivery**...causes the audience to smile,

↓ so 连接的并列句，表因果

so speak slowly and **remember**（祈使句：谓1+and+谓2+宾从）

that 引导的宾语从句，↑作 remember 的宾语

[that] a raised eyebrow or an unbelieving look may help to **show**

that 引导的宾语从句，作 show 的宾语 ↑

[that] you are making a light-hearted remark.

Washington, who had begun to believe that all men were created equal after observing the bravery of the black soldiers during the Revolutionary War, overcame the strong opposition of his relatives to grant his slaves their freedom in his will. 华盛顿在目睹了美国独立战争中黑人士兵的英勇表现之后，开始相信人人生来平等，于是他不顾亲属们的强烈反对，在遗嘱中赋予了他的奴隶自由。【英语（一）2008 Text 4】

【难句类型】嵌套结构 + 非谓语动词 + 分隔结构　　　　难度：★★★★☆

【结构分析】

句子主干

Washington,...overcame the...**opposition** of...relatives（主 + 谓 + 宾）

动词不定式短语作目的状语

to grant his slaves their freedom in his will.

who 引导的非限定性定语从句，修饰 Washington

一级修饰

[who] had begun to **believe**...after observing...black soldiers

that 引导的宾语从句，作 believe 的宾语

[that] all men were created equal

介词短语作时间状语

二级修饰

during the Revolutionary War,

210

Together with another two scientists, he is publishing a paper which not only suggests that one group of humanity is more intelligent than the others, but explains the process that has brought this about. 他将要和另外两名科学家联名发表一篇论文，这篇论文不仅表明人类的某一族群比其它族群更聪明，还解释了导致这一结果的过程。【英语（一）2008 完形】

【难句类型】嵌套结构 + 比较结构 + 平行结构　　　　　　　难度：★★★★☆

【结构分析】

一级修饰　　Together **with** another two scientists,

　　　　　　↓ 介词短语作状语

句子主干　　he is publishing **a paper**（主 + 谓 + 宾）

　　　　　　↑ which 引导的定语从句，修饰 a paper

[which] not only suggests

　　　　　　↑ that 引导的宾语从句，作 suggests 的宾语

一级修饰　　**[that] one group of...the others,**

　　　　　　not only...but 连接的并列谓宾

but explains the process

　　　　　　↑ that 引导的定语从句，修饰 the process

二级修饰　　**[that] has brought this about.**

They could still invalidate Fourth Amendment protections when facing severe, urgent circumstances, and they could take reasonable measures to ensure that phone data are not erased or altered while waiting for a warrant. 在面对严峻且紧迫的情况时，他们仍然可以使第四修正案失效。此外，在等待搜查令期间，他们还可以采取合理的措施确保手机中的数据不被删除或修改。【英语（一）2015 Text 2】

【难句类型】

从句 + 嵌套结构 + 非谓语动词 + 平行结构 + 否定结构　难度：★★★★☆

一级修饰　[**when**] (they are) facing severe, urgent circumstances,

　　　　　　│ when 引导的时间状语从句

句子主干　They could still invalidate Fourth...protections（主＋谓＋宾）

　　　　　　│ and 连接的并列句

　　　　　and they could take reasonable measures（主＋谓＋宾）

　　　　　　↑ 动词不定式短语作目的状语

一级修饰　**to** ensure [that] phone data are not erased or altered

　　　　　　↑ while 引导的时间状语从句

二级修饰　[**while**] (they are) waiting for a warrant.

三　冲刺演练

实例26 ››››

Finally, because the ultimate stakeholders are patients, the health research community should actively recruit to its cause not only well-known personalities such as Stephen Cooper, who has made courageous statements about the value of animal research, but all who receive medical treatment. 最后，由于最终的利益相关者是病人，医疗研究界不仅应该积极争取像斯蒂芬·库伯这样敢于肯定动物实验价值的名人来支持自己的事业，还要争取所有接受药物治疗的病人的支持。【英语（一）2003 Text 2】

【难句类型】平行结构＋从句＋分隔结构　　　　　　难度：★★★★★

【结构分析】

一级修饰　[**because**] the ultimate stakeholders are patients,

　　　　　　│ because 引导的原因状语从句，作句子主干的原因状语

　　　　　Finally,...community **should** actively **recruit** to...cause（主＋谓＋宾）

　　　　│ should...recruit 的宾语 ↑

句子主干　　　　　**not only** well-known **personalities**

　　　　　　│ not only...but 连接的并列宾语

　　　but all [who] receive medical treatment.

　　　　　such as... 举例说明 personalities

一级修饰　　　　　　**such as Stephen Cooper**,

　　　　who 引导的非限定性定语从句，↑ 补充说明 Stephen Cooper

二级修饰　[**who**] has made courageous **statements**

　　　　　　介词短语作后置定语，↑ 修饰 statements

三级修饰　　　　　　**about** the value of animal research,

If railroads charged all customers the same average rate, they argue, shippers who have the option of switching to trucks or other forms of transportation would do so, leaving remaining customers to shoulder the cost of keeping up the line. 他们认为，如果铁路公司向所有客户收取同样的平均费率，那些有选择余地的客户将会转而使用公路运输或其他运输方式，使剩下的客户来承担铁路正常运作的开销。【英语（一）2003 Text 3】

【难句类型】虚拟 + 非谓语动词 + 从句 + 分隔结构   难度：★★★★★

【结构分析】

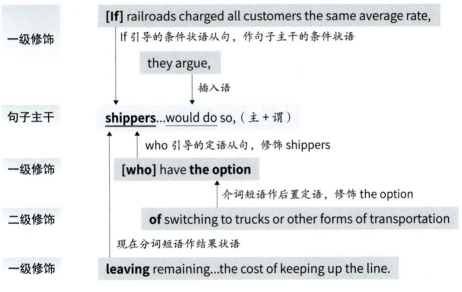

一级修饰	[If] railroads charged all customers the same average rate,
	If 引导的条件状语从句，作句子主干的条件状语
	they argue,
	插入语
句子主干	shippers...would do so,（主 + 谓）
	who 引导的定语从句，修饰 shippers
一级修饰	[who] have the option
	介词短语作后置定语，修饰 the option
二级修饰	of switching to trucks or other forms of transportation
	现在分词短语作结果状语
一级修饰	leaving remaining...the cost of keeping up the line.

Pushed by polls that show health care is one of his main domestic problems and by forecasts showing that the retiring baby-boomers will crush the government's finances, George Bush is to unveil a reform plan in next week's state-of-the-union address. 民意调查显示，医疗问题是美国国内主要问题之一，并有预测表明生育高峰期出生的一代人的退休问题将会拖垮政府的财政。在这种双重压力之下，乔治·布什将在下周的国情咨文演讲中公布一项改革计划。【英语（二）2007 Text 2】

【难句类型】嵌套结构 + 平行结构 + 非谓语动词 + 省略   难度：★★★★★

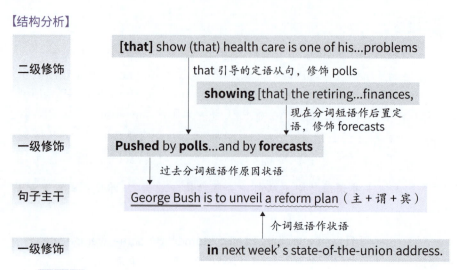

二级修饰　[that] show (that) health care is one of his...problems
　　　　　that 引导的定语从句，修饰 polls

　　　　　showing [that] the retiring...finances,
　　　　　现在分词短语作后置定语，修饰 forecasts

一级修饰　Pushed by polls...and by forecasts
　　　　　过去分词短语作原因状语

句子主干　George Bush is to unveil a reform plan（主＋谓＋宾）
　　　　　介词短语作状语

一级修饰　in next week's state-of-the-union address.

实例 29

To encourage innovation and competition, the report calls for increased investment in research, the crafting of coherent curricula that improve students' ability to solve problems and communicate effectively in the 21st century, increased funding for teachers and the encouragement of scholars to bring their learning to bear on the great challenges of the day. 为了鼓励创新和竞争，该报告呼吁增加对科研的投资，精心制定连贯的课程来提高 21 世纪学生解决问题和有效沟通的能力，增加对教师的资助，鼓励学者用他们的学识来应对当今的巨大挑战。【英语（一）2014 Text 4】

【难句类型】平行结构＋非谓语动词＋从句　　　　　难度：★★★★★
【结构分析】

一级修饰　To encourage innovation and competition,
　　　　　动词不定式短语作目的状语

句子主干　the report calls for increased investment in research,（主＋谓＋宾）
　　　　　并列宾语

　　　　　the crafting of coherent curricula...encouragement of scholars

that引导的定语从句，修饰curricula
一级修饰　[that] improve students' ability
　　　　　　　　　　动词不定式短语作后置定语，修饰 encouragement

　　　　　to bring their learning...of the day.
　　　　　动词不定式短语作后置定语，修饰 ability

二级修饰　to solve problems and communicate effectively in the 21st century,

"So few authors have brains enough or literary gift enough to keep their own end up in journalism," Newman wrote, "that I am tempted to define 'journalism' as 'a term of contempt applied by writers who are not read to writers who are'." "具有足够智慧或文学天赋并最终将新闻写作坚持到底的作家很少，"纽曼写道，"以至于我不禁想把'新闻工作'定义为'无人问津的作家对拥有大批读者的作家的蔑称'。"【英语（一）2010 Text 1】

【难句类型】嵌套结构＋非谓语动词＋平行结构＋分隔结构 难度：★★★★★
【结构分析】

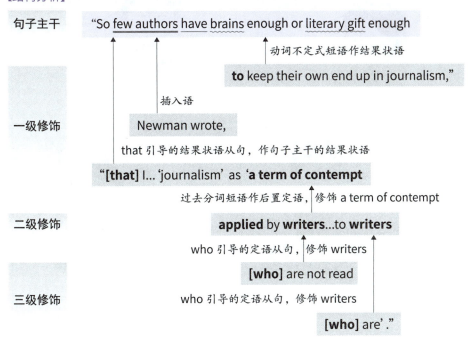

句子主干
"So few authors have brains enough or literary gift enough

动词不定式短语作结果状语

to keep their own end up in journalism,"

插入语

一级修饰
Newman wrote,

that 引导的结果状语从句，作句子主干的结果状语

"[that] I... 'journalism' as 'a term of contempt

过去分词短语作后置定语，修饰 a term of contempt

二级修饰
applied by writers...to writers

who 引导的定语从句，修饰 writers

[who] are not read

三级修饰
who 引导的定语从句，修饰 writers

[who] are'."

Before	After

基础弱复习搭档

考研词汇用闪过
划重点，省时间

逐词逐句讲透真题
专注基础薄弱17年

注：《考研真相》系列含英语（一）和英语（二）